# WOMEN WHO SEXUALLY ABUSE CHILDREN

# THE NSPCC/WILEY SERIES

in

# PROTECTING CHILDREN

The multi-professional approach

*Series Editors:* Christopher Cloke,
NSPCC, 42 Curtain Road,
London EC2A 3NX

Jan Horwath,
Department of Sociological Studies,
University of Sheffield,
Sheffield S10 2TU

Peter Sidebotham,
Warwick Medical School,
University of Warwick,
Coventry CV4 7AL

This NSPCC/Wiley series explores current issues relating to the prevention of child abuse and the protection of children. The series aims to publish titles that focus on professional practice and policy, and the practical application of research. The books are leading edge and innovative and reflect a multi-disciplinary and inter-agency approach to the prevention of child abuse and the protection of children.

All books have a policy or practice orientation with referenced information from theory and research. The series is essential reading for all professionals and researchers concerned with the prevention of child abuse and the protection of children.

For other titles in the NSPCC/Wiley Series, please see www.wiley.com/go/nspcc

# WOMEN WHO SEXUALLY ABUSE CHILDREN

Hannah Ford

John Wiley & Sons, Ltd

*Other Wiley Editorial Offices*

John Wiley & Sons Inc., 111 River Street, Hoboken, NJ 07030, USA

Jossey-Bass, 989 Market Street, San Francisco, CA 94103-1741, USA

Wiley-VCH Verlag GmbH, Boschstr. 12, D-69469 Weinheim, Germany

John Wiley & Sons Australia Ltd, 42 McDougall Street, Milton, Queensland 4064, Australia

John Wiley & Sons (Asia) Pte Ltd, 2 Clementi Loop #02-01, Jin Xing Distripark, Singapore 129809

John Wiley & Sons Canada Ltd, 6045 Freemont Blvd, Mississauga, Ontario, Canada L5R 4J3

Wiley also publishes its books in a variety of electronic formats. Some content that appears in
print may not be available in electronic books.

*Library of Congress Cataloging-in-Publication Data*

Ford, Hannah.
    Women who sexually abuse children / Hannah Ford.
        p.   cm.
    Includes bibliographical references and index.
    ISBN-13: 978-0-470-01573-5 (cloth : alk. paper)
    ISBN-10: 0-470-01573-X (cloth : alk. paper)
    ISBN-13: 978-0-470-01574-2 (pbk. : alk. paper)
    ISBN-10: 0-470-01574-8 (pbk. : alk. paper)
    1. Women child molesters.   2. Child sexual abuse.   I. Title.
HV6570.F67 2006
362.76'2—dc22                                    2006012746

*British Library Cataloguing in Publication Data*

A catalogue record for this book is available from the British Library

ISBN 13  978-0-470-01573-5 (hbk)      978-0-470-01574-2 (pbk)
ISBN 10  0-470-01573-X (hbk)          0-470-01574-8 (pbk)

Typeset in 10/12pt Palatino by TechBooks, New Delhi, India
Printed and bound in Great Britain by TJ International Ltd, Padstow, Cornwall
This book is printed on acid-free paper responsibly manufactured from sustainable forestry
in which at least two trees are planted for each one used for paper production.

*For Mum, Dad, Lindsey and Andrew*

# CONTENTS

# FOREWORD

Cultural schema in any society that enable the majority of its citizens to feel psychologically comfortable are often maintained by a process of shared minimisation and denial. This is the means by which the long held "secret" of the sexual abuse of children by women has been ignored. Should this "secret" be explored and fully accepted then the seeming social security of having women as "sexually safe" primary carers and protectors of our children would be irretrievably damaged. Therefore, despite at least a century of knowledge pointing to a significant number of women engaging in sexually abusive behaviours towards children, it is still a phenomenon that has not been sufficiently accepted.

If sexual abuse by women is accepted at all it is most often in the context of the woman being coerced into those acts by a man for his sexual gratification. The woman in this situation therefore becomes another victim of the male. Consideration is rarely given to the possibility that these women acted as equal partners or even that they may have coerced a male into offending. Women who are convicted of sexual abuse against adolescent boys can also be seen as "victims" of those boys in a society where adolescent males are seen as more sexually dominant and powerful than adult women. Those women who have acknowledged acting as sole perpetrator of sexual abuse against younger children are often seen as "mentally unwell". Whereas men committing the exact same offence would be prosecuted, women are most often referred to psychiatric services.

The failure to accept that women can be initiators of sexual abuse is perhaps a relic of a now archaic view of women as passive or weak, which has been rejected in many activities in society. If we accept that women can take responsibility to run corporations why is it that society finds it so difficult to accept negative traits in women?

Looking at the gender of convicted sexual offenders against children, the very low percentage (1 % to 2 %) of these that are female could almost justify societal beliefs and attitudes. One possible cause of these seemingly low rates is that judges are generally in the later decades of life and therefore may reflect attitudes to women of decades earlier.

However, when research in relation to the gender of the perpetrators alleged by adult survivors of childhood sexual abuse is considered, much higher percentages are found (between approximately 6 % and 60 %) depending on the population surveyed. Considering the vast numbers of adults who describe sexual abuse in childhood, even if the lower percentages were the most accurate representation of reality, that is a vast number of victims who have been sexually abused by women in childhood. As Allen (1991, p. 21) states ". . . it does not really matter to the victims of female sexual abusers that theirs was a low-probability event. What does matter is the possibility that they may experience further stigmatisation when professionals disbelieve them". Indeed, the disbelief that women can and do perpetrate sexual abuse against children can exacerbate the distress caused by that abuse.

The 1990s saw a considerable increase in the number of books, academic papers and conference presentations relating to the issue of women as sexual offenders against children. Despite these efforts, there is still a general tenet of disbelief, even among professionals (see, for example, Denov, 2004a) and this disbelief reduces the likelihood that victims will disclose their experiences of sexual abuse by women. Thus the belief that this is a very rare phenomenon is perpetuated and society's mistaken construction of women as highly unlikely to engage in such behaviour is maintained.

Clinical work and research with abusers, males and females, adults and adolescents, have shown that sexual assaults on children are rarely impetuous or impulsive events. In most cases the child is "targeted" to fit the needs or desires of the abuser. The child and any others in the environment are "groomed" or manipulated to facilitate the abuser's access to the child and to ensure compliance. Threats and coercion are imposed on the child to prevent disclosure. The acts take place in secrecy and only the abuser(s) shares the child's experience. The only view or interpretation that the child has is that which is imposed on it by the perpetrator(s). Thus the child internalises the beliefs of the perpetrator(s). Salter (1995) working with male offenders describes how adult survivors very frequently have cognitive distortions that reflect those of their abuser/s. She argues that these cognitive distortions exist not only in the content of their thoughts but also the process of their thinking. There have been similar findings when studying the beliefs of women sexual offenders and those of their victims (Saradjian, 1997). Moreover, it is clear that victims of women perpetrators of abuse also internalise society's construction of women in relation to females as perpetrators of childhood sexual abuse (Saradjian, 1997).

Thus, the belief that this is a rare phenomenon is also internalised by victims. This can compound their distress as not only does it increase the stigmatisation, as Allen (1991) rightly suggests, but it also increases the traumatic sexualisation, betrayal and powerlessness, those factors that have been found to be the traumagenic dynamics that lead to the numerous symptoms displayed by children and young people who have experienced childhood sexual abuse

(Browne & Finkelhor, 1986). Society's construction of women and the general denial, disbelief and misunderstanding about women who sexually abuse children, is argued to actually compound the impact of the abuse for the victim (Hunter, 1990). With the social construction of women as carers, nurturers and asexual beings, particularly, as is often the case, if that female abuser is the mother or primary carer of the child, the link between care-getting, care-giving and sex is likely to be even more distorted, as is the confusion in areas of sexuality and sexual norms. With abuse by women being perceived as very rare, and women, particularly mothers, construed as generally "good", both boys and girls may conclude that they bear even greater guilt in relation to the abuse, and a greater "shame and a greater sense of their own 'badness'". Victims of female perpetrators frequently describe very damaging reactions of shock, disbelief and minimalisation when they disclose sexual abuse by a woman perpetrator. Thus the victims will feel yet more "different" and "separate" from other human beings. Society's construction of females as "trustworthy" and nonabusers means that sexual abuse by a woman is likely to be perceived, as a greater betrayal than that by a man. While in no way arguing that to be sexually abused by a woman is in itself worse than being sexually abused by a man who is in a similar relationship to the child, clinical experience and the small amount of research to date on this issue (Sgroi & Sargent, 1993; Lind, 1995; Saradjian, 1997) would support the hypothesis that the social construction of women and the general denial of sexual abuse by women actually increases the distress for these survivors. Moreover, perpetrators will go unseen, unrecognised and consequently their behaviours will go unaddressed, thus increasing the potential number of untreated victims.

Despite this ongoing denial and disbelief, a body of research evidence is being collected that helps those of us working in this field to understand more about the women who sexually abuse children and the impact of that abuse on their victims.

In this book Hannah Ford takes us on a journey through the literature, breaking it down into bearable sections. She looks not only at the facts but also how these facts are both interpreted and distorted in a society that is resisting accepting them. She considers what is currently known and also highlights areas of research that need further exploration. Thus she provides an excellent overview of this evidence and gives an erudite snapshot of the current state of our knowledge in this field.

J. Saradjian

# ACKNOWLEDGEMENTS

There are several people who have helped and encouraged me in creating this book and I would like to express my gratitude to all of them.

First of all I would like to thank Hilary Eldridge and Sheila Brotherstone from the Lucy Faithfull Foundation for their interest in the earlier work I had done in this area, for their support, encouragement and help in the preparation of this book and for continuing to alert me to developments in this field and include me in their work.

I would also like to thank Jacqui Saradjian for her positive comments on an earlier draft of this book and for encouraging me to pursue publication.

I wish to express my thanks to Peter Sidebotham, my editor, for ploughing through an onslaught of draft chapters and whose thoughts and suggestions have been gratefully received and, I think, added significantly to the final product.

Although they probably do not realise their contribution, I want to thank Danielle Harris for our conversations and shared experiences and for generating the idea of writing a book (even though it was about a different topic!) and David Shaw for his support, encouragement and confidence-boosting.

Finally, I particularly want to thank Professor Tony Beech from the University of Birmingham who set the ball rolling in terms of getting this book published and I would like to take this opportunity to say how grateful I am for all the help and support he has given me over the past few years.

# INTRODUCTION

Researchers have only given serious consideration to women as sexual abusers since the mid-1990s, probably reflecting the fact that until recently there was often denial that women could behave in such a way, particularly towards children. When female sexual offenders were mentioned by researchers this was often limited to a sentence or two stating that very few females sexually abused children. Yet history reveals that sexual abuse of children is not an entirely new aspect of female behaviour. Although they do not feature as significantly as males, historical sources cite reports of women involved in the sexual abuse of children. For example, Atlas (2000, p. 118) cites Petronius' description of "clapping women encircling the bed as a seven-year old girl was raped". In discussing child sexual abuse in Victorian England, Jackson (2000) reports that although 99 % of the cases of rape or sexual abuse involved male defendants, the remaining 1 % were female, which is similar to the proportion of females imprisoned for sexual offences today. Thus although women have not appeared as frequent perpetrators of sexual abuse it would seem that such behaviour was not entirely unknown in the past.

In the last few years, however, reports from victims and recent media coverage of cases of sexual abuse by women have necessitated an acknowledgement that women do sexually abuse children and that they do so in numbers larger than previously believed. Despite increasing interest in this field and an upsurge in research studies, it remains the case that comparatively little is known about women who molest children when considered against the large body of knowledge gathered about their male counterparts. Furthermore, when compared with the volume of work examining females who commit crimes generally, information on this group remains limited (Minasian & Lewis, 1999).

The research so far has also tended to focus on specific areas. Eldridge and Saradjian (2000) suggest that because sexual abuse by women is such a transgression of our expectations of female behaviour, researchers have found it difficult to understand why women behave in this way. Perhaps as a consequence of this, they suggest, research has tended to examine these women's life histories, relationships, beliefs and motivations in greater depth than much of the research carried out with male abusers. However, this narrow focus leaves many areas largely unstudied, including the psychometric profiles of these women, the ways in which they differ from nonoffending women, factors related to their reoffending and treatment targets and outcomes.[1]

As our knowledge in this area accumulates, some of our previous suppositions, such as a belief that women do not sexually abuse children or that, if they do, they do not really cause any harm, are being broken down. This is clearly of benefit to the victims of sexual abuse by women who may now be more likely to find themselves believed and their disclosures taken seriously. However, continued study is important in order to help them further, to tackle sexual offending by women and particularly to inform us of how best to intervene and prevent further offending.

This book aims to bring together the expanding body of knowledge about female sexual abusers. Taking heed of Eldridge and Saradjian's (2000) comments about the specific focus of some of the previous research, this book aims to highlight some of the less well researched areas and to link female sexual abuse of children with research developing in other areas, including women who sexually assault adult males, sexually abusive adolescent females and the nonoffending partners of male abusers. In so doing, it is hoped that this will help in broadening our thinking about female perpetrators.

The book is organised into five main parts. The first discusses the rates of sexually abusive behaviour in females and how such behaviour is conceptualised and understood within the criminal justice system and other relevant professions, as well as within the general population. It then moves on to consider the specific nature of sexual abuse committed by females, including the acts committed and the process of offending, as well as considering how this may or may not be similar to sexual offending by men. The second part considers some of the relevant factors in female sexual offending, which in Eldridge and Saradjian's (2000) view have been most strongly focused upon. These chapters include discussion of the personal factors and previous experiences that may influence female sexual abuse of children, as well as examining the question of whether females are most likely to abuse others under the coercion and duress of a male partner. The final chapter in this section examines possible motivations for sexual offending by females and the work to develop female abuser typologies. The third part examines the consequences of female abuse for the victims and challenges earlier beliefs that sexual abuse by females is generally not harmful.

Having described the extant research in this area, the fourth part of the book moves on to consider the gaps in the current literature and offers suggestions for areas in need of further study. This is followed by a discussion

---

[1] Hilary Eldridge at the Tools to Take Home Conference: "Treating women who sexually abuse children". Birmingham, April 2003.

of treatment issues and approaches for sexually abusive women and the formulation of appropriate treatment for such women in the context of current knowledge. The final part of the book aims to broaden awareness of other areas related to child sexual abuse committed by women. Although not offering a fully comprehensive review of the literature, the first chapter in this final part examines what is known about the nonoffending partners of male abusers, critically examines the suggestion that such women collude with the sexual abuse of their children, and considers the many issues facing women in this situation. The final chapter outlines the knowledge base relating to female adolescents and children who abuse children, considering their specific characteristics and treatment needs and, where appropriate, drawing parallels with their adult female counterparts.

# The Nature and Prevalence of Sexual Abuse by Women and our Understanding of it

# 1

# THE PREVALENCE OF SEXUAL ABUSE BY WOMEN

Although research attention is now being directed towards women who sexually abuse children, this is a comparatively recent development, initially hindered by disbelief that women would behave in this way towards children and supported by the low rates of sexual abuse by women in official statistics. This first chapter therefore examines these issues more fully, outlining some possible reasons for the disbelief surrounding women as abusers and evaluating the low rates of female sexual abuse. In evaluating these low rates it is essential to consider some of the methodological issues in estimating rates of abuse, and this discussion forms the basis of the second part of the chapter.

Estimating the prevalence of sexual abuse by women has been difficult as the issue is one that until recently has been insufficiently researched. Part of the reason for this has been the comparatively slow rate at which society has come to accept females as abusers. There are a number of possible reasons for this, the first being that the role defined for women – that of child carers – does not encompass the possibility that a woman may abuse a child sexually. As Allen (1990, p. 111) states, "women are socialised to be the victims of child sexual abuse, not the perpetrators". It is only since the mid-1970s or so that there has been widespread acknowledgement of child sexual abuse by men (Olafson, Corwin & Summit, 1993), or universal acknowledgement of child sexual abuse as a problematic behaviour. McConaghy (1998) cites a survey by Hunt (1974) which found that 25 % of boys and 13 % of girls in the USA aged between 13 and 19 did not agree with the statement "a parent and child having sex with each other is something I would consider abnormal or unnatural, even if both of them wanted to do it". Acknowledgement of abuse by women has appeared still more recently; Rowan, Rowan and Langelier (1990) report that no data were available on female sexual abuse of children before 1986. Furthermore, many attempts to explain child sexual abuse have focused on theories of male power and the subordination of women and children. Discussing sexual abuse by females may raise concern that we are trying to deny the importance of patriarchy (Koonin, 1995).

The paradox, however, as Elliott[1] points out, is that we can accept that women physically abuse their children but not that they may sexually abuse them. Featherstone (1996) and Parker (1995), for example, reported figures suggesting that women perpetrate 50 % of the physical violence inflicted on children (cited in FitzRoy, 1998). Similarly, Cawson, Wattam, Brooker and Kelly (2000) found that in their sample of young adults reporting physical violence at home, the mother was most frequently reported to be responsible (49 % of cases), followed by the father (40 % of cases). Elliott goes on to suggest some reasons why sexual abuse by females is minimised. First, sexual abuse by women may be seen as more threatening. Women are expected to love children and care for them, not to hurt them. Accepting that women can sexually abuse children changes how we view women. As she says, children are often told that if they are in trouble, they should ask a woman for help, presumably because she is thought to be "safe". By accepting that women may sexually abuse, however, what advice should we offer to children? Acknowledging that women can abuse children shatters feelings of security and safety for children and thus makes it more difficult to accept. This may be true even for those working in professions dealing with abuse issues. Denov (2001, p. 322) quotes one psychiatrist who commented, "Psychiatrists feel uncomfortable dealing with female sex offenders . . . a lot of [my colleagues] are more offended and more grossed out by females doing this [sexual assault] than they are by males – partly because they don't think of females as being sexual predators". The attitudes of professionals will be examined in the next chapter.

Another possible reason for denying sexual abuse by women is the difficulty in understanding how women may sexually abuse children without possessing a penis. This may have contributed to beliefs that even if women do abuse they are unlikely to cause significant harm, which is discussed in Chapter 7. As women are also usually the primary caregivers, Elliott[2] reports, it is easier to hide their abuse under the guise of childcare. Pizzey (1997)[3] describes one mother who forced her sons to hold down their brother while she placed suppositories into his anus. She had also given him enemas when he was younger. Whilst abusive, the behaviour was disguised as medical care, which was very confusing for the victim and may have made it more difficult for others to detect. Even if healthcare professionals recognise females as abusers, the fact that women, as the primary caregivers, are most likely to accompany their children on visits to the doctor means that a child abused by

---

[1] Michele Elliott. Kidscape conference: "Female sexual abuse of children – what we know now". London, May 8, 1997.

[2] See note 1.

[3] Erin Pizzey. "Some observations on female abusers." Notes from Kidscape conference. London, May 8, 1997.

their mother, for example, will have difficulty in revealing what is happening and the abuse is likely to remain undetected (Elliott & Peterson, 1993).

In addition to beliefs that abuse by women causes less harm, sexual relations between an older woman and younger male child or, particularly, an adolescent may be viewed as acceptable. A young male who has sex with an older woman may be viewed enviously by his peers who think he is "lucky" for having been "initiated" by an older woman. Mendel (1995) notes that many films differ in their portrayal of male and female victims of sexual assault. Portrayals of sexual abuse of females are often filmed with sensitivity, he states, but several films depicting sexual relations between boys and adult women portray the event as neutral, positive or even humorous. Such views may extend to professionals working in the field. Saradjian (1996, p. 7) quotes an officer investigating the case of a 14-year-old runaway boy who was being sexually abused by a woman in return for somewhere to stay: "He fell right on his feet there didn't he... lucky sod". Similarly, Weber (1999) writes of cases in which women had sexually abused both their sons and daughters but were prosecuted only for abusing their daughters. Perpetuation of these stereotypes prevents a deeper understanding of the damage female abusers can cause. However, as awareness of female-perpetrated abuse increases, we should not assume that such stereotypes remain; heightened awareness may help to challenge these beliefs.

## HOW MANY WOMEN SEXUALLY ABUSE?

A further barrier to accepting sexual abuse by women is that many studies have suggested such abuse to be rare. McConaghy (1998) reports that in the USA, as increased attention was given to the problem of adult–child sexual contact, there was a rapid rise in the reported prevalence of such contact and a corresponding increase in community concern. Mayer (1992) observes that during the two previous decades, as awareness of male sexual offending grew, it was predicted that the figures would also rise for female offenders. However, this is not reflected in many of the studies. Grubin (1998) reports criminal statistics showing that less than 1 % of sexual offences are committed by women. Freel (1995), summarising a number of studies, suggests an incidence rate for female perpetrators of between 1 % and 4 %. Official data continue to suggest that the number of female abusers is low. Vandiver and Kercher (2004) reported that in 2001 adult females constituted 1.6 % of the registered sexual offenders in the state of Texas. Denov (2003a) quotes similar figures from both the UK and Canada, with 1.5 % of adults convicted of sexual assault in Canada in 2000 being female, while in the UK, 2 % of adults convicted of a sexual offence were female. It is important to note, however, that statistics such as these are likely to be influenced by beliefs about females as abusers in criminal justice system (CJS) agencies. Chapter 2 focuses on this.

In the light of these figures, it is not surprising that female sex offenders make up only about 0.5 % of all sex offenders in prison and a tiny proportion of the UK female prison population. As shown in Table 1.1, this proportion (around 1 %) has remained fairly stable over time and is considerably smaller than the proportion of male sex offenders comprising the male prison population. However, the figures in Table 1.1 do not specify the type of sexual crime for which women were imprisoned and could therefore include offences against adults as well as children.

Some studies present a slightly different picture, although the rates are often still quite low. Allen (1990) cites Finkelhor's (1986) conclusion that in the general population, women commit 5 % of abuse of girls and 20 % of abuse of boys. Harrison and Cobham (1993) reported that 9 % of abusers reported to ChildLine were female and that boys were more likely than girls to be abused. ChildLine figures for the year 2004/5 reveal that overall 11 % of callers about sexual abuse were calling about a female abuser. Further breakdown of these figures indicated that 3 % of 6,538 girls calling about sexual abuse were calling about a female and that 2 % of the girls calling about a female abuser were calling about their mothers. Meanwhile, 35 % of the 2,099 boys calling about sexual abuse were calling about a female abuser and 17 % of the boys calling about a female were calling about their mothers (ChildLine, personal communication). However, as many victims of female abusers are young, possibly too young to be able to use a telephone or gain access to one, this could potentially distort the picture presented to the organisation. White (1992) found that the rate of reported sexual abuse of boys by women is higher in the USA than in the UK. However, this potentially reflects differences in reporting rates; the USA may simply have become receptive to disclosures of abuse by women at an earlier stage, encouraging more victims to report their experiences. This suggestion is endorsed to some degree by Blues, Moffat and Telford (1999, p. 169) who stated that, "whilst there has been a developing awareness of women as sexual abusers in the USA from around 1984... it was only some eight years later that this knowledge base crystallised into a national UK conference".

## METHODOLOGICAL ISSUES IN ESTABLISHING RATES OF ABUSE BY WOMEN

Perhaps the key question, then, is whether abuse by women is rare or just underreported. It is certainly significant, as Mendel (1995) notes, that self-report studies find higher rates of female abuse than those relying on officially reported cases. Kasl (1990) asked therapists in Minneapolis to estimate the percentage of their clients who had been sexually abused by women. Their

**Table 1.1** Comparison of male and female sex offenders in the UK prison population between 1996 and 2005

| Year | Number of females in prison for sex offences | As percentage of total sentenced adult female prison population (total N) | Number of males in prison for sex offences | As percentage of total sentenced adult male prison population (total N) |
| --- | --- | --- | --- | --- |
| 1996 | 14 | 0.96 (1,464) | 3,939 | 11.3 (34,856) |
| 1997 | 12 | 0.68 (1,774) | 4,069 | 10.5 (38,805) |
| 1998 | 24 | 1.17 (2,047) | 4,780 | 11.5 (41,624) |
| 1999 | 25 | 1.17 (2,142) | 4,910 | 11.9 (41,205) |
| 2000 | 26 | 1.15 (2,258) | 5,080 | 12.1 (41,987) |
| 2001 | 28 | 1.10 (2,535) | 5,090 | 11.9 (42,951) |
| 2002 | 22 | 0.77 (2,842) | 5,283 | 11.6 (45,601) |
| 2003 | 26 | 0.84 (3,078) | 5,472 | 11.4 (47,798) |
| 2004 | 27 | 0.88 (3,063) | 5,471 | 11.0 (49,555) |
| 2005 | 37 | 1.19 (3,121) | 5,854 | 11.5 (50,769) |

*Source:* These statistics were compiled from the Prison Statistics for England and Wales 2002, available from the Home Office Stationary Office, London and from the monthly prison population bulletins available at: http://www.homeoffice.gov.uk/rds.omcsa.html.

responses ranged from 10 % to 39 %. Studying a sample of African-American men, Duncan and Williams (1998) reported that 51 % of the men described sexual abuse by a female while 57 % reported being abused by a male. Denov (2003a) emphasises the disparity between the two sources of data with, she notes, official data suggesting prevalence rates for female sexual abuse of between 1.2 % and 8 %, while some self-report data suggest a prevalence rate of 58 %.

Taking a different approach, Fromuth and Conn (1997) asked college women about their perpetration of behaviours that would constitute the sexual molestation of a child. Four per cent reported at least one incident that met the criteria for child sexual abuse. While this is not a large proportion, as the authors state, "this figure is likely to be an underestimate given that the women may have forgotten these experiences and had little reason for reporting such socially unacceptable behaviour" (Fromuth & Conn, 1997, p. 462). The issue of recall may be an important one; McConaghy (1998) cites work by Williams (1994), which found that over one-third of women with a documented history of sexual victimisation in childhood failed to report this when interviewed 17 years later, most apparently because of an absent or impoverished memory of it. The extent to which such recall failure results from "blocking out" past traumatic events remains to be determined.

The context of sexual abuse may also influence the likelihood of it being reported. Faller (1987) suggested that underreporting of abuse by women is likely to occur in single-parent families in which the child has no other significant adult to tell. In a study of the rape and sexual assault of adult women, Myhill and Allen (2002) noted that offences perpetrated by a close relation are less likely to be reported than those involving an offender who is not well known or a stranger to the victim. A similar dynamic could operate in the sexual abuse of children and, as Chapter 3 describes, female offenders may be more likely to target victims who are well known to them, and often related. Victim gender may also be influential. Meston, Heiman and Trapnell (1999) summarise the work of several researchers suggesting that there is a tendency for males to underreport their sexual abuse experiences, which is perhaps emphasised by Robertiello's (1998) comment that in 50 years of practice he has accumulated information about only three cases of incestuous abuse of males by female offenders. King, Coxell and Mezey (2000) describe their work from the late 1980s, which constituted the first British study of men who had survived sexual assaults. They found that although all the men felt the assault had had a major impact on their lives, less than half reported it in the immediate aftermath, and over one-quarter disclosed it for the first time by responding to the research. However, they present no comparable findings for female victims. Hetherton (1999) suggests that disclosure of abuse is less likely if victims believe their experiences to be extraordinary in any way or that their claims will not be taken seriously. Thus, underreporting may also be likely as a result of the denial of female abuse. Survivors who describe their experiences may find themselves disbelieved or accused of fantasising. Longdon (1993) reports that survivors have received disbelieving or negative statements from therapists when they disclosed their abuser was a woman. So desperate were these survivors to get help that some eventually said their abuser was a man.

However, victims may also attempt to deny female abuse to themselves. As Hetherton (1999, p. 163) states, "processes that construct women as caring and nurturant may prompt victims to reframe dubious activities, inhibiting disclosure of ambiguous behaviours". Peluso and Putnam (1996) describe earlier work by Crewdson (1988) which found that when an agency asked to hear from men who had been sexually abused as children it received very few responses. When the agency changed from using the term "sexual abuse" to "sexual experiences", more than 100 men responded. Peluso and Putnam suggest that, perhaps like society in general, some boys may try to reframe abuse experiences as rites of passage or "getting lucky".

The method used to elicit information about abuse experiences may influence the ease with which it is obtained. In discussing incest, Demause (1991) reports that disclosures increase as the researcher moves from using simple questionnaires to detailed face-to-face interviews. This may be true for abuse by females, but, as this may be particularly difficult to reveal, victims may be more willing to reveal such experiences in anonymous questionnaires. There may be subtle differences in the nature of the information obtained from these different methods. Nelson and Oliver (1998) report that while boys' reactions to sexual experiences with women remained generally positive, their responses in interviews revealed more ambivalent feelings than they had expressed in questionnaires.

Other features of interview situations may influence the information obtained. Kasl (1990) cites work by Carlson (1990) which asked male perpetrators in therapy about their experiences of abuse. She reports that at the start of the treatment programme few revealed abuse by a woman but that this figure rose to 39 % at the end of the programme. She suggests these findings indicate that length of time in therapy may be an important factor in discovering sexual abuse by females. A one-off research interview, then, may not be sufficient to obtain such information, although this could be true for those abused by perpetrators of either gender. Even the gender of the interviewer may exert influences. Coxell, King, Mezey and Gordon (1999) reported that male subjects recruited by a male researcher were more likely to report sexual molestation as adults and children, or consensual sexual experiences as children, than subjects recruited by the female researcher. This could be an anomaly of this particular study but is interesting nonetheless. It appears to contrast with findings reported by Duncan and Williams (1998) that sexually abused and sexually abusive males are more comfortable talking about sex with a female rather than male interviewer. The extent to which this depends on the sex of their abuser is unknown, however.

Incorporating technology into research may overcome some of these potentially confounding gender effects. Coxell et al. (1999) interviewed participants by computer, asking them to enter their own data and stated that this method has been shown to increase the reporting of sensitive information. However, this is very impersonal and may be similar to asking people to complete questionnaires, the effect of which has already been discussed. The most appropriate methodologies for gathering such information are therefore yet to be determined.

## Defining Sexual Abuse

Another difficulty lies in defining sexual abuse. Studies of abuse by males have used many definitions – some exclude noncontact abuse, some require that force be used, some include single abusive episodes and so on. Other variants in the definition of child sexual abuse include victim age, the age differential between perpetrator and victim, the relationship between the perpetrator and victim and issues of consent or legality (Cawson et al., 2000). The definition of abuse is perhaps even more important in the case of female perpetrators as their abuse may be disguised as childcare. Banning (1989) agrees with this, suggesting that a woman's behaviour is more likely to be seen as affectionate than as intentionally abusive. Mayer (1992) suggests that society is likely to tolerate more affectionate displays of behaviour by females, again leading to potential difficulties in determining whether boundaries have been breached.

The breadth and consistency of the definition used will influence the rates of sexual abuse obtained. Kasl (1990) illustrates this through work by Carlson (1990), who described four levels of sexual abuse by women:

- Chargeable offences such as oral sex, intercourse or masturbation.
- Offences such as voyeurism, exposure, seductive touching, sexualised hugging or kissing, extended nursing or flirting.
- Invasions of privacy including enemas, bathing together, washing the child beyond a reasonable age, excessive cleaning of the foreskin or asking intrusive questions about bodily functions.
- Inappropriate relationships created by the adult such as substituting the child for an absent partner, sleeping with the child, unloading emotional problems on the child or using them as a confidant for personal or sexual matters.

Carlson's data indicated that 31 % of male sex offenders on a treatment programme experienced the first level of abuse. The proportion rose to 50 % when the second form of abuse was also considered. If all four levels were considered, nearly all the men had experienced some form of sexual abuse by women. This aptly demonstrates how reported rates of abuse by women may differ depending on the behaviours included in the definition.

The victim's reaction is also important in establishing rates of abuse by male and female perpetrators. If a teenage boy enjoyed sex with an older woman, for example, he is unlikely to report it as abuse. Therefore, as Dube and Herbert (1988) (cited in Briggs & Hawkins, 1996) suggest, researchers may fail to uncover abuse because they ask the wrong kind of questions. Mendel (1995) reports that studies asking about "sexual activity in childhood" and those asking about "sexual activity in childhood construed as abusive" yield different results; the first type reveals a broader range of sexual activity and a higher rate of abuse by females. This is supported by Coxell et al.'s (1999) study of men attending general practices who described sexual experiences before the age of 16. Of 126 men who responded, 21 % reported non-consensual sexual experiences with a female perpetrator before the age of 16. The mean age of the victim in these cases was 11. Sexual experiences were reported by 193 men which they perceived as consensual but which happened when they were under 16 and the perpetrator was more than 5 years older. Of these men, 91 % reported a female perpetrator and the mean age of the victims at the first consensual experience was 14.

It is important to recognise, then, that the language employed in research questions can influence the outcomes. It is also important to be clear about the consequences of including or not including particular components in any definition of abuse. Duncan and Williams (1998, p. 769) emphasise this:

> Combining cases which the teen does not define as abuse with cases which involve force, threat or coercion may confuse or muddy statistical findings. On the other hand, removing these cases from analyses altogether may ignore an important type of early sexual contact that might have negative consequences similar to those more traditionally defined cases of childhood sexual abuse.

It is therefore not difficult to see why there are so many different estimates of rates of abuse by women.

The intention of this chapter has not been to suggest that females abuse in the same numbers as males. However, it seems plausible that rates of female abuse may be higher than official data have indicated. Several authors (Allen, 1990; Krug, 1989; Lawson, 1993) proffer additional arguments as to why sexual abuse by females is underreported. The interested reader should refer to these papers.

## SUMMARY OF MAIN POINTS

- There are a number of possible reasons why sexual abuse by women has not been readily acknowledged. These include societal expectations of women as carers of children, as well as stereotypical beliefs about sexual activity between older women and younger males.

- Official data tend to suggest that few sexual offences are committed by women. However, self-report studies indicate higher rates of female perpetration.
- A number of methodological variations may influence the estimated rates of sexual abuse by women. These include the specific language and acts incorporated in a definition of abuse and the methods used to ask people about abuse experiences.
- Reporting rates are also likely to be influenced by the context of the abuse, the victims' feelings about the experience and whether they think they are likely to be believed.

# 2

# HOW IS SEXUAL ABUSE BY WOMEN CONCEPTUALISED AND UNDERSTOOD?

As the previous chapter described, some of the difficulty in acknowledging women as sexual abusers of children is that such behaviour is antithetical to our concepts of women and female behaviour. Thinking about a woman as a sexual offender opposes the traditional sexual scripts of women (Denov, 2003a). Such thinking, she argues, has extended to professionals working in the field of child sexual abuse, including those in the CJS, which clearly has implications for the extent to which victims of female abuse are believed and action is taken against the perpetrator. This chapter discusses more fully how sexual abuse by women may be perceived by professionals, as well as the general population.

## PERCEPTIONS OF FEMALE SEXUAL ABUSE WITHIN THE CJS

There may be some failure to fully recognise sexual abuse by women within the CJS. Certainly until recently, this was emphasised by the gendered nature of the law in the UK, with a number of sexual crimes specifying that the perpetrator could only be male and the victim only female (Denov, 2003a). The changes brought about by new legislation (Sexual Offences Act 2003) have largely redressed these gender inequalities, however. Denov reports similar gender bias in US law, with some states defining rape as a male-perpetrated crime or stating that while a woman can be charged with assisting a male in committing rape, she cannot commit rape on her own. In 2004, Kite and Tyson noted that in New Zealand it was not an offence for a woman to have sex with an underage male, and this was only changed after new legislation appeared in May 2005 (Ages of Consent in Various Countries, 2005).

Even with greater equality in the statutes, Vandiver and Kercher (2002) suggest that many female offenders are not charged with a sexual offence or convicted of such charges if a report is made. Allen (1990, p. 117) cites a district judge justifying dropping the charges against a mother accused of sexually abusing her children: "Women don't do those kinds of things, especially in this community. Besides, the children need their mother". Finkelhor, Williams and Burns (1988) reported that cases involving female perpetrators were the least likely to result in criminal charges. Faller (1995) reported that only three women of the 72 in her sample had criminal charges filed against them and none of the prosecutions were successful even though some of their male co-offenders were prosecuted. Wolfers (1993) reported that the Crown Prosecution Service tends to decriminalise sexual offending by women and jurors too may minimise such behaviour, perhaps reducing the likelihood of conviction (Mayer, 1992).

Banning (1989) suggested that there might be a bias towards incarcerating men, one possible explanation for the small number of female sex offenders in prison described in Chapter 1. However, this may also reflect differences in how men and women are perceived within the CJS. As Gelsthorpe (1989) (cited in Stephen, 1993) reports, girls' delinquency is defined differently to that of boys; girls are seen as less criminal and more in need of care and protection. A report undertaken for the Iowa Commission on the Status of Women (1997) describes the "paternal" attitude shown towards girls in the CJS and suggests that the authorities are often less likely to recognise that females may be as violent or dangerous as males. Viki, Massey and Masser (2005) support this, citing a number of studies suggesting that females may be treated with comparative leniency, perhaps because of stereotypical expectations that female offenders present less danger.

Fehrenbach and Monastersky (1988) expand on these different perceptions in relation to sexual behaviour. They suggest that exhibitionism in a female teenager, for example, might be labelled as promiscuity rather than as indecent exposure as it might be in males. However, as we live in a society that tolerates and arguably encourages more nudity among females than males (Minasian & Lewis, 1999) this may also influence how female sexual behaviour is viewed. Fehrenbach and Monastersky report that unlike males, no females were referred for exhibitionism, peeping or making indecent telephone calls. Perhaps then, females are reported only for more "serious" offences. This is echoed by Mathews, Matthews and Speltz (1990, p. 289) who suggest that stereotypes and cultural expectations of male and female sexuality influence which behaviours are seen as offences. They state: "Few female offenders appear in clinical and research populations for exposing, stealing men's underwear, making obscene phone calls or window peeping. Do females not engage in these nontouch types of behaviours, or are they not considered offences when committed by females, or both?"

Unlike males, "lesser" offending by females may be ignored or dealt with in an alternative manner. Gender differences may be evident, even if a female abuser passes through the CJS. Freel (1995) describes the case of a male and female who abused a child and were incarcerated. Upon the male's release, a case conference was called and a Supervision Order sought. However, no action was taken when the woman left prison and the case conference minutes and court report did not mention her offence. Aylward, Christopher, Newell and Gordon (2002) describe other differences in postrelease supervision requirements between male and female offenders. For example 71 % of male offenders were required to have no contact with minors, compared with 53 % of the female offenders. Sixty-eight per cent of the female offenders were to have no contact with their victim or victim's family, compared with 86 % of the male offenders. In addition, 66 % of the male offenders were required to undertake sexual deviancy treatment or evaluation compared with 24 % of the females, although this could reflect the more limited availability of such facilities for females. Even so, the fewer postrelease restrictions placed on females implies that their risk is viewed less seriously, despite the fact that these authors reported the males and females to score similarly on a measure of risk of reoffending.

Stephen (1993) reports that women are more likely to be judged on their moral character, way of life and sexual behaviour than on their offence. The author also suggests that a woman's sentence might be influenced by the extent to which her offence deviates from female norms. This accords with Daly (1989) (cited in Viki et al., 2005) who found that "preferential" treatment by the CJS extended only to women who had committed stereotypically female crimes, such as shoplifting. A woman appearing in court charged with sexual offences could therefore fare worse than a male. She has doubly transgressed, first by committing a sexual offence and secondly by being a woman who committed a sexual offence. It may therefore be, as Worrall (1990, p. 54) suggests, that women "who do draw attention to themselves as a result of 'unusual' offences, behaviour, or personal circumstances are always and already marked out as 'unfeminine'". Furthermore, if, as Search (1988) reports, courts take a very stern view when the abuser is the mother, this may be because a mother abusing her own child deviates most greatly from the accepted norms of female behaviour. This is probably a longstanding and deeply rooted view. In 1905, a woman appeared in court charged with aiding and abetting the sexual assault of her 11-year-old daughter. In describing this woman, the judge stated that "of all the mothers that he had come across, she was the most cruel and the most wicked" (Jackson, 2000, p.109). Wolfers (1992) therefore suggested that the CJS may be a double-edged sword for women; if they *are* prosecuted they may receive harsher sentences than men committing similar offences. This is not entirely borne out in statistics. The Home Office (2002) report that in 2001, the average sentence length for principal offences was

41.2 months for males committing sexual offences and 22.2 months for females who had sexually offended. However, these figures are not separated according to sexual offence type.

Implicit in the above comments is a suggestion that women who sexually abuse are not feminine, or do not display female behaviour. This may reflect beliefs that criminality is primarily a masculine trait and that women who commit crimes are therefore either "not criminals" or "not women" (Worrall, 1990), although the increasing female prison population (see Chapter 1) may pour some doubt on this. Nonetheless, Matthews' (1998, p. 259) candid admission of her expectations upon first meeting a female sexual abuser perhaps reflects such beliefs. She acknowledges that she had expected to meet "a hostile, unrepentant monster". The woman she met instead was "a tiny woman curled in the corner of a large leather sofa. She looked almost childlike herself, with her knees tucked up close to her and her feet to her side".

Banning (1989) suggested that women abusers may identify with male roles and values. This contrasts with Pothast and Allen (1994), however, who found that both male and female sex offenders had a higher average score on the Bem Sex Role Inventory Femininity Scale than did male and female comparison groups. Offenders of both sexes scored highest on the item "loves children" and lowest on the item "forceful". This suggests that rather than being less feminine, female abusers actually possess more "feminine traits" than comparison women. Of course, as offenders rated themselves on these scales, they may have been producing socially desirable responses or rating themselves as gentle, affectionate and loving in an effort to justify their offending. This finding is interesting, however, and may warrant further investigation.

## PERCEPTIONS OF FEMALE SEXUAL ABUSE AMONG PROFESSIONALS IN THE CHILD SEXUAL ABUSE FIELD

As with the CJS, there may be a failure among other agencies to recognise female sexual offending fully. Bunting (2005) notes that national child protection policy in the UK does not refer to sexual offending by females and that few Area Child Protection Committees (ACPCs) have policies and procedures for dealing with female sexual abuse of children. It is perhaps not surprising, therefore, that some research has suggested professionals working in child abuse related fields to have differing views about male and female sex offenders. Eisenberg, Owens and Dewey (1987), for example, reported that in their sample of health professionals (comprising health visitors, nursing staff and medical students), for both adult–child and sibling incestuous relationships, cases with male perpetrators were seen as more harmful than those with female perpetrators. Williams and Farrell (1990) examined the responses of legal agencies to alleged cases of sexual abuse in day care centres.

When cases fitted the stereotypical image of a male perpetrator with a white female victim, arrest and conviction of those involved was more likely. Once a case departed from this stereotype any formal response was less likely. For a woman to be arrested for the sexual abuse of a male child, more deviant sex acts needed to have been committed.

Perhaps reflecting the increased awareness of female-perpetrated abuse in recent years, Hetherton and Beardsall (1998) found that the social workers and police forming their sample did recognise female sexual abuse of children as a serious problem that required action. However, some differences according to perpetrator gender remained. In particular, social service involvement and investigation were considered significantly more appropriate by male social workers if the perpetrator was male rather than female. All participants thought the incidents were more appropriately registered as cases of child sexual abuse when the abuser was male rather than female. Also, all participants, but particularly the policemen, viewed imprisonment as more appropriate for male than female perpetrators. Kite and Tyson (2004) conducted a similar study among police officers in Australia. Although they found no significant differences between male and female police officers in terms of the perceived seriousness of the sexual abuse scenario, the vignette describing sexual abuse by a male was regarded as significantly more serious, more serious action was recommended and the victim was thought to suffer a greater impact than when the vignette described a female perpetrator. However, abuse scenarios were perceived as serious and as having an impact on the victim, regardless of the perpetrator gender.

Denov (2001) also found different attitudes towards female abusers in some professionals. Her research included interviews with police and psychiatrists specialising in sexual offending as well as a period of observation in the police sexual assault unit. She reported that both groups of professionals had "an informal yet well-established way of 'seeing' sexual assault" with males as perpetrators and females as victims. This was supported by their professional discourse, which appeared to exclude the possibility of women being sexually abusive. As one police officer stated: "A woman doesn't have the capacity to sexually assault... it's not in their nature" (Denov, 2001, p. 315). Even when presented with evidence of sexual abuse by a woman, this group of professionals made efforts to portray the female offender as harmless. They achieved this by providing explanations that exonerated her, by minimising her future risk to the community or, in cases involving a male victim, by viewing the victim as more blameworthy while giving the female abuser the benefit of the doubt. Nelson (1994) (cited in Denov, 2003a) also found that police officers dealing with female abusers tended to "reconstruct" the offender and the offence into an image that conformed to societal conventions of gender and sexuality. Although based on very small numbers, Kite and Tyson (2004) similarly noted attempts to provide alternative explanations for female abuse vignettes. Twelve of their police officers commented that the touching in the female abuser vignette could be accidental and one queried whether the female abuser could have been checking a medical complaint. Only two participants made such comments for the male abuser vignette. The views expressed in Denov's (2001) study were more extreme, however. At least as far as cases involving male victims were concerned, abuse by a female seemed not to be viewed seriously and was perhaps even risible. The author quotes one detective saying to her and laughing, "how are those dangerous, violent, scary female rapists who are on our streets sexually assaulting? . . . I only wish they would sexually assault me" (Denov, 2001, p. 319).

However, the existence of such attitudes is perhaps not surprising. Denov's (2001) research revealed that the training of both groups of professionals had portrayed sexual abuse as behaviour committed by males against female victims – sexual abuse by a woman had never been discussed. Bunting (2005) found that about half of the ACPC's responding to her survey provided some form of training about female sex offenders but much of this seemed to consist only of a "passing reference" to women abusers. Furthermore, such training may not be prioritised; Bunting found that one of the most commonly cited reasons for not offering such training was competition with other training priorities and female abusers were not regarded as a primary training need. Hetherton and Beardsall (1998, p. 1280) suggest that "until professionals are personally confronted with the realities of female child sexual abuse, they may sustain the belief that it is not sufficient to warrant serious punishment". Thus recognition of its existence alone may not be enough to change beliefs about its seriousness, which has important implications for those who disclose sexual abuse by a female.

## PERCEPTIONS OF FEMALE SEXUAL ABUSE AMONG THE GENERAL POPULATION

Given the lack of professional acknowledgement of abuse by females it should not be surprising to find such attitudes within the general population. Consideration of public attitudes are important for a number of reasons; Broussard, Wagner and Kazelskis (1991) suggest that public attitudes influence those serving as jurors in sexual abuse cases and the public willingness to continue financing offender treatment programmes from public money. Public perceptions of the severity of particular sexual acts with children and their definition of what constitutes abuse may also influence which acts are reported to child protection or legal agencies. Furthermore, public opinion is important in the formation of laws and in developing education and awareness-raising programmes (Calvert & Munsie-Benson, 1999).

Work with nonoffending samples has tried to determine the types of abuse scenario deemed to be most serious and most clearly examples of sexual abuse. Rather than finding that any adult–child sexual interaction is viewed seriously, this work has revealed factors that moderate whether particular scenarios are viewed as serious and abusive. Among others, important factors are the sex of the perpetrator and the sex of the child victim. The research shows a pattern in which scenarios involving male perpetrators are viewed as more serious and more clearly examples of abuse than scenarios with female perpetrators. Finkelhor and Redfield (1984) reported that both male and female respondents believed that vignettes involving fathers and daughters or male relatives and girls were highly abusive. However, the scenarios seen as least abusive were those involving female perpetrators. This accords with Broussard et al. (1991) who found that undergraduate students were less likely to view a sexual interaction between a female adult and a male child as sexual abuse. Interestingly, Finkelhor (1984) asked respondents to estimate the number of child abusers who might be women. Their median estimate was 20%. Thus, these respondents were prepared to label a sizeable proportion of women who have sex with children as "abusers" whereas in other studies sex between a woman and a child is seen as less abusive.

Other work has suggested that same-sex adult–child pairings are seen as more abusive than mixed-sex relations. Maynard and Wiederman (1997) reported that their student sample rated adult–child sexual interactions as less abusive when they depicted opposite-sex interactions compared to same-sex interactions. Broussard et al. (1991) also found that students rated male perpetrators to be significantly more harmful to male victims and female perpetrators as significantly more harmful to female victims. However, this stands somewhat in contrast with the findings of Finkelhor and Redfield (1984); while a male perpetrator and male victim was rated as more abusive than any scenario with a female perpetrator, the ratings of abusiveness for male adult/female victim were much higher. The female perpetrator/female victim pairing was viewed as the least abusive.

More recently, Fontes, Cruz and Tabachnick (2001) examined beliefs about child sexual abuse in Latino and African-American communities. In a similar vein to the above studies, their results indicated that while participants were generally able to describe and acknowledge child sexual abuse, none of them mentioned the possibility of women abusing girls and they tended to express less concern about cases involving a female abuser and male victim, usually describing this as "seduction" rather than as abuse.

In Calvert and Munsie-Benson's (1999) general population survey, only 2% of respondents suggested that females could be likely perpetrators of sexual abuse, which was even smaller than the proportion of those who identified another child as a possible perpetrator. However, as respondents were asked about "likely perpetrators", the statistics presented in Chapter 1 would agree that a male perpetrator is more likely. Whether the proportion would have been greater if respondents were asked to describe anyone who may be a perpetrator remains open to investigation. However, this links with Gavin's

(2005) research, which used a story completion methodology to elicit the narratives people use in their thinking about sex offenders. Although she only had a small sample (N = 20), 70 % constructed the sex offender as male in their stories and when female abusers were included the stories expressed surprise or disbelief that women would commit this type of offence. Thus, she argues, the dominant societal narrative constructs sex offenders as male. This is not to say that society is unable to consider women as abusers, but that peoples' first thoughts would be that a sex offender is male. This, Gavin notes, has implications for those in positions of authority, such as professionals or legislators, who are not separate from the dominant narrative of society and may hold some of the same beliefs.

Woghiren (2002), meanwhile, examined public attitudes about child sexual abuse in a sample of the population from Surrey, UK. Participants were asked to rate a series of vignettes as to whether they were examples of sexual abuse. One vignette described an 18-year-old woman having sexual intercourse with a 14-year-old boy and 42.2 % of the sample rated this as "definitely sexual abuse". A further 40.5 % stated that this "might be sexual abuse", indicating that just over 80 % of the sample identified some problematic aspects in this behaviour. This finding may result from the fact that there had been a high-profile case involving a female abuser in Surrey at the time of the study. However, it may also reflect a gradual shift in public awareness of sexual abuse and those who perpetrate it. Either way, it is a fruitful area for further research.

## SUMMARY OF MAIN POINTS

- Research has suggested that there may be a lack of acknowledgement of female sexual abusers among professionals working in the field, as well as in the general population.
- Some researchers have suggested that female abusers may be treated differently within the CJS and that the same sexual acts by males and females may sometimes be viewed differently.
- Recent studies continue to suggest that professionals may perceive sexual abuse by male perpetrators as more serious than that by female perpetrators.
- Professionals may sometimes attempt to downplay the harm caused by female abusers or to reframe their behaviour in more gender-consistent terms.
- General population studies have suggested that males are thought most likely to be the abusers of children and that sexual abuse by females is perceived less seriously. Whether this is now beginning to change could be a subject for further research.

# 3

# THE NATURE OF CHILD SEXUAL ABUSE COMMITTED BY WOMEN

Miller (2003) argues that the research literature on female sexual abusers is inconsistent in its approach to gender. On one side, she states, are gender-biased approaches, which are rooted in stereotypical beliefs about females and tend to view female abusers as very different from male abusers in terms of their offences and motivations. On the other side are gender-blind approaches, which begin from an assumption that female abusers are no different from males and thereby disregard the concept of gender. Such polarised views could affect both our responses to male and female abusers and the interventions we offer them. Bearing in mind these possible biases, this chapter examines what we know about abuse by women considering both the extent to which female abusers differ from their male counterparts and also identifying areas of similarity. It is important to note, however, that much of the research in this area has used small samples, does not always include comparison groups and considers primarily Caucasian samples (Johansson-Love & Fremouw, 2006), all of which may limit the generalisability of the findings.

## THE ABUSIVE ACTS COMMITTED

Some evidence suggests that abuse committed by women is not substantially different from abuse by men, at least in overt behavioural terms. Kaufman, Wallace, Johnson and Reeder (1995) found that the types of acts committed did not differ significantly between male and female perpetrators and that female abusers participated in the full range of sexual acts. Male abusers, however, were more likely to engage in anal intercourse with victims and males were also more likely to elicit oral–genital contact by the victim. Pothast and Allen (1994) reported that almost half the female offenders in their sample had engaged in oral, vaginal or anal intercourse with victims, compared with one-third of the male offenders. However, there were twice as many males as females in their sample. Allen (1991) described female offenders engaging in more acts at both ends of the spectrum, from voyeurism to penetrative abuse. Nathan and Ward (2002) reported that 7 of 12 female offenders penetrated their victims with objects as well as digitally. Rudin, Zalewski and Bodmer-Turner (1995) found no significant differences between lone female perpetrators, lone male perpetrators and male/female coperpetrators in terms of severity of abuse, with the greatest number of offenders committing "very severe abuse" (defined as all acts of genital penetration), regardless of gender. Thus, they conclude, abuse by females is not necessarily any less severe than that by males.

Finkelhor, Williams and Burns (1988) reported that abuse by women was more likely to involve multiple perpetrators, multiple victims, ritualistic abuse, penetrative acts and threats of force. Kaufman et al. (1995) reported penetration with foreign objects to be significantly more likely among female perpetrators. Condy, Templer, Brown and Veaco (1987) reported that, in cases of sexual acts between older women and younger boys, at least half involved intercourse. However, this seemingly severe abuse by women may reflect reporting bias. "Lesser" acts such as fondling could be disguised as child care so that victims only report acts such as oral sex, which are not so easily masked. Howitt (1992), for example, considers the case of breast-feeding, which is clearly an important part of childcare. However, if a mother weans her child very late, he asks, is she sexually abusing the child? Is she continuing with breast-feeding for the sexual pleasure it affords her? It may be difficult to disentangle the motives of the female abuser and victims may not realise that they have been abused, resulting in less reporting of such activities.

Search (1988) suggested that it is less common for women abusers to force victims to masturbate them. Kaufman et al.'s (1995) data also show fewer cases of genital fondling or oral–genital contact by the victims of female abusers, but differences were only significant for oral–genital contact by the victim. Mayer (1992) reports work by Wolfe (1985) which found that female offenders tended not to make victims manipulate their genitals, possibly suggesting that these women were less interested in obtaining their own sexual gratification. More recently, King, Coxell and Mezey (2000) described similar patterns, although not all male victims in their study were children. They found that a smaller proportion of victims were made to masturbate the perpetrator or touch their genitals when the perpetrator was female rather than male.

Victim gender may also have a bearing on the acts committed by female abusers. Aylward, Christopher, Newell and Gordon (2002) reported that against female victims, female abusers are most likely to have the child engage in sexual behaviour with another person, followed by themselves touching the child. With male victims, however, female abusers are most likely to engage in sexual intercourse or to force children into sexual activity with each other.

Female perpetrators may also engage in noncontact or exploitative sexual acts with children. Wolfers (1993) reported that women can be involved in using children for pornographic purposes. Kelley, Brant and Waterman (1993) reported that women offenders were more likely to force children into engaging in sexual acts with other children, a finding also noted by Finkelhor et al. (1988). Kaufman et al. (1995) found that female perpetrators were significantly more likely than males to allow others to use a child sexually. One survivor describes her experience:

> a mother took her three year old daughter to visit a friend who worked for an important man . . . subsequently, and after a period of instruction and training in the child's house, the child provided services for gentlemen, who would visit her at home. These services were paid for, the mother being the recipient. (Elliott, 1993b, p. 159)

However, these findings could also reflect differential access to children between men and women. While it is important to examine the acts committed by male and female offenders, Kasl (1990) warns of the dangers of categorising types of abuse, suggesting that it then becomes easy to describe one as more serious than another. The belief that sexual abuse by women is less harmful will be examined in Chapter 7.

## VICTIM CHARACTERISTICS

Some researchers have suggested that the victims of female abusers are often very young. Elliott (1993a) reports that most female victims were under the age of 5, whereas approximately equal numbers of male victims were above and below age 5. Rudin et al. (1995) reported that the victims of females abusing alone were the youngest of all (mean age of 6 years), while the victims of male/female co-perpetrators were very slightly older (mean = 6.4 years). The victims of lone male perpetrators were somewhat older (mean = 9.3 years). Finkelhor (1984) reported that victims of abusive mothers are younger than children abused by fathers but victims of mother–son incest are the youngest of all. More recent research has presented slightly different findings, however. Aylward et al. (2002) found that the female offenders in their sample more frequently offended against victims aged between 9 and 15 (67% of cases) whereas males were more likely to abuse younger children (60% of their offences were against children aged between 5 and 12). Nathan and Ward (2002) also reported victims to be older; the average age of victims abused by the women in their sample was 11, although victim ages ranged from 1 to 15 and there was no comparison data for male offenders. Vandiver and Kercher (2004) stated that just over half the victims of the female offenders in their sample were aged between 12 and 17. They queried the representativeness of this finding, however, noting that their sample consisted of offenders brought to the attention of criminal justice agencies. As they state, younger victims may be less likely or less able to report abuse. Despite research variation, then, it is clear that women sexually abuse children across the age range.

Kaplan and Green (1995) noted that the ages of the victims of female abusers closely mirrored the ages at which the offenders themselves had been abused. Maison and Larson (1995) identified a similar theme, stating that the age the offenders felt themselves to be "inside" was very similar to the ages of their victims. They also stated that similar patterns have been found in male abusers. Eldridge and Saradjian (2000) reported that almost all female abusers who had been sexually abused as children re-enacted some aspect of that abuse in the sexual acts they perpetrated.

Saradjian (1996) reports that women tend to target children who are closest to them, often their own. Elliott's[1] UK figures accord with this. She found that the mother was the abuser in 73 % of cases with male victims and in 70 % of cases with female victims. Even if the abuser was not the mother, she was likely to be a relative. Family members committed 94 % of cases of abuse in male victims. The figure was slightly lower for female victims (87 %), probably because non-family members such as babysitters and teachers were also abusers. No victims reported abuse by a female stranger. Allen (1991) similarly reported that victims were most likely to be members of the immediate family, whether the abuser was male or female, but 70 % of the victims of female abusers came from the immediate family, compared with 59 % for male abusers. Male abusers were more than twice as likely as females to abuse victims from their extended families but equal proportions of male and female abusers targeted victims who were neighbours or acquaintances. Thus, there may not be great differences between male and female perpetrators in terms of victimising children known to them. Aylward et al. (2002) similarly reported that most abuse by females was directed towards known children, although they found lower rates of abuse by relatives (38 %). These authors also reported three cases of female sexual abuse of a stranger, although it is not clear whether the victims were children or adults.

Jennings (1993) suggests that female abusers have fewer victims than male offenders. This could, however, reflect the intrafamilial nature of female-perpetrated abuse; male intrafamilial offenders tend to have fewer victims (Hayashino, Wurtele & Klebe, 1995) as they concentrate on forming a "relationship" with 1 or 2 victims. Jennings also suggests that male abusers continue offending until a much later point in their lives. Supporting this, Faller (1987) noted a significant difference between the ages of male and female perpetrators, with the oldest female in her sample being 47, whilst the

---

[1] Michele Elliott. Kidscape conference: "Female sexual abuse of children – what we know now". London, May 8, 1997.

oldest male was 75. Faller's later work (1995) included some older abusive women (the oldest was 68) but overall, female offenders were still reported to be significantly younger than males. Allen (1991) also found differences in the ages of male and female offenders and suggested that while most female offenders were aged between 20 and 39, the age range for male abusers was broader. However, these findings could simply reflect more limited recognition of sexual abuse by older women.

Some researchers have suggested that women primarily abuse male victims. Adshead, Howett and Mason (1994, p. 47), for example, state "it seems very clear that boys are more likely to be abused by female offenders than girls". Finkelhor, Hotaling, Lewis and Smith (1990) also found that a greater proportion (and greater absolute number) of boys (17%) had been abused by a female than had girls (1%). In reviewing the literature, Denov (2003a) notes that female offenders seem to be abusing male victims at a higher rate than female victims and that studies of female victim populations report low numbers of female perpetrators.

Faller (1995), however, reported that abuse of boys only was the least common pattern amongst female abusers; women were most likely to abuse victims of both sexes. Vandiver and Kercher (2004) reported that nearly half the victims in their large sample of female offenders were female. Elliott[2] reports 110 cases of abuse of boys by females but has 288 cases of women abusing girls. Aylward et al. (2002) reported that comparison of male and female offenders found that both primarily abused female victims, whereas Nathan and Ward (2002) found that 11 of their 12 female abusers had victimised female rather than male children. Thus, girls may be just as likely as boys to be abused by women and possibly more so, although males may be underrepresented in these figures because they have not revealed their experiences or viewed them as abusive. Some abusing women may have specific gender preferences. Vandiver and Kercher (2004) found that the majority of female offenders who had abused more than one victim appeared to have a preference for either male or female victims. The woman's sexual orientation may also be related to the sex of her victim, particularly when victims are adolescents (Saradjian, 1996).

Establishing the gender of victims most likely to be abused by females may not seem particularly important but this could have implications for future reoffending rates. Friendship and Thornton (2002) reported data from male child abusers that suggested that those abusing male victims were at greater risk of being reconvicted for further sexual offences and that those targeting young male victims presented a similar level of risk to females as those who initially offended against females. As this was based on male offenders it is not known whether having a male victim is a similar risk factor for female abusers. Clearly, however, this is an area meriting further investigation.

[2] See note 1.

Female abusers, then, share some similarities with males – they engage in many of the same sexual acts and abuse children of both sexes. They may be slightly more likely than males to abuse children from their immediate family and perhaps less likely to abuse a stranger. However, this last finding may simply reflect difficulties for a victim in reporting abuse by an unknown woman. Research suggesting that male abusers continue abusing later in life may also be a "false" finding, dependent on reporting and acceptance of older women as abusers. One further difference that Saradjian[3] notes, is that unlike for male offenders, we do not have much knowledge or many cases of women who target children between the ages of about six and ten.

## THE OFFENDING PROCESS

Further similarities between male and female offenders are apparent in the offending process. Saradjian (1996) states that women offenders use similar tactics to males to groom children and set up the abusive situation, although those abusing very young children may start to abuse them at such an early age that they know no other form of treatment and grooming is unnecessary. Toon[4] illustrates the process in a grandmother who groomed her grandson by buying him gifts and showing strong favouritism that she showed to no other family member. The victim's parents and siblings came to dislike him for this reason, leaving him isolated (thereby limiting the opportunities for disclosure) and making him yearn for affection. Saradjian also provides a detailed example of the grooming undertaken by one female offender, including bribery, normalising the keeping of secrets between herself and the victim, gradually increasing their levels of physical touch, grooming the parents and attributing blame and responsibility to the victim. Minasian and Lewis (1999), however, suggest that offering the victim material gifts for participating in abuse is more typical of male than female offenders.

Once the abusive situation has been set up, women, like male offenders, may overcome their inhibitions and feelings of guilt through cognitive distortions and there is ample evidence of such beliefs. In some early work, Barnett, Corder and Jehu (1990) gave the Abel and Becker Cognition Scale to a group of six female abusers and found that they did hold some distorted beliefs, although their scores varied considerably. More detailed study of a larger sample was carried out by Saradjian (1996) and examples of the distorted beliefs expressed by women offenders appear throughout her work. One woman described the sexual abuse of her son as, "an extension of our love for one another. It satisfied both our needs" (Saradjian, 1996, p. 117).

---

[3] Jacqui Saradjian at Kidscape conference. London, May 8, 1997.
[4] Kay Toon: "Working with the victims of women perpetrators". Notes from Kidscape conference. London, May 8, 1997.

Another woman claimed that her 11-year-old son wanted to have sex with her because when he went into the bathroom in the evening, she felt that he was teasing her and so she would bath and then masturbate him (Saradjian, 1996, p. 130). Many of the women who abused young children rated the children as having a high sex drive and interpreted the children's behaviour as an indication that they wanted to have sex. This is similar to Eldridge and Saradjian's (2000) finding that many women who abuse their own children sexualise all the child's behaviours. Other women tell themselves they are "helping" the child by having sexual contact with them. O'Connor (1987, p. 618) describes one female offender who believed "she was educating the child by exposing her to loving sex rather than the violent variety she had experienced before". Similarly, women may minimise the effects of the abuse; Matthews (1993, p. 75) reports one male-coerced woman, often violently sexually assaulted by her partner, who stated of his sexual abuse of her daughter, "at least he was kind and gentle with her".

La Fontaine (1989) suggests that women are more likely than men to view child sexual abuse as a serious problem and this has been supported by other studies. Harnett (1997) reported that female care workers perceived a greater difference between the seriousness of hypothetical sexual and physical assaults on a child than male workers, and that females rated the perpetrators as more dangerous than did males. Kite and Tyson (2004) cite other studies that have suggested that women view child sexual abuse more seriously than men and believe the impact on the victim to be greater. This raises interesting questions about how female abusers perceive child sexual abuse. It may be that female abusers do not see it as such a problem, perhaps because they themselves were abused. Another possibility is that female offenders do recognise that abuse is serious and therefore have more extensive cognitive distortions than male offenders to counter this. Allen (1991) examined acknowledgement of guilt and beliefs about the appropriate punishments for those who sexually abuse children in male and female abusers. There was a significant difference between the numbers of male and female abusers who admitted offending, with almost half of the male abusers (49 %) admitting their guilt but only just over a quarter of the women (27 %). When asked to describe appropriate penalties for perpetrators, overall female abusers chose harsher penalties for child sexual abusers than did the male offenders. More male than female offenders recommended the least severe punishments, whereas more female than male offenders believed that the most severe consequences were appropriate. Considered together, these findings suggest that if female offenders see sexual abuse as a more serious, punishable offence, greater distorted thinking may be required to initiate abusive behaviour and then reframe it, in order to lessen the guilt that might otherwise be felt after abusing. Some support for this may come from Ring's (2005) finding that women abusing alone had significantly higher levels of cognitive distortions (as measured by psychometric tests) than women who were brought into offending by males.

Victim empathy may be lacking in some female sexual abusers as it is for some males. Mathews, Matthews and Speltz (1990) cite work by Grier and Clark (1987) which found that incarcerated female offenders were often unaware of the consequences to their victims. This is largely supported by Fromuth and Conn (1997) who found that among college women who self-reported sexually molesting children, two-thirds believed the effects would have been neutral and only one-third perceived the effects on the child to be negative. Ring (2005) reported that in her sample, women abusing on their own had poorer scores on a measure of victim empathy than "high deviance" male offenders described in other research, although she qualifies this by noting that as many of these women were abusing adolescents, they may have been particularly likely to report that the victim enjoyed or encouraged the abuse.

Aspects of the offending process described here may be more applicable to women who abuse children alone. When women are coerced by men, the grooming of the child is perhaps more likely to be done by the male partner and the woman herself may be groomed. The coercive male may suggest, for example, that by abusing the child herself, the woman is protecting the child from being abused by him. Whether coerced women develop their own distorted thinking patterns and, if so, the content of these beliefs is an area for future research. Ring (2005) noted that women who coabused with males did not differ from nonoffending women on measures of cognitive distortions and victim empathy, but it is possible that the thinking patterns of these women are qualitatively different from the items on the measures used in Ring's research, which may explain the lack of difference from nonoffending women. Equally, Ring questions whether the women in her sample were really coerced by males, which may also have influenced her findings. Further investigation of this issue is important as, without challenging the distorted thinking of female offenders, their abusive behaviour cannot be satisfactorily addressed.

This chapter has suggested that female abusers are committing many of the same abusive acts as male offenders and in similar ways. However, in order to avoid the gender-blind thinking described at the start of this chapter it is important to give further consideration to the motivations and dynamics underlying sexual abuse by women and whether these differ from male offenders. The next section of the book explores some of these issues.

## SUMMARY OF MAIN POINTS

- Female abusers commit all types of sexual offences against children, including noncontact or exploitative acts.
- Research findings are not consistent as to whether female offenders are more likely to abuse younger or older victims. However, women abuse

children across the age range. There may also be parallels between the age of her victims and the age at which the offender was abused.

- In general, females appear most likely to abuse a child known to them, often from their immediate family.
- Evidence is conflicting as to whether female offenders are more likely to abuse male or female victims. However, some females may have a specific gender preference for victims, perhaps related to their own sexual orientation.
- Female offenders share similarities with male abusers in terms of the offending process, such as grooming their victims, displaying distorted thinking about their behaviour and lacking empathy for their victims.
- Some research has suggested that women generally view child sexual abuse more seriously than men. Whether this is also true of sexually abusive women and, if so, its clinical implications, requires further study.

# II

# Contextualising Sexual Abuse by Women

# 4

# POTENTIALLY RELEVANT FACTORS IN SEXUAL ABUSE BY WOMEN

Although sexual abuse by women has not been studied in the same depth as abuse by males, researchers have begun to identify areas that may be related to sexual offending in women. Some of these overlap with well recognised risk factors for other types of child maltreatment and with factors associated with more general female offending. Those discussed in this chapter include psychiatric disorder, substance misuse, sociodemographic factors, personal experiences of victimisation and other aspects of early life, which have also been identified as risk factors in the literature discussing other types of child maltreatment. While such factors may be pertinent to sexual offending, it is important not to prematurely assign a more causal role to them, as some may reflect societal assumptions and biases more than actually contributing to sexual abuse by women. Additionally, as there is overlap with risk factors for other types of child maltreatment, the presence of these factors does not explain why women perpetrate specifically *sexual* abuse.

## GENERAL LIFE SITUATIONS OF FEMALE SEXUAL ABUSERS

### Sociodemographic Factors in Sexual Abuse by Women

There is a well recognised social class bias in much of the general child maltreatment literature. Hall, Sachs and Rayens (1998), for example, note that reported cases of child maltreatment are most prevalent among low-income families. Similarly, Cawson, Wattam, Brooker and Kelly (2000) state that the clinical literature has linked neglect of children with poverty, while their own study found a markedly greater use of violence towards children in social classes D and E. Hamilton and Browne (2002) further suggest that socioeconomic problems are associated with higher rates of physical abuse and neglect of children.

Similar findings have been reported when examining the characteristics of female sexual abusers. Grayston and De Luca (1999), for example, note that despite some variation between studies in terms of educational attainment, the socioeconomic status of female sexual abusers tends to be low. Nathan and Ward (2002) reported that female sex offenders are often poorly educated, of lower socioeconomic status, frequently unemployed and tend to follow traditional female roles, such as homemakers. A tendency towards traditional female occupations was also noted by Allen (1991), who additionally found that sexual abusers of both genders tended to have lower incomes. Saradjian (1996) stated that irrespective of education level, the majority of employed sexually abusive women worked in poorly paid, unskilled jobs, and Tardif, Auclair, Jacob and Carpentier (2005) described over two-thirds of the female abusers in their sample as living on welfare benefits. Such findings suggest that these women face a number of social disadvantages and difficulties, which may contribute to the feelings of powerlessness discussed in Chapter 6.

However, as suggested in other child maltreatment literature, these findings may reflect practice biases, as abusive women in lower social groups may be more likely to come into contact with agencies alerted to the possibility of sexual abuse in these groups (Saradjian, 1996). In fact, Saradjian's sample of female abusers consisted of women from all social classes and victim disclosures of sexual abuse have not been restricted to those from the lower social groupings. In discussing child maltreatment generally, Cawson et al. (2000) suggest that one of its most underreported aspects is the abuse of children in the upper or middle classes and, if the findings above are accepted at face value, this also seems true of female sexual abuse. Interestingly, despite the association between abuse and lower socioeconomic status, Gavin (2005) found that when participants constructed stories about sexual offenders, the perpetrators were described as being in middle-class occupations rather than from the lower classes. This may simply be an artefact of her small sample, or the fact that the perpetrators in the stories were primarily men but could reflect a gradual shift in public perceptions of abuse, which would be important to investigate further.

Another suggested risk factor in the child maltreatment literature is that of parental youth; Hamilton and Browne (2002) noted that a mother being aged less than 21 at the time of her child's birth is associated with higher rates of physical abuse and neglect of children. Saradjian (1996) found that sexually abusive females tended to become pregnant at an earlier age than nonoffenders and, although not all these pregnancies came to term, there was a trend for abusive women to have their first child at a younger age. However, while the offenders were most likely to abuse their own children, this was not the case for all, and so the extent to which this is relevant is debatable. Similarly, as described in the previous chapter, these findings may be confounded by the fact that sexual abuse by older women is less well recognised, potentially skewing the figures towards younger offenders.

## Are there High Levels of Psychiatric Disorder in Sexually Abusive Women?

Abel and Rouleau (1995, p. 140) suggested that when women sexually abuse, they "are more likely to have concomitant psychiatric or organic disease contributing to their molesting". It is perhaps more comfortable to think of women who abuse children as having psychiatric difficulties. If their offending can be explained in this way it prevents us having to acknowledge that women may abuse children through choice or even sexual desire. Such thinking may extend to the CJS; Worrall (1990, p. 58) notes that "psychiatric reports... comfortingly reassure magistrates that 'normal' women do not commit crime". Furthermore, if female offenders have committed crimes that deviate from stereotypically female crimes but they can be shown to be psychiatrically unwell, this reinforces paternalism in the CJS and the need to care for these women rather than punish them (Viki, Massey & Masser, 2005). It is perhaps unsurprising that psychiatric conditions are referred to; female offending (sexual or otherwise) has often been explained by biological or medical conditions. As Gibbens (1971, p. 281) reported, "medical problems play a large part in the offences of women". Indeed, sexual abuse by women was once thought so rare that such behaviour in itself was taken to indicate psychiatric disturbance (Allen, 1991).

Some researchers have found high levels of psychiatric difficulty in female sex offenders. O'Connor (1987) reported that of women convicted of gross indecency with children and indecent assault on persons under 16, 48 % had a psychiatric diagnosis and history of psychiatric treatment. Green and Kaplan (1994) found that their female sex offenders were highly psychiatrically disordered. Sex offenders had a mean of 3.6 personality disorders each, compared with 2.4 for comparison women (imprisoned for non-sex offences), and were most likely to have a diagnosis of avoidant or dependent personality disorder. All the female abusers showed PTSD symptoms, which were attributed to physical or sexual victimisation in their past. Even if some female abusers are diagnosed with psychiatric disorders, however, it cannot be concluded that this *caused* the offence. Faller (1995) reported that of 23 women coded as being mentally ill, in only three cases could their difficulties have been deemed to directly precipitate their offending.

Other researchers have failed to find high rates of psychiatric disorder. Faller (1987) reported that female abusers are not generally highly disturbed or psychotic when abusing children, although Faller's (1995) work coded nearly one-third of sexually abusive women as mentally ill. In Saradjian's (1996) study, only three women abused children while in a psychotic state and were described as "atypical perpetrators". The more "typical" female abusers did not demonstrate psychotic symptoms. Interestingly, this author also found that it was when the women were not abusing children that many showed symptoms of psychological distress including self-harm, depression and anxiety. She therefore hypothesised that these women abuse children as a means of coping. Eldridge and Saradjian (2000) develop this, suggesting that sexual abuse may become a coping mechanism to avoid negative feelings such as anger, fear or loneliness. Typically, studies have tended to consider samples of abusive women as a whole. However, some researchers have suggested rates of psychiatric disorder to be greater in some types of abusive women than others. Nathan and Ward (2002) report work by Davin, Hislop and Dunbar (1999), for example, which found that women who offended independently were more psychologically disturbed than those offending with others.

Methodological differences may account for some of the discrepant findings. Different results may arise from the diagnostic tools used or the definitions of psychiatric disorder. O'Connor (1987), for example, included mental handicap in the definition of psychiatric disorder. Different samples may also yield different results. The O'Connor and Green and Kaplan (1994) studies both used incarcerated samples. Abusive women with psychiatric disorders may perhaps be more likely to be convicted so that they can be more easily assessed and treated. Abusive women with psychiatric disorders could also be more likely to be convicted owing to a belief that women could only do such things if they were disordered; in the past, at least, women without psychiatric difficulties may simply not have been thought capable of abusing children and their cases may have been dropped. A further possibility is that women with psychiatric difficulties may be more likely to be detected or may commit more severe abuse, perhaps increasing their likelihood of being convicted and imprisoned. All these factors could inflate figures of psychiatric disorder in women abusers in prison.

It is worth noting that studies of female non-sex offenders have similarly identified high rates of psychiatric disorder. While these have again tended to focus on imprisoned women, studies have suggested substance dependency to be common in this group as well as high lifetime prevalence rates of psychiatric disorder, particularly for depressive and neurotic disorders (Messer, Maughan, Quinton & Taylor, 2004). In this respect, then, women who sexually abuse children may share similarities with other female offenders. Whether incarcerated women are representative of female offenders generally, however, remains questionable.

### Substance Misuse Problems

A frequently reported finding is that of high levels of substance misuse in abusive women. Adshead, Howett and Mason (1994) report substance abuse to be common in female abusers although, they note, it is also a problem for some male abusers. Faller (1995) found that just over half of her female abusers had histories of substance abuse, although this does not necessarily imply current usage. Aylward, Christopher, Newell and Gordon (2002) also reported that 53 % of the abusive women in their sample had substance abuse problems. As suggested previously, however, this may not be a characteristic exclusive to female sexual offenders as substance dependency disorders have been reported in the general female prison population (Messer et al., 2004). In interpreting these findings, it is important to distinguish between women who use drugs or alcohol purely to facilitate their offending and those who use these substances more generally in their lives. Wilkins (1990) suggested that alcohol or drugs are facilitating factors when women abuse children in- dependently and McCarty (1986) proposed that substance abuse could be more important for independent female abusers. However, these suggestions could reflect attitudes that women must be unable to abuse independently without consuming psychotropic substances. Mendel (1995), conversely, re- ported that abusive mothers were twice as *unlikely* to combine substance and sexual abuse as were fathers, grandparents, aunts and uncles who abused children. Allen (1991) found that the majority of female offenders did not consider themselves substance abusers, although they could be denying a problem. If they did use such substances, however, women were more likely to use drugs than alcohol. Saradjian (1996) reported that substance abuse rates did not differ between women abusers and the comparison group. In fact, there was a tendency for the comparison women to be heavier users. Substance abuse has been viewed as escapism and if Saradjian's hypothesis of abuse being a coping strategy is valid, perhaps women who abuse children have less need of these substances. However, some women in the study ad- mitted using alcohol to disinhibit victims and some coercive males gave the coerced women alcohol before they jointly abused the children.

## CHILDHOOD AND EARLY LIFE

### Victimisation History in Female Sexual Abusers

That some female abusers show symptoms of psychiatric disorder, particu- larly PTSD, is perhaps not surprising, given the often severe victimisation reported to have occurred in their lives. Travin, Cullen and Protter (1990) re- ported that all the female abusers in their sample had suffered physical, sexual or psychological abuse and often a combination of these. In many cases, the abuse had been ignored or minimised by their caregivers and the victims themselves had been blamed. Similarly, Matthews, Mathews and Speltz (1991) reported that by adolescence, almost all the abusive women in their sample had been sexually abused and many had also been physically abused. Lewis and Stanley (2000) found that 80 % of their small sample of female offenders (N = 15) reported a history of sexual abuse, three-quarters of this involving penetrative acts. Eighty per cent of the sample also reported physical victim-isation by a parent or parental figure. Saradjian (1996) similarly found high levels of sexual and physical abuse in the women in her sample. All the women who were lone perpetrators had been sexually abused and 75 % of those co-erced by men were sexually abused as children. In comparison, 19 % of the nonoffending women suffered sexual abuse. Women who abused young chil-dren reported that their own abuse began at a very early age and, in half the cases, continued into adulthood. McCarty (1986) reported that women abus-ing independently were primarily abused by older brothers while women who co-offended with men were usually victimised by adult caregivers. Female abusers were more likely than nonoffending women to have been physically abused and unless their injuries were very serious, less than half re-ceived appropriate treatment for them (Saradjian, 1996). Similarly, Saradjian[1] suggested that a major difference between female abusers and nonoffenders was the greater amount of emotional abuse and neglect in the offenders' lives.

Not all research has found such high levels of childhood abuse. Fehrenbach and Monastersky (1988) reported that only half their sample of female ado-lescent sex offenders disclosed sexual abuse. Barnett, Corder and Jehu (1990) had only 1 female abuser of the 6 in their treatment programme report sexual, physical and emotional abuse and 1 other reported emotional abuse. These authors do, however, acknowledge that this information is probably incom-plete. Their treatment programme consisted of only 10 sessions, a timescale probably not sufficient for some women to reveal their own abuse. In the Fehrenbach and Monastersky study, the offenders were adolescents and so it is possible that some were still being abused and were fearful of disclosing. Of the female offenders incarcerated by the Correctional Service of Canada in 1995, only half indicated a history of sexual victimisation. However, when other forms of victimisation were included, over 90 % reported a history of abuse. Thus, although there are exceptions, studies appear fairly consistent in documenting high levels of abuse in the childhoods of female sexual of-fenders and if some women are misusing substances as described previously this may be a means of coping with their own victimisation experiences.

## The Intergenerational Transmission of
## Sexual Violence: a Brief Note

Given the high rates of sexual victimisation reported by many sexually abusive women, it may be tempting to explain their offending in terms of their own abuse experiences. Put simply, the intergenerational transmission hypothesis proposes that abused children are at greater risk of becoming abusive or violent as adults. Widom (2000) presents evidence suggesting that

---

[1] Jacqui Saradjian at Kidscape conference. London, May 8, 1997.

physical abuse as a child increases the likelihood of being arrested for violence in adulthood and that being neglected also increases the likelihood of later violent behaviour. A similar process has been suggested for later perpetration of child sexual abuse, perhaps because victims have "normalised" their experience or abusing others enables them to work through and take control of their own abuse experiences. This could involve them becoming direct perpetrators of abuse; Egeland (1993) reports that 61 % of mothers who reported sexual abuse as children were maltreating their own children although the type of maltreatment is not described. Alternatively, women who have been abused could perhaps be more likely to somehow set up a situation in which their child may be abused, or fail to act to prevent abuse from occurring. Although their sample was small, Perrott, Morris, Martin and Romans (1998) found that over half of the women who reported that their own children had been sexually abused were themselves sexually abused by either their father or stepfather. However, caution is necessary as such statements may be redolent of the mother-blaming attitudes discussed in Chapter 10.

Glasser et al. (2001) state that although there is widely believed to be a link between sexual abuse as a child and later sexual offending in males there is limited empirical evidence for this relationship. Their work identified two groups of child sexual offenders, a larger group who reported no childhood victimisation and a smaller group who did report such experiences and for whom the concept of intergenerational transmission could be relevant. Of particular interest was the fact that abuse of males by a female relative seemed more likely to contribute to the male victim becoming an offender than did abuse by male relatives or people outside the family. However, they found no evidence of a similar cycle for female victims becoming abusers, although their female sample was smaller.

Although some evidence suggests a link between experiencing abuse as a child and later perpetration, the strength and directness of this link is uncertain and some researchers are suggesting that attention be directed instead to understanding how this link can be broken (Egeland, 1993; Kaufman & Zigler, 1993). Kaufman and Zigler (1993, p. 218) indicate why we should not accept the intergenerational hypothesis as inevitable. They describe a case known to them in which

> a woman nearly lost custody of her children in a routine child custody case when it came up in her divorce trial that she had been badly abused as a child. Even though her own parenting practices were reportedly exemplar, the judge feared that at some point she would resort to abusing her children because she had been abused.

Propagation of this theory may also lead to fear among victims. Ogilvie and Daniluk (1995) describe the fears of daughters abused by their mothers that they would become like their mothers and abuse any children they had or experience other difficulties in mothering.

Egeland (1993) cites a number of factors that appear to have helped abused women "break out" of this cycle of abuse so that they have not gone on to abuse others. While his suggestions are not specific to sexual abuse, many are relevant to sexually abusive women. The first is that although women who "broke out" of the cycle were abused as children, they received emotional support from another adult. This support seemed to continue into adulthood as, he reports, most women who broke the cycle were in intact, stable and satisfying relationships with adult partners. In addition, women who did not break the cycle of abuse tended to dissociate themselves from their abuse experiences, idealise their pasts and describe their parents and childhoods unrealistically positively. Many sexually abusive women do not have these "protective factors" and so attending to such factors in any intervention with these women could help prevent them repeating the cycle. However, not all sexually abusive women have been abused as children and not all sexually abused females go on to abuse others. Thus the intergenerational hypothesis is not sufficient to explain sexual offending by women.

### Family and Other Interpersonal Relationships

In addition to experiencing abuse in childhood, the backgrounds of sexually abusive women appear chaotic in other ways. Green and Kaplan (1994) reported that only 4 of their 11 women sexual abusers grew up in intact families. Two-thirds of the women in Freel's (1995) study were in care during their early lives, although the actual numbers were small. Harper (1993) also found that all of the mothers abusing children alone had been placed in either foster or residential care at some point in their lives although again the actual numbers are small. In contrast, Allen (1991) reported that most sex offenders (male and female) came from intact homes, although female offenders were more likely than males to come from families in which parents had more than one partner. These women, then, generally had two parental figures, even if the adults changed over time and were not the biological parents.

Relationships with parents were often poor (Saradjian, 1996). She found that women offenders used words such as "cold", "rejecting" or "unloving" in describing their mothers and either negative or probably idealised terms to describe their fathers. Allen (1991) reported similar findings. When asked about the parenting style of their parents, female abusers reported higher levels of negative interactions with their parents than male abusers and this was particularly true of their interactions with their mothers, who were most likely to be described as being critical of their daughters. However, unlike Saradjian's findings, women in his sample also tended to view interactions with their fathers negatively. Green and Kaplan (1994) similarly reported that female offenders saw their relationships with primary caretakers as overwhelmingly negative and predominantly abusive. These difficult interactions with parents and, in some cases, separations from them as children may be connected to the psychiatric difficulties of some female abusers. Greenberg (1999) suggests that there is copious research linking poor parental bonding and events such as separation or trauma in childhood with a greater risk of psychopathology in later life (cited in Platts, Tyson & Mason, 2002).

Perhaps unsurprisingly given their backgrounds, many female offenders in Saradjian's (1996) study had very poor self-concepts and low self-esteem. They rated themselves as lacking power and control in most aspects of their lives and held overwhelmingly negative views about themselves. In addition to poor parental relationships, relations with peers tended to be superficial or non-existent, resulting in poor social skills and difficulties in forming close relationships with adults. Saradjian, for example, notes that one of the most striking differences between the female abusers and the nonoffenders in her sample was that at the time they were abusing children, none of the offenders could name anybody who was a friend. McCarty (1986) reported that many female offenders had rushed into early and brief marriages, perhaps in an effort to escape from their home situation, Saradjian suggests, and many women who cooffended with men had had more than one marriage (McCarty). Saradjian further states that the sexual relationships of all the women in her sample had been abusive, adding to the negativity experienced by these women. Lewis and Stanley (2000) reported that 80 % of their female offenders experienced physical abuse or threats from their current partners. Miccio-Fonseca (2000) reported that half the female sex offenders in the sample reported relationship difficulties compared with just over one-quarter of the female non-sex offenders, although the nature of these difficulties was not specified. The negative self-views held by the women in Saradjian's sample had therefore not been challenged by positive peer relationships, leading these women to expect nothing better and to try to gain control over their lives in any way they could. Such relationship difficulties also have implications for these women's ability to "break out" of the cycle of abuse as, in many cases, they lack the protective factor of stable and supportive relationships with others.

A number of these findings again have similarities with risk factors identified in the general child maltreatment literature and with the characteristics of female non-sex offenders. Messer et al's. (2004) study found that female non-sex offenders tended to establish relationships earlier than nonoffenders and if they were still in relationships by their mid-thirties, offenders were more likely to have an unsupportive partner and difficulties in their relationships. They also reported that women who experienced family disruption as children, or who spent time in institutional care, were at greater risk of involvement in crime. These data suggest an association between such factors and later criminal behaviour but they do not indicate direct causation. It is also clearly important to consider why women who sexually abuse children engage specifically in this behaviour rather than or in addition to other types of offending.

## SUMMARY OF MAIN POINTS

- Several factors have been suggested to be relevant to sexual offending by women.
- Some of the sociodemographic factors identified in the general child maltreatment literature have also been found in female sexual abusers. However, there is little evidence to suggest a direct causal role for these factors and they may be more a reflection of biased thinking in society and among practitioners.
- Some researchers have found high levels of psychiatric disorder and substance misuse in female sex offenders although other studies have failed to find such high rates. Methodological variation may partially explain these different findings.
- The literature fairly consistently reports high levels of physical, sexual or psychological victimisation in the backgrounds of female sex offenders. There is little evidence to suggest a direct link between this and later abuse perpetration in females, but abusers may lack the factors suggested to help women escape from the cycle of abuse and it would be useful to address these in any treatment programme offered.
- The early lives of female sexual abusers may have been chaotic in many ways, including disruptions to the family unit or poor relationships with parents and peers.
- There are some similarities between sexually abusive women and other female non-sex offenders in terms of high levels of psychiatric disorder, substance misuse issues and difficulties in familial and other interpersonal relationships.

# 5

# MALE COERCION OF FEMALES INTO SEXUALLY ABUSIVE BEHAVIOUR

It may be easier to accept that women sexually abuse children if we conceptualise these women as having been coerced into the behaviour by males. Amongst other things, sexual abuse has been explained by male power and aggression and, according to this theory, women do not abuse unless powerful, aggressive males have forced or persuaded them into it.

Forbes (1993, p. 104) maintains that if women are involved in the sexual abuse of children it is the result of "men's predominance in initiating and perpetrating abuse on children, and very often, on the women themselves". Faller (1990), describing sexual abuse in day care centres, reports that in her experience all offenders who were coerced into abusing were women. This was corroborated by the victims, who reported that the coerced women were often less abusive and were forced into sexual acts by the primary perpetrator. However, while all the coerced offenders in this study were women, this does not indicate that *all* women abusers are coerced. Nor does it suggest that those who coerce others into abuse are always men; women may also coerce others into abuse.

Wolfers (1992) studied 10 women who had sexually abused children and reported that in 7 cases male partners rather than the women precipitated the abuse. Many such women are often very dependent on their male partners and have low self-esteem, perhaps leading them to believe it better to yield to the partner's wishes than resist. In some cases coercive men may use grooming methods akin to those used with victims to gain the female's compliance. Saradjian (1996) reports that some males, for example, told their female partners that if they joined in the abuse the child would not suffer as much as if the male abused the child alone. Thus women can be drawn into abuse believing that they are indirectly "protecting" the child.

However, while most cases in Wolfers' (1992) sample did involve coercion by males, three women appeared to abuse independently. It is possible that these three women were attempting to protect their male partner from being identified as an abuser; Saradjian (1996) reported that in her group of male-coerced women there was a tendency for the women to see the relationship with their male partner as more important than the relationship with their children. McCarty (1986) also reported that women who offended with men were more concerned not to lose their partner than to protect their child. However, this may reflect concern not just about losing the male partner himself but some of the other aspects of the relationship, such as financial security.

If women were trying to protect partners by describing themselves as sole perpetrators this suggests these women are more willing to take responsibility for their actions and are not denying their abusive behaviour. Certainly, Matthews (1993, 1998) suggested that women are less likely to deny abusive acts and are more willing to take responsibility for their behaviour. Faller (1995) also reported that two-thirds of the women in her sample admitted the abuse at some level. Koonin (1995), meanwhile, cites work by McCary (no date given) who reports that because women make a greater investment in childcare, they are more likely to deny abuse. Allen (1991) also found that women offenders were more reluctant to admit abusing children, even when there was supporting evidence, and felt that they had been wrongly accused. They also had lower levels of guilt than male offenders. This suggests that they were denying the abuse both to the authorities and also to themselves. However, a woman's willingness to admit the abuse may depend upon the person to whom she must admit it. The context of the abuse may also influence the extent of denial; Faller (1995) reported that women involved in extrafamilial abuse with multiple perpetrators were the least likely to admit the abuse. If women are less likely to admit responsibility for abuse, it is possible that some reports of male coercion could be an excuse to remove some responsibility from the woman herself. However, some women may have suffered at the hands of male partners and claims of coercion should be fully examined.

Some characteristics of women coerced into offending by men have already been described, such as dependency on the male partner or viewing the relationship with him as more important than the relationship with the children. However, this could be related to the social isolation experienced by such women. Saradjian (1996), for example, found that women who had initially been coerced into abusing by men lacked social support and several felt that their ability to form relationships with others had been destroyed by their coercive male partners. Furthermore, she reported a trend for such women to believe that they had even less control over their lives than other female abusers, which they largely attributed to the relationship with their coercive male partner. Many similar characteristics are reported by Matthews (1993), who additionally described male-coerced women as feeling unloved and unloveable, expecting to be rejected and as staying in abusive relationships because they do not believe that anyone else will want them. Ring (2005) administered psychometric test batteries to female abusers and found that all reported difficulties with emotional loneliness, self-esteem and beliefs about their level of control over events in their lives. However, she also noted that women abusing with males tended to have more difficulties in these respects. Saradjian suggests that many of these characteristics seem primarily to result from being in a relationship with a coercive male, rather than reflecting pre-existing traits. However, there may also be links with their past; Saradjian noted that all coerced women in her sample construed their partners as being similar to their fathers and, initially at least, had ignored or minimised negative characteristics in their partners in the same way that they had frequently idealised their fathers. This dependency, she states, was exploited by the coercive partners, to ensure that the women would do anything to maintain the relationship, even abusing their children.

It is also important to consider what might lead males to coerce women into sexual activity with children. Martín, Vergeles, Acevedo, Sánchez and Visa (2005) note that sociocultural theories have emphasised socialisation processes in males to support and justify their engagement in sexually coercive behaviour, although they note that not all studies have found evidence for such a link. Malamuth's Confluence Model (described in Wheeler, George & Dahl, 2002) postulates that sexual aggression or coercion is the result of an interaction between two pathways linked to childhood experiences and relationships. The first pathway (Hostile Masculinity) is hypothesised to be associated with hostile or abusive family environments that lead to the development of adversarial or hostile beliefs about male-female relationships. The second pathway (Impersonal Sex) suggests that family and peer influences can hinder the development of prosocial skills and the ability to develop or sustain intimacy, particularly sexually. Wheeler et al.'s own study supported the Confluence Model, finding that men with high levels of both Hostile Masculinity and Impersonal Sex were at greater risk of sexually aggressing against women, although this was moderated by high levels of empathy. Martín et al. reported similar findings, noting that a need to control and dominate women was the greatest predictor of involvement in sexually coercive behaviour. However, empathic capabilities were also important and the effects of other variables could be reduced by greater levels of empathy. However, both these studies relate to men coercing women into engaging in sexual activity with them. Whether the same factors are relevant to males who coerce women into sexually abusing children is an area for further research.

## ARE SEXUALLY ABUSIVE FEMALES ALWAYS COERCED BY MALES?

While the actual extent of male coercion of female offenders is unclear, studies are repeatedly suggesting that women also abuse as equals with men or in the absence of a male offender. The Correctional Service of Canada (1995) found that only 4 of 9 women who offended with males could be described as having been coerced by those males. For the remaining 5 women there was no evidence of coercion and 3 appeared to have been very active or even initiatory perpetrators. Aylward, Christopher, Newell and Gordon (2002) stated that 38 % of their female offenders abused with a male partner, suggesting that the remaining 62 % did not. The picture may be further confused by the fact that some women who are initially coerced by men may go on to abuse independently. Although their sample size was extremely small, Kalders, Inkster and Britt (1997) reported that although all identified female sex offenders had cooffended with a male at some point, 25 % had gone on to abuse independently. Why some women should go on to abuse on their own is not certain. However, one offender reported by Mathews, Matthews and Speltz (1990, p. 283) gave the following reason: "I was unwilling at first . . . I was afraid he was going to hurt me so I did it willingly, even though I knew it was wrong. But then after a while, it got to the point where I liked it".

Perhaps there are similar attitude changes in other women who progress to abusing alone. Although not referring specifically to sexual offending, Weerman (2003) notes that while some offenders switch between cooffending and solo offending, many in fact have a preference and usually offend either alone or with others. Whether this is true for sexual abuse and what may lead to any change in preference is an interesting area for further consideration. However, if the woman has initially been coerced, perhaps this cannot really be described as "cooffending" per se.

Elliott (1993a) analysed 127 victim reports of abuse by females and found that three-quarters were abused by a woman acting alone. Subsequent figures by Elliott[1] found that many more mothers abused alone (225 mothers abused victims of both sexes alone, compared with 48 mothers abusing victims of both sexes in conjunction with another male offender). She also reported female babysitters to be more likely to abuse children of both sexes alone (N = 23) than in conjunction with another male (N = 2). However, perhaps this reflects the fact that babysitting is more likely to be a solitary occupation. Briggs and Hawkins (1996) likewise reported that their female offenders often abused alone and were not influenced or accompanied by males.

However, as discussed earlier, the lack of acknowledgement of women as perpetrators makes it difficult for victims to disclose such abuse. Sgroi and Sargent (1993) suggest that victims are more willing to report abuse by males and any disclosure of abuse by females is likely to occur later in therapy, if at all. Peterson, Colebank and Motta (2001) (cited in Vandiver & Kercher, 2004) note that females abusing with male offenders are often not reported. Therefore, if both a man and a woman abused a child, the child might report only the male offender and the woman's participation would not be represented in

---

[1] Michele Elliott. Kidscape conference: "Female sexual abuse of children – what we know now". London, May 8, 1997.

abuse statistics. If a lone woman abused a child, however, only that woman could be named as the perpetrator. If this occurred repeatedly, the figures for lone female perpetration may be inflated compared with figures for joint abuse by men and women. It would be interesting to examine the CJS response to this issue. Worrall (1990) notes that in non-sexual offences such as burglary, the focus has been on prosecuting men, and if women commit such offences with men, there is an assumption that these women "cannot be as dangerous as their male companions" (Worrall, 1990, p. 79). Whether such attitudes exist in the sexual offence arena may benefit from further study.

Thus it is not clear whether women are more likely to abuse alone or in conjunction with another male. Some researchers, however, are reporting additional scenarios, such as women coercing men into abusing children. Saradjian (1996) describes one woman who coerced her husband into abusing a teenage girl. Pizzey[2] reports the case of a woman coercing her husband and a male neighbour into abusing the husband's daughter. Gallagher (2000) describes another female who appeared to initiate the sexual assaults and involve others in them, although whether this was coercion is unclear. The case:

> centred around a female childminder who sexually abused her neighbour's four children and two of her own children. She appeared to be the "ring-leader" of a group of abusers comprising her adult daughter and her own cohabitee, and four other abusers living in the same town to whose homes she took the children to be abused. (Gallagher, 2000, p. 806)

Women may abuse with men as equal coperpetrators. Saradjian (1996) describes one female offender who had married her husband knowing that he had a sexual interest in children. When this woman was herself imprisoned for sexual offences she wrote to other men in prison for similar offences, declaring her love for them and promising to marry them. It is as if she sought out men with whom she could abuse children. There have also been reports of women abusing together. Elliott (1993a) describes cases of mothers abusing in conjunction with sisters, aunts and grandmothers and Longdon (1993) reports a female survivor being "gang-raped" by her mother and the mother's female friends. Mathews et al. (1990) describe the case of an adolescent female offender who was pressured into having oral sex with her younger brother by a female peer. Finkelhor, Williams and Burns (1988) found that in 17% of multiple perpetrator cases of abuse in day care the abusers were all female.

Therefore, it is important to make a distinction between women who abuse *in conjunction with* men and those who are *coerced* by men. Kaufman, Wallace, Johnson and Reeder (1995) reported that cases of abuse by females were

---

[2] Erin Pizzey: "Some observations on female abusers". Notes from Kidscape conference, May 8, 1997.

significantly more likely to involve multiple perpetrators and that three-quarters of these "other offenders" were males. Jennings (1993) states that it is rare for men to offend against children in the presence of others but that women are much more likely to abuse in conjunction with another. This accords with Finkelhor et al. (1988) who reported that abuse by women was most frequently committed with others. The most common scenario was a group of several women with one or two male abusers. This may have some relationship with Eldridge and Saradjian's (2000) finding that women involved in multiperpetrator groups derived positive feelings not just from the actual abuse but from being part of the group.

Nathan and Ward (2002) reported that most of the abusive women in their sample co-offended with men, but less than half of these women reported being "coerced". In fact, the women were more likely to report offending because of rejection or jealousy or to seek revenge than as the result of coercion. Thus while women may be more likely to offend with a male, it cannot always be assumed that he coerced her into abusing.

## FEMALE COERCION OF ADULT MALES INTO SEXUAL ACTIVITY

> One man reports a sexual assault after being picked up and taken to a flat by two (female) prostitutes. Before this he relates how he was taken to his own flat which was ransacked, and his sound system disappeared. They also found a bank book, took him to a bank and forced him to withdraw around £1000.... Although his description of the prostitutes' flat was accurate, and his pen was found behind a sofa cushion, the CPS would not proceed with a prosecution. Reportedly, this was in part because of doubts about the possibility of women sexually assaulting a man. (Williams, 1995, p. 3)

At this point it may be useful to examine briefly the literature related to adult female sexual coercion of adult males. While not directly related to the sexual abuse of children, this work has clearly demonstrated that women can be sexual initiators, sexually powerful and sexually demanding. By examining this work it is hoped to further dispel beliefs that females are incapable of sexually coercive or aggressive behaviour.

Until comparatively recently, the sexual assault of adult males was largely ignored in the clinical and research literature (Stermac, Sheridan, Davidson & Dunn, 1996), perhaps, they suggest, reflecting popular beliefs that males were rarely sexually assaulted. In light both of this and the initial reluctance to recognise females as perpetrators, it may not be surprising that studies have generally found that adult female sexual assault of adult males is perceived as less harmful. LaRocca and Kromrey (1999), for example, found that when rating sexual harassment vignettes in which perpetrator and victim genders were manipulated, both male and female subjects rated an incident involving female perpetrators as less harassing than the same incident with a male perpetrator. In fact, the women perpetrators' actions were more likely to be interpreted as "harmless flirtation". Smith, Pine and Hawley (1988) also asked participants to make judgements about a sexual assault scenario in which the gender of the perpetrator and victim were manipulated. Despite the seriousness of the behaviour described in the scenario, the male victim of a sexual assault by females was perceived to have been more likely to encourage or initiate the incident, to have derived more pleasure from it and to have experienced less stress. They additionally report that this belief was particularly pronounced among male subjects. These findings suggest that sexually assaultive behaviour by women is not viewed as being particularly abusive or harmful and the same behaviours may be seen differently depending on whether they are committed by a male or female. Struckman-Johnson and Anderson (1998) cite earlier work by Struckman-Johnson and Struckman-Johnson (1991) which found that when asked to rate the acceptability of different coercive sexual strategies (ranging from verbal pressure to physical force), male participants rated all acts as more acceptable when perpetrated by a woman against a man than the other way round. The authors suggest this indicates that sexual violations by women are "seen as romantic and motivated by intimacy, whereas the identical behaviours by men are viewed as threatening, aggressive, and motivated by power and control". As has been suggested of women who abuse children, then, even pressuring or forcing behaviours in women could be reinterpreted in a manner more concordant with female roles so that such behaviour could be viewed as "a method of foreplay and not aggression" (Anderson & Melson, 2002). Struckman-Johnson and Anderson further report having sometimes encountered similar views when presenting their findings at professional forums. This shares similarities with some of the general feelings and double standards related to female sexual abuse of children.

A number of studies have reported significant proportions of female coercion of males into sexual activity, although many of these focus on the context of dating relationships. The Struckman-Johnsons (1994), for example, cite an earlier study by Sorenson, Stein, Siegel, Golding and Burnam (1987). This study reported that in a sample of 1,480 men, 7.2 % reported being pressured or forced into sexual contact and that the majority of these incidents were perpetrated by a female acquaintance. Their own study asked college males about experiences of pressured or forced sexual touch or intercourse since the age of 16. Twenty-four per cent reported coercive sexual contact from women, compared with 4 % from men and 6 % from both sexes. Russell and Oswald (2001) classified 18 % of a sample of female students as sexually coercive, based on their anonymous self-report. Strike, Myers, Calzavara and Haubrich (2001) studied sexual coercion in dating situations among adults aged between 18 and 25. Among the women in the sample, 58 % reported that they had been pressured to have sex while 42 % had been both pressured and had pressured someone else. However, the participants of this study were described as "street-involved", that is they had experienced homelessness, lived in shelters and/or participated in the sex or drug trade and so these vulnerable people may not be representative of the wider population. Nonetheless, King, Coxell and Mezey (2000) reported that in their sample of men recruited through general practices in the UK, women were perpetrators of nonconsensual sexual acts against males over the age of 16 in almost half of the reported cases. Krahé, Waizenhöfer and Möller (2003), meanwhile, reported almost 1 in 10 women to use aggressive strategies to obtain sexual contact with a man against his will on at least one occasion.

Strike et al. (2001) point out that research has tended to suggest that heterosexual women are less physically coercive than men. However this should not rule out the possibility of violence; Harned (2001) reports that findings have generally indicated women to be at least equally as likely to use physical aggression towards dating partners as men. The use of violence by women offending against children is discussed in Chapter 7. However, Struckman-Johnson (1988) reports that most men coerced into sex by women describe the women using psychological tactics such as verbal pressuring, being made to feel guilty or threatening to end the relationship. Strike et al. (2001, p. 543) documented additional strategies women used to coerce others into sex: "... and I hadn't been with him in quite a while and all I did was I brought over a 12-pack of beer and a joint and we, you know, smoked and drank and I got what I wanted, I got what I went there for." They also describe a female coercing another female who "admitted that she had offered to pay her partner's rent if they went away for the weekend together. Once they had reached their destination, the participant demanded sex and threatened to leave her stranded if she did not give her sex" (Strike et al. 2001, p. 546).

Russell and Oswald (2001) found that sexually coercive women reported using both verbal and physical strategies, although verbal strategies were more frequently reported. Struckman-Johnson and Struckman-Johnson (1994) reported that the strategy most frequently employed by females was persuasion of their "partner". However, they reported some men as saying that females had physically restrained them, threatened harm or bribed them to have sex. Anderson (1998) reports that in his sample, 20 % of the women used physical force, 27 % threatened physical force and 9 % used a weapon to obtain sexual contact. Krahé et al. (2003) report lower rates of physical aggression, citing exploitation of a man's incapacitated state as the most frequently used strategy.

Women may also hold attitudes that condone coercive sexual behaviour and include a sense of "entitlement". Anderson and Melson (2002) cite work by Shea (1998) that concluded that coercive women differed from noncoercive women in that they were more likely to view traditional female roles as restrictive, were more likely to acknowledge an acceptance of forced sex, to believe that it is acceptable for women to have and act on sexual thoughts or desires and to acknowledge a wish for power in their sexual activities. Russell and Oswald (2001) similarly found that coercive women were more tolerant of sexual harassment than non-coercive females and more likely to adopt a "Ludic lovestyle", which they defined as being emotionally uninvolved and manipulative in relationships and preferring to be in control. However, they also found that women high in femininity were more likely to be sexually coercive and question whether such women may use their exaggerated femininity to manipulate others.

Female sexual aggression is not directed solely towards adult males. Vandiver and Kercher (2004) identified a sub-group of female offenders who had primarily sexually abused other adult females. However, this seems an underresearched area and Muehlenhard (1998) suggests that many factors contribute to the "invisibility" of sexual aggression within lesbian relationships. Perhaps reflecting this, Byers and O'Sullivan (1998) suggest that the incidence of sexual coercion among lesbian women may be similar to that of heterosexual couples but that the research on sexual violence within same-sex relationships is too limited to reach firm conclusions. This is beyond the scope of the present review but is an important area for future research.

Much of this work has studied female coercion in the context of relationships. However, some researchers have also considered sexual harassment of males by females in the workplace. Lee (2000) cites the findings of telephone interviews conducted in 1995, which found that 7 % of men and women were aware of men being sexually harassed by women in their workplace. Her own study highlights the case of a male harassed by a female at work. Perhaps because he had previously had a relationship with her, her actions were not recognised as harassment and no action was taken by the management. The man eventually took his own life.

Although this brief review of the literature cannot hope to be comprehensive, it highlights parallels between female coercion of adult males and female sexual abuse of children. In general, there appears to be a lack of acknowledgement of the seriousness of abuse by women either against adults or children and a perception that victims are not overly harmed by such contact. Research suggests that women are most likely to sexually offend against a child known to them and also to coerce an adult they know. Struckman-Johnson and Struckman-Johnson (1994) report that in at least 90 % of cases of female-initiated contact against adult males the woman was known by the man, either as a casual acquaintance or a girlfriend. However, this brief discussion of the research is above all useful in that it further raises our awareness of sexually aggressive activity by females and helps dispel notions that women are incapable of such behaviour.

## SUMMARY OF MAIN POINTS

- Some research has suggested that many female sexual abusers are coerced into offending by males. Some of the characteristics of women coerced into abuse by males, such as social isolation or feelings of powerlessness, could increase their vulnerability to coercion or being targeted by coercive males, although they may also be a consequence of being in relationships with coercive males. Their childhood relationships with parents, particularly their father, could also increase their vulnerability to exploitation.
- It is not known whether the research examining the characteristics of men who coerce women into engaging in sexual activity with them is applicable to men who coerce women into abusing children. This would benefit from further study.
- However, women may also abuse children as equals with males or in the absence of a male perpetrator. Some women who are initially coerced into abuse by men may go on to abuse children alone although the specific reasons for this transition are yet to be established.
- Although several research studies have found that female sexual assault of adult males is not viewed particularly seriously, a significant proportion of females have been reported to coerce males into sexual activity against their will. Many of these women are reported to use tactics such as verbal pressure but some violence is also reported.
- Female sexual coercion of other females is reported but this remains a relatively underresearched area.
- The research has highlighted some parallels between female sexual abuse of children and sexual coercion of adult males.

# 6

# WHAT MIGHT MOTIVATE WOMEN TO SEXUALLY ABUSE CHILDREN?

As research attention has increasingly been directed towards sexual abuse by women, the findings have suggested many different motivations for why women may abuse children. Furthermore, the findings have made clear that there is no one overall motivation for why women sexually abuse others. However, through the study of progressively larger samples of female abusers, researchers have started to develop typologies of sexually abusive women and suggest particular types of motivations among the different groups. While there will still be individual motives and needs for each offender, these typologies may be useful in helping treatment providers identify broad areas of need to address in intervention. The first part of this chapter therefore outlines some of these typologies and motivations suggested to be associated with them. It is important to recognise that such work is in its early stages, however, and different researchers have suggested different numbers of offender groups. The earliest typology described in this chapter, for example, proposed three categories (Matthews, Mathews & Speltz, 1991). Saradjian's (1996) typology also described three categories, but recognised that not all women fell within these and so added an "atypical perpetrators" category, and recent work (Vandiver & Kercher, 2004) identified six categories of offender. There are also themes that seem to transcend offender categories, as will be described later in this chapter. The second part of the chapter considers whether sexual abuse by women is simply loving, affectionate behaviour that has been misinterpreted by others as abusive and contends that there is no basis for believing this. Indeed, unless such a suggestion is eliminated it will help perpetuate denial and minimisation of female offending.

Returning to the issue of male coercion discussed in the previous chapter, one consequence of assuming that women abuse only when coerced by men is that the primary motivation for abusing ascribed to such women is to placate or please their male coercer or to somehow protect themselves from him. That is, the woman's motivation to abuse is connected to the motivations of the male (Saradjian, 1996). This may be limiting when undertaking therapeutic work with female abusers, suggesting that their primary treatment needs are simply to increase their levels of assertiveness and independence.

Kaufman, Wallace, Johnson and Reeder (1995) suggest that male and female abusers may have different motives. They propose that male offenders may be more likely to focus on obtaining sexual gratification whereas females may be seeking nonsexual needs such as emotional or physical closeness. In support of this, Allen and Pothast (1994) found that female abusers have the highest level of emotional needs. However, it is not clear whether this results from these women being innately more needy, perhaps as a consequence of their childhood experiences, or whether they are simply in poorer quality relationships which are failing to meet their needs. Equally, however, focusing on the emotional needs of female offenders may also reflect a reluctance to acknowledge female sexual desire, which is discussed again in Chapter 8.

It is unlikely, however, that any one motivation can be ascribed to most women who abuse children. Each abuser may have a number of motivations that differ according to environmental factors. Some may be conscious and others unconscious. As one offender stated, "there were different reasons at different times . . . if I'd feel her slipping away, I'd need to be sexual with her. At other times I was just so angry I wanted to hurt someone, anyone, so I hurt her, sexually" (Saradjian, 1996, p. 137).

## FEMALE OFFENDER TYPOLOGIES

As the female offender research base has expanded, researchers have begun to develop offender typologies, which suggest different general motivating factors for each offender type. These typologies have utility in helping to understand the differential development of sexually abusive behaviour and in identifying areas of need for intervention programmes. As Vandiver and Kercher (2004) note, however, much of the female abuser typology work is in its early stages and has been limited by small sample sizes.

Discussion of this work here will be structured around the typology described by Saradjian (1996), who reported 3 main offender types in her sample of women abusers: those who abuse young children, those who abuse adolescents and those initially coerced into abuse by men. This has been selected as it is based on a comparatively large sample of female abusers and also has detailed information about the women in each of the groups. However, it overlaps to some extent with Matthews et al.'s (1991) typology of three female offender types: the teacher/lover, the intergenerationally predisposed offender and the male-coerced offender, which will be described more fully when discussing Saradjian's work. Most recently, Vandiver and

Kercher (2004) have used a significantly larger sample (N = 471) and identified six categories of female sexual offenders. Interestingly, although they hypothesise that one of their female abuser groups abusing primarily female victims may have been acting with a male accomplice, they did not identify a specific category of women coerced into abuse by males. However, they note that they did not have sufficient information to draw firm conclusions about this or their other groups and their sample was not restricted to offenders against children. As their work is still in its early stages, it will not be discussed in detail. However, Table 6.1 outlines their six categories and illustrates where they might overlap with other typologies.

Based on their responses to questionnaires, Saradjian (1996) was able to suggest some broad motivating factors among the women in her different offender groups.

**Table 6.1** The six categories of female sexual offenders identified by Vandiver and Kercher (2004) including possible motives for offending as identified by the authors

| Female offender category | Possible motivations for offending |
|---|---|
| Heterosexual nurturer (N = 146) *Male victims only with average age of 12* | Generally likely to perceive relationship with victim as nonabusive *Similar to "teacher/lover" and "women who abuse adolescents" categories?* |
| Noncriminal homosexual offenders (N = 114) *Primarily female victims with average age of 13* | Insufficient information available to be certain but query whether these women were acting with a male accomplice |
| Female sexual predators (N = 112) *High number of offences; 60 % of victims male with average age of 11* | Has similar characteristics to other female criminals so sex offending may be part of her criminal disposition |
| Young adult child exploiters (N = 50) *Victims young with average age of 7; half the victims related to the offender* | May include mothers abusing their own children but more information needed *Similar to "women who abuse young children" category?* |
| Homosexual criminals (N = 22) *Mostly female victims, average age of 11. High proportion of "forcing behaviour" such as compelling prostitution* | For at least some, motivation appears related more to economics than other reasons |
| Aggressive homosexual offenders (N = 17) *Assaulted adult victims, primarily female* | No motivations suggested |

Adapted from Vandiver and Kercher (2004). Offender and victim characteristics of registered female sex offenders in Texas: a proposed typology of female sexual offenders. *Sexual Abuse: A Journal of Research and Treatment, 16*(2), 121–137.

## I   Women who Initially Abuse Young Children

When women initially abuse young children, Saradjian (1996) suggests that major reasons for the abuse are to obtain physical gratification and increase feelings of power and control. It may also help the women to feel that they have bonded more closely with their child, which perhaps partly accords with the suggestion of Chasnoff et al. (1986) that maternal-neonatal incest is likely to be motivated by loneliness and isolation. Saradjian suggests that in some cases, abuse may be the only way mothers feel they can "connect" with their child. Faller (1987) reported that in single-parent families, the oldest children are often abused to serve as surrogate partners. However, rather than simply using them as surrogates, another interpretation of this finding is possible. It may be that by abusing their first-born child inexperienced mothers are trying to connect with that child. If this is so, however, we need to consider why such a mother may later have other children that she does not abuse. This would suggest that either the mother is not trying to bond with subsequent children or that she has found alternative ways of doing so.

Difficulties in connecting to their children may be linked to these women's own experience of being parented or to their poor understanding of child behaviour. Saradjian (1996) reports that many abusive women had difficulty in appropriately disciplining their child, particularly when the child sought more independence. Many had poor understanding of age-appropriate behaviours and abilities in young children and became angry when the child was not able to respond in the required manner, the expected behaviour being beyond the child's years. This may have some relationship with the offender's own history of abuse, however. Ruscio (2001) reported that sexually abused mothers find it difficult to provide their children with clear structure, behavioural expectations and consistent discipline. In keeping with Saradjian's findings, Ruscio notes that survivors of sexual abuse make fewer age-appropriate demands on their children than nonabused mothers. Therefore, this may be not so much a characteristic of being an offender as being a survivor of sexual abuse and so what then distinguishes survivors who do and do not sexually abuse children is an area in need of further consideration.

Perhaps as a consequence of the difficulties in providing structure and discipline, sexual acts may be used by some women as a means of controlling children or "punishing" them for disobedience. FitzRoy (1998, p. 186) quotes one victim sexually abused by her mother: "As I grew up, it became violent – used as a punitive, disciplinary measure . . . my mother told me that all mothers 'did these things to naughty girls' and if I was to tell, then everyone would know what a wicked child I was."

Through these words, the sexual abuse is portrayed as punishment, but they are also a means of blaming and silencing the victim, transferring responsibility on to her by stating that it happened because of her "misbehaviour".

As an interesting aside, the suggestion of sexual abuse as punishment or discipline is also present in some offences against adults. Aylward, Christopher, Newell and Gordon (2002) describe four cases of sexual assaults by females against adult victims. In two cases, the offences appeared to be sexually motivated but the other two cases were described as "punishment" and occurred within the context of nonsexual assaults.

## 2  Women who Abuse Adolescents

Saradjian (1996) suggests that power and control issues may motivate some women who sexually abuse adolescents. However, this group tend to idealise their "relationships" with adolescents and see the victims as providing the support as well as the sex that an adult partner should give (Saradjian, 1996) but these relationships differ from those with adults in that the women feel they have the power (Eldridge & Saradjian, 2000). Nonetheless, some women speak of the abuse in terms that suggest it is an attempt to meet their emotional needs. One offender described her abuse of a 13-year-old boy in the following way: "I'd never met another man I could talk to the way I could talk to him . . . I was never lonely when he was around, we'd share everything together, we were so close . . . he'd look after me if I was feeling low . . . he'd do the shopping, help me out with the kids" (Saradjian, 1996, p. 92).

This woman seems to value the victim for his ability to raise her self-esteem and listen to her problems. She views the "relationship" as not based on sexual desire but on support, affection and closeness. Many sexually abusive women have previously had poor or nonexistent relationships with husbands, families or peers and so, in some cases, the abusive relationship may meet needs for personal relationships and social support that are not being met elsewhere.

This grouping is similar to Matthews et al.'s (1991) category of the "teacher/lover" offender, who they describe as a woman who falls in love with an adolescent (usually male), viewing him as an equal and believing that he wants the sexual contact. Such offenders, they suggest, could therefore be motivated by the desire for a loving relationship.

## 3  Women Initially Coerced into Abuse by Men

Saradjian (1996) suggests that the initial motivation for this group of offenders was connected to the motivations of their male partners, and may have been a way of preventing their partner behaving aggressively towards them by going along with his wishes, or a means of alleviating fears that their partner would otherwise leave. While Saradjian notes that this remains the motivation for some women in this group she suggests that others gradually begin to associate the sexual abuse with feelings of power and control, which counter-balance feelings of being powerless and lacking control in most other aspects of their lives. This may then either exist alongside the male's motivations, or perhaps supersede them in the case of women who go on to abuse alone.

Matthews et al.'s (1991) male-coerced typology similarly comprises women who were brought into the abuse by a male. Lacking power and control were important issues for this group, who were typically very passive, fearful of being alone and remained in abusive relationships owing to a belief that no one else would have them (Matthews, 1998). Their motivations are therefore likely to be tied into their fear and a desire not to antagonise their male partners (Matthews et al., 1991).

What is striking is how the theme of power pervades all these typologies and so perhaps for many women, sexual abuse of children somehow satisfies their needs for power and control. Liem, O'Toole and James (1992) reported that women abused as children have greater needs for power than nonabused women, and this finding could clearly be relevant to the abusive women who were themselves victims of abuse. In addition to their individual past experiences, Eldridge and Saradjian (2000) suggested that women abusers' feelings of powerlessness could be exacerbated by the stereotypical role of women in society. The abusive women in Saradjian's (1996) sample rated themselves as powerless and lacking any real control over their lives. Abusing others, then, may give women a perceived element of control in their lives and domination of a child may give immense feelings of power. When answering a questionnaire about what sex meant to them, almost all the abusers in Saradjian's sample stated that sex with children gave them at least some feelings of power and control, a somewhat different response to their reports of sex with adults. As one offender said, "it felt so good to be able to do something sexually I actually chose to do, to have my sexual needs met as I wanted them to be" (Saradjian, 1996, p. 139).

However, Liem et al. (1992) also found that abused women sometimes feared power and so children could be preferred targets for this reason. Perhaps to such women, power over a child is less threatening than power over an adult. However, this does not explain why some abused women seek power by abusing others whereas other survivors adopt nonabusive methods for meeting their need for power (Liem et al., 1992). Nor does it fully explain why women use sex as a means of gaining power in preference to physical abuse, for example.

Matthews et al.'s (1991) final typology, the predisposed offender, may apply to many of the women across Saradjian's (1996) categories, as she reports many of the women in her sample to have been abused as children. Predisposed offenders, Matthews et al. report, tend to describe lengthy histories of childhood sexual abuse and later relationships in which they may also have been used sexually. Such women, then, may be motivated by the anger and distress of being abused throughout their lives. Certainly, some of the women in Saradjian's sample said that offending gave them a way to hurt someone and feel that they had "got their own back". Many of these women had suffered terrible physical and sexual trauma and by abusing another may have felt that they could "avenge" their own abuse. One offender said of her victims, "I want to ruin his or her childhood as mine was ruined" (Saradjian, 1996, p. 129). Another abuser reported by Eldridge and Saradjian (2000) fantasised about inflicting damage to the genitals of men who had abused her during her childhood while she sexually abused her eldest son.

It is also possible that sadistic motivations exist in certain types of abuse. For women involved in ritualistic abuse, Saradjian (1996) reported that anger, tension or the desire to hurt others were primary motivating factors. Furthermore, all admitted to having sexual fantasies that involved inflicting pain on adults or, more usually, children. While ritual abuse is exceptional, some sadistic feelings could be present in women who are not involved in such abuse, such as those who punish children sexually and Matthews (1998) notes that predisposed offenders may experience deviant sexual fantasies when they feel angry, hurt or lonely, which could play a role in their offending.

While Matthews (1998) contends that she has consistently seen female offenders falling into one of the three types reported by Matthews et al. (1991), other research suggests that current typologies do not "fit" all female abusers. Saradjian (1996) reported some "atypical" perpetrators in her sample, including women who abused as equal co-perpetrators, one woman who coerced a man, women who abused while psychotic or in a dissociative state and women who breached sexual boundaries but did not apparently intend to sexually abuse children. The Correctional Service of Canada (1995) suggested that a category of "angry-impulsive" should be added to Matthews et al.'s (1991) typologies, to accommodate the female offender in their sample who acted alone and appeared to be motivated by feelings of anger. Nathan and Ward (2002) reported that only a minority of female abusers with male co-offenders were actually coerced by them and suggested extending the "angry-impulsive" classification to include women with co-offenders who were motivated by anger, jealousy or feelings of revenge. Vandiver and Kercher's (2004) work identifies further categories of offender not described in other research, which may reflect their larger sample size, the particular composition of the sample (offences against adults were also included) or the fact that development and refinement of extant offender typologies will be required to accommodate our growing knowledge of female abusers.

This need to develop additional categories to encompass the specific motivations of small numbers of offenders emphasises the importance of recognising that whatever a general motivating factor might be for a particular offender type, each woman will have her own personal motivations, which may be quite specific and unique. Eldridge and Saradjian (2000) stress the importance of examining the particular needs that sexual abuse meets for each abuser. As they state, "unmet needs are associated with aversive emotional states to which the woman may have responded by sexually abusing" (Eldridge & Saradjian, 2000, p. 403). Therefore, these individual needs must be identified and worked upon if meaningful intervention is to occur.

## DISMISSING THE IDEA THAT ABUSE BY WOMEN IS JUST "MOTHERLY LOVE"

Linked with the previous discussion that sexually abusive behaviour might be a means by which some women attempt to connect with their child, sexually abusive behaviour by women has often been explained away as "inappropriate affection" (Saradjian, 1996). The belief that abuse is just an expression of motherly love or affection that is either inappropriate or has been misinterpreted by others may be expressed by both offenders and nonoffenders. It need not be restricted to women who abuse their own children but could also be applied to other abusive women, who may be viewed as being loving and affectionate to children, in accordance with the female role. In the case of offenders, this distorted belief justifies their behaviour, preventing them from facing the harm they are doing to the victim. Mathews, Matthews and Speltz (1990) reported that a quarter of the women in their sample (4/16) saw their abusive behaviour as expressions of love, in 3 cases as love for the victim and in 1 as love for her husband. Nathan and Ward (2002) also reported that a quarter of their sample (3/12) cited affection as a motivating factor for their offending. Some female abusers may capitalise on this belief in their offending, telling victims that by abusing them they are demonstrating how much they love them. Elliott (1993b) reports one male survivor abused by his aunt. The aunt performed fellatio on the victim to "show him how much she loved him": "She said that now she had proved how much she loved me, I had to show her how much I loved her ... after this, she would often get me to show her how much I loved her" (Elliott, 1993b, p. 171).

This may make victims uncertain about whether they have been abused and, as Eldridge (1993) points out, if victims do not recognise their experiences as abuse their sense of normality may have been abused – they no longer know what is acceptable behaviour and what is not. A further possible consequence, Briggs and Hawkins (1996) suggest, is that, in males at least, those who normalise their experience of sexual abuse may be more likely to go on to abuse others. Whether this is also true for female victims and whether this depends on the gender of the perpetrator may warrant further investigation.

The idea that abuse is just "love or affection" could be used by those who hear disclosures of abuse but do not want to believe them, perhaps particularly likely when a woman is the abuser. Another survivor states, "when I tried to tell them why I was so unhappy all I ever got in reply was, 'but she is your mummy dear, of course she wants a cuddle'. They could not, or would not understand" (Elliott, 1993b, p. 129).

However, the idea that abuse is an inappropriate expression of love and one that has been misinterpreted by others does not stand up to scrutiny. As already discussed, some female abusers describe wanting to hurt children or use sexual abuse as a means of controlling or punishing victims. Mathews et al. (1990) reported that 7 of the 16 offenders in their sample stated feelings of anger, revenge, power, jealousy and rejection towards people other than their victims to be their reasons for abusing. Thus these women may be expressing their negative feelings using their victims as the targets; the authors report that the majority of the women viewed their own or other children as safe targets for these displaced feelings. This tendency may also be present in nonabusing women, however. When Saradjian (1996) asked the women in her sample who they would be most likely to direct aggression, anger and frustration towards, the majority (including nonoffending women) named the recipient as a child.

Far from being an expression of affection, some women, particularly those involved in ritualistic abuse, reported sexual arousal to pain and suffering in their victims (Saradjian, 1996). She also found that female abusers in her sample generally had negative views about the children they abused. Both women who initially targeted very young children and those who were co-erced by men rated their victims negatively and said that they were very different from their ideal child. Some of the women also believed that certain behaviours in the child were personal attacks against them. One woman who abused her son from soon after birth said, "I hated him . . . he'd do anything to get at me . . . always crying, crying, crying . . . I'd tell him to 'shut up' and he wouldn't . . . he does it to wind me up" (Saradjian, 1996, p. 107). This is simi-lar to findings by Newberger and White (1989) (cited in Buchanan, 1996) that parents who mistreated their children were more likely to attribute the child's behaviour negatively. For example, they would attribute difficult behaviour to "badness" in the child rather than a consequence perhaps of tiredness. In such cases, then, rather than an expression of "motherly love", the abuse seems either to express the mother's dislike and disapproval of the child or other negative emotions which are vented on a "safe" target – a child.

The abuse of adolescents may involve the female abuser expressing her love for the victim and romanticising the abuse as a "love affair" (Saradjian, 1996). However, this is not an expression of motherly love. Women who abuse adolescents describe their "relationship" with the victim in terms of an adult partnership. The abuser views the victim not as a child but as an adult and claims to love the victim in an adult, not parental way.

A mother showing love for her child would be expected to have empathy to-wards that child. Such empathy is lacking in some female abusers (Saradjian, 1996). Even in women who were initially coerced into abusing by men, em-pathy for the victim diminished as the abusive episodes continued. These women seemed either not to understand or not to care about the distress and suffering they caused. This is not the image of a woman expressing love for a child. Women may demonstrate affection in different ways but it is hard to imagine that this would be done by hurting a child both physically and emotionally.

Perhaps such beliefs reflect our psychological processes. Hetherton (1999) describes how sexual abuse by a woman falls outside the range of behaviours predicted by our schema of women. As abusive behaviour does not fit with our expectations of female behaviour it produces psychological discomfort which we attempt to reduce by "reframing" the behaviour whenever possible. Similar processes may exist in the offenders themselves who attempt to justify and minimise their behaviour, thereby overcoming any guilt they feel or inhibitions they have. This discussion, however, indicates that the suggestion of abuse being love and affection that has been misinterpreted by others is simply an excuse for female offenders to deny responsibility and minimise the harm they have caused and a means for society to pretend that women do not sexually abuse children.

## SUMMARY OF MAIN POINTS

- Work has begun to develop typologies of female abusers, based on their characteristics and offence patterns. General sets of motivating factors have also been identified among the different offender types. However, this work is in the early stages, has typically been conducted with small samples and has found that not all female offenders fit neatly into these typologies.
- Themes of power and control appear frequently in some of the typologies.
- However, each offender will have her own specific motives, which may differ according to the situation, or even the particular victim being abused. Focusing on the specific needs that abuse serves for each woman is important and should be addressed in treatment.
- Offenders may tell their victims that the abuse is an expression of their love. This is likely to confuse or silence victims and perhaps make them feel responsible for the abuse.
- There is no evidence to suggest that sexual abuse by women is an expression of love or affection that has been misinterpreted by others as abusive behaviour.

# III

# The Consequences of Sexual Abuse by Women

# 7

# IS SEXUAL ABUSE BY WOMEN HARMFUL?

McConaghy (1998) believes there has been a general reversal in thought from viewing child sexual abuse as not particularly serious to viewing it as universally and inevitably harmful. He states: "workers whose research findings conflicted with this belief [that child sexual abuse is always harmful] have been labelled sceptics and risked being considered not opposed to, or even covert supporters of, sexual activity of children with older subjects" (McConaghy, 1998, p. 254). Given this, and the fact that the sexually abusive acts that women perpetrate are often similar to those of male offenders (as discussed in Chapter 3), there seems little reason to suggest that women have less potential to inflict severe and long-lasting harm.

Nonetheless, some of the earlier literature, at least, suggests that if women do abuse children, the abuse they perpetrate is less serious and harmful or, in the case of male victims, that the sexual contact may even be beneficial (Mars, 1998). The words of Mathis (1972) typify this: "that she might seduce a helpless child into sexplay is unthinkable, and even if she did so, what harm can be done without a penis?" (cited in Allen, 1991 p. 12). Gelinas (1983) suggested that abuse by women usually consists of overstimulating physical games or prolonged physical care, this language implying that female abuse is less serious and less abusive. Even in 1998, Robertiello reported that there was comparatively little information about "the results of seduction of boys by their mothers or older sisters" (Robertiello, 1998, p. 235), the word "seduction" perhaps detracting from the potentially abusive nature of these interactions. Finkelhor (1984) found that the general population also perceived abuse by a woman to be the least abusive of a range of scenarios.

Some researchers have reported that sexual relations between women and children produce less harmful outcomes for victims. Finkelhor, Williams and Burns (1988) reported that when the perpetrator was a woman victims had fewer sequelae. However, they did not state that victims of female abusers had no symptoms. In terms of responses to abuse by women, some research has suggested that not all victims perceive their abuse negatively, perhaps reducing the likelihood that such experiences would produce harmful effects. Condy, Templer, Brown and Veaco (1987), for example, found many boys to report good feelings about sex with an older woman, although the feelings tended to be positive if the female was a friend but negative if she was a relative. Fromuth and Burkhart (1989) reported that in their sample of college males abused as children, the majority of abusers were woman. Sixty per cent of the subjects reported interest or pleasure at the time of the abuse and only 12 % reported negative feelings such as shock or fear. However, there are no details of the type of abuse they experienced. These authors note that despite their generally positive perceptions of the abuse, one of their two samples was slightly less well psychologically adjusted than the nonabused sample, which, they suggest, could indicate that these experiences affected later psychological functioning. They conclude, however, that the majority of the sexually abused men did not experience any demonstrable serious long-term effects. However, these studies refer generally to young boys being abused by older women. In keeping with stereotypes surrounding such scenarios, victims may have felt compelled to report enjoying the abuse, or at least indifference to it, whether that was the case or not.

The difficulty in carrying out and interpreting studies such as these is in operationalising the term "harm". Should the focus be on observable, measurable harm such as physical damage or the presence of psychiatric disorders, or should researchers try to record harm such as relationship problems or low self-esteem? Furthermore, if harmful effects are found, can we be sure they result from the earlier sexual abuse? This chapter considers a broad range of types of harm, but the difficulties in defining and measuring this should be remembered throughout.

## WHAT ASPECTS OF FEMALE SEXUAL ABUSE MIGHT CAUSE HARM TO VICTIMS?

Several authors have described the heightened presence of psychiatric disorder in adults sexually abused as children (e.g. Browne & Finkelhor, 1986; Mullen, Martin, Anderson, Romans & Herbison, 1993). While a number of these studies asked clinical samples about sexually abusive experiences in childhood, some studied non-clinical samples (e.g. Burnam, Stein, Golding, Siegel, Sorenson et al., 1988) and also reported poorer psychological adjustment in survivors. These studies referred primarily to abuse by males but there is little reason to suppose that abuse by females could not produce similar consequences. More work needs to examine the consequences for survivors of abuse and whether there are differences depending on perpetrator gender, victim gender and the perpetrator–victim relationship.

Some studies have attempted to identify aspects of the abusive experience that are most likely to produce harm. The results are sometimes contradictory and by no means conclusive but some factors identified as producing the most negative effects are equally applicable to male and female offenders. Chandler (1982) (cited in Kendall-Tackett & Simon, 1987) found that the closer the relationship between victim and perpetrator, the more severe the molestation seemed to the victim. Although not referring specifically to female abusers, this finding may be particularly relevant given that women may be most likely to abuse a known victim and often one who is related to them (see Chapter 3). Briere (1988) found that "bizarre" abuse (incorporating ritual abuse, penetration with foreign objects or sex with animals), multiple perpetrators and abuse involving intercourse were likely to lead to psychological problems for survivors. Bizarre abuse was particularly likely to produce negative effects. As discussed in previous chapters, abuse by women may be more likely to use foreign objects, involve multiple perpetrators & possibly also be more likely to involve intercourse. Browne and Finkelhor (1986) describe further factors that might produce more negative effects in victims. Of most relevance to abuse by females are their suggestions that harm is more likely when the abuse is committed by a closely related person, involves penetration and when there is an unsupportive reaction to disclosure. This last factor is a possibility if the abuser is a woman, as will be discussed later in this chapter. Children may be particularly traumatised if they are forced to abuse each other (Browne & Finkelhor, 1986) and, as described previously, women may be more likely to engage in this type of abuse.

Other difficulties may occur for survivors of female abuse. Condy et al. (1987) reported that if a boy was forced into sexual activity by a woman then not only could his feeling at the time of the abuse be unfavourable but so too could its effect on his adult sex life. Sarrel and Masters (1982) reported that despite feelings of fear and panic, men sexually abused by women had had erections and half had ejaculated. This may have confused and distressed the victim who might believe that however afraid he was, at some level he must have enjoyed the abuse. These authors also reported that sexual molestation by females produced extensive sexual dysfunction in victims although this may be an artefact of all the men in their sample being drawn from programmes offering help for sexual difficulties. Krug (1989) found that all his male victims of abuse by mothers had later relationship problems, 88 % reported depression and almost two-thirds had drug problems although these cases were drawn from males presenting for psychotherapy. Coxell, King, Mezey and Gordon (1999) reported that nonconsensual sexual experience in childhood was a significant predictor in men for further nonconsensual sexual experience in adulthood. This was not specific to experiences with females but it would be interesting to examine any differences according to the gender of the perpetrator. Furthermore, these studies have only considered male victims. Whether similar findings exist for female victims of female abuse requires further study.

## VICTIM REPORTS OF HARM CAUSED

Toon[1] argued that female and male abusers cause similar harm to their victims. In an analysis of male victims' accounts of their abuse, Lisak (1994) found little difference in the emerging themes irrespective of perpetrator gender. However, themes of shame or humiliation occurred more frequently in accounts of abuse by women while abuse by men was more likely to produce concerns about homosexuality. Johnson and Shrier (1987) reported that victims tended to describe the abuse as traumatic whether the abuser was male or female. Even before differentiating between perpetrator gender, over two-thirds of victims stated the immediate impact of abuse to be strong or devastating. This was slightly greater for those abused by women (73 % rated the impact as strong/devastating) compared with those abused by males (64 % rated the impact as strong/devastating) but was not statistically significant. Almost all male and female participants in Denov's (2004b) sample reported their sexual abuse by women to be highly damaging and difficult to recover from and only one male reported that his abuse by a female perpetrator did not damage him. Furthermore, of those who had been abused by both male and female perpetrators, all felt that the abuse by a woman was more harmful and damaging.

However, the impact of sexual abuse may depend less on the actual event and more upon how it is perceived and appraised by the victim (Woodward & Joseph, 2003). As Margolin (1987, p. 113) states, "it is these symbolic meanings, not the sex act itself, which are seen as producing the response to incest". Some of the men in Kelly, Wood, Gonzalez, MacDonald and Waterman's (2002) sample reported feeling "especially deviant" as they had experienced pleasurable feelings while being abused by their mother. Mars (1998) also reports three male patients who felt extremely gratified by sexual contact with their mothers, the sexual excitement in some cases surpassing that felt in sexual activity with other women. Kelly et al. (2002) suggest that pleasurable feelings during a sexual activity that is "taboo" may lead to guilt, shame and self-recrimination, which then trigger other negative emotions. Thus, initial responses at the time of the abuse do not necessarily predict the later effects on victims, which links with Fromuth and Burkhart's (1989) findings described earlier in this chapter. There may also be individual differences in when symptoms start to appear, with some victims showing little initial symptomatology but demonstrating "sleeper" effects later in life (Noll, 2005).

---

[1] Kay Toon: "Working with victims of women perpetrators". London, May 8, 1997.

## VICTIM GENDER AND HARM CAUSED BY ABUSE: IS THERE A DIFFERENCE?

There is no consensus in the research as to whether males and females are similarly affected by sexual abuse, although Noll (2005) notes that males are still not adequately represented in sexual abuse research. Nelson and Oliver (1998) cite work by Kilpatrick and Himelein (1986) who argued that males have more difficulty integrating their experiences of victimisation because they are inconsistent with their self-perceptions of strength and dominance. This may perhaps be compounded if their abuser is female. However, this does not indicate whether males are likely to experience more distress than female victims.

Watkins and Bentovim (2000) state that one of the myths surrounding sexual abuse of males is that when males are abused they are less psychologically affected than females in both the short term and long term. Other researchers, however, have suggested that perhaps male victims *are* less harmed by their experiences. Kelly et al. (2002) report a meta-analysis by Rind, Tromovitch and Basuerman (1998), which suggested that the positive initial perceptions of sexual abuse experiences often reported by male college students might indicate that most are not negatively affected by sexual abuse as children although, as stated previously, initial perceptions of abuse experiences may not predict later outcomes. Nelson and Oliver (1998) found that in their sample of college students, females were more likely to interpret abuse experiences as coercive and harmful, whereas males were more likely to interpret such experiences, particularly those with women, as consensual and not harmful. However, this work only details the boys' feelings at the time of the abuse and did not record their present feelings. The female abusers of the men in this study were also relatively young themselves and the boys' responses might have been different had the female abusers been significantly older than they were. The studies described here have focused on college samples and so cannot be generalised to other populations. Further work with clinical populations may therefore be important.

However, Denov's (2004b) work suggests a number of similarities in how male and female victims responded to sexual abuse by a woman. All the participants reported feelings of rage as a result of the abuse, all reported strongly mistrusting women and all reported some discomfort or difficulty in sexual relationships. Although not reported by all participants, approximately equal numbers of male and female victims of female abuse reported depression and suicidal ideation throughout their lives and, in a small number of cases, sexually abusing children themselves. Denov found that the majority of female participants abused by women reported difficulties with their sense of identity and self-concept, in many cases trying to deny a female identity from childhood through to adulthood. Issues of self-concept were less prominent in male victims but some reported feelings of humiliation and of being "failures" as men. Many male victims in an earlier study by Dimock (1988) voiced feelings of failure as men; one man stated that, "I think that deep down if I were a real man I should have been able to stop the abuse" (Dimock, 1988, p. 209). Not all these men were abused by women but it may be even more difficult for a male to accept that he could not stop himself being abused by a woman.

It is not clear whether professionals working with victims anticipate different effects according to perpetrator and/or victim gender. Eisenberg, Owens and Dewey (1987) found that while health visitors believed male and female victims would be similarly affected, the medical students in their sample felt that female victims would be more affected. These differences may result from differential experience in dealing with abuse victims; health visitors may have an important role in detecting potential child abuse in high-risk families (Browne, 1989) and therefore may be more experienced in understanding the effects of victimisation than relatively inexperienced medical students. However, Eisenberg et al. also cite work by Pierce and Pierce (1985), which found that male victims were given significantly fewer hours in treatment. Some treatment providers, then, may also believe that abuse is less serious for male victims. It could be argued that these results reflect outdated attitudes, from a time when the abuse of boys was not properly recognised. How much these attitudes have changed remains to be examined. Broussard, Wagner and Kazelskis (1991) reported that undergraduate students were less likely to believe that sexual interactions between a female adult and male child constituted abuse. Furthermore, the students believed that it was more realistic for a male victim to respond encouragingly to a female abuser than a male abuser and also more realistic than female victims responding encouragingly to any perpetrators.

It is important to emphasise that studies such as these are not suggesting that males are never affected by sexual abuse. Duncan and Williams (1998) describe work examining the effects of sexual abuse on males. This has found that, as with sexually abused women, male victims of child sexual abuse are more likely than nonabused males to have negative self-views, low self-esteem and difficulties in developing and maintaining satisfying adult relationships. As the authors state, however, little research has examined the different long-term effects on males of being abused by a male or female. This also seems true for female victims; there is little work specifically examining the effects on girls of being abused by a female compared with a male.

## WHAT MIGHT MEDIATE ANY RELATIONSHIP BETWEEN VICTIM GENDER AND HARM CAUSED BY SEXUAL ABUSE?

A child's age at the time of the abuse may influence its effects. DiGiorgio-Miller (1998) suggests that children perceive sexual abuse differently according to their stage of development. Very young children, she writes, may not know the activity to be wrong but are often confused by it and may begin to incorporate it into their own behavioural repertoire. From ages 6 to 13, children are able to conceptualise the abuse as "wrong" and may develop feelings of guilt, shame, worthlessness or "dirtiness". She suggests that teenagers experience similar feelings but that they may also experience sexual feelings that can lead to further confusion and related symptomatology. This is echoed in work by Friedrich (1988, 1995) (cited in Watkins & Bentovim, 2000), which suggested that young children will only perceive their abuse as abuse if they experience pain whereas an older child can conceptualise abuse in more abstract terms. King et al. (2000) reported that for their male victims of sexual assault, the effects were most devastating when the men were sexually inexperienced before the assault. This does not separate the effects according to perpetrator gender but presumably the majority of child victims are sexually inexperienced and the effects could therefore be compounded.

Nelson and Oliver (1998) reported that for the girls in their study, 88 % aged under 13 at the time felt they were coerced or abused compared with 60 % of the girls aged 14 or 15 at the time. Only 2 boys in the sample who were abused by women were aged below 12 at the time of the abuse; they both stated that the contact with a woman was coercive. All the other boys were aged 12 or more at the time of sexual contact with a woman and all of these said they agreed to the contact or wanted it. King, Coxell and Mezey (2000) found that of the men reporting "consensual" sex before the age of 16 with someone 5 or more years older than them, 90 % of cases involved a female perpetrator and the mean age at which these "consensual" experiences occurred was 14, that is after puberty. A possible implication of these studies, then, is that younger, prepubertal children may be more likely to view sexual abuse as coercive.

Of course, these age effects could themselves be mediated by increasing awareness and absorption of social pressures and stereotypes by older children. Males are socialised to seek out sexual encounters and value sexual contact and so, as Nelson and Oliver (1998, p. 573) state: "The boys could have felt manipulated and abused, but they usually did not. Instead the positive-status enhancement of having 'sex with a woman' seemed to predominate. Even if they had been manipulated, their sense of masculine potency had been enhanced by the encounter." However, such processes make it more difficult for a boy to admit that he did not enjoy sexual contact with an older woman and that he felt coerced or abused.

The victim's own interpretation of the abuse is likely to have an important influence on its long-term effects and this may also be influenced by socialisation processes. Nelson and Oliver (1998, p. 573) state that for female victims the stereotypical passive female identities reinforce a sense of helplessness and victimisation whereas for male victims, "dominant masculine identities seemed to provide most boys with potent self-images to counter the impotence they might have felt in victimisation". Duncan and Williams (1998) reported that there were different effects for male victims of female sexual abuse depending on whether or not their experiences were interpreted as coercive. Males experiencing coerced sexual contact with females reported higher levels of violence in their intimate adult relationships and were more likely to have committed sex offences. In contrast, males who reported no coercion in their sexual contacts with older women showed no such long-term negative effects.

A possible influence on the interpretations a victim makes of the abuse is the way in which that abuse was committed. As Leahy, Pretty and Tenenbaum (2004, p. 523) state, "what may be more salient for sexually abused individuals is their subjective experience of the abuse – not what was done, nor by whom, but rather how it was done". Nelson and Oliver (1998) report interesting findings, suggesting that whether or not victims interpret their abuse experiences as coercive depends partly on the "style" adopted by the perpetrator and whether the adult had "asked" or persuaded the child into sexual activity or "taken", which was done without any pretence of gaining the child's cooperation. In their sample, male perpetrators were more likely than females to "take" (76 % of cases with male perpetrators involved "taking"). Female perpetrators were more likely to "ask", however, persuading or manipulating the child into the sexual activity (women "asked" in 75 % of cases). Thus, women who had sexual contact with boys generally "asked" for their participation and therefore the boys felt as if they had consented to the behaviour. Consequently, the authors suggest, the boys tended to view the experience in a less coercive and more positive light. Leahy et al.'s work, meanwhile, found that the use of emotionally manipulative strategies by the perpetrator (gender not specified) differentiated between survivors with clinical or nonclinical levels of posttraumatic and dissociative symptomatology. Significantly more survivors in the group with clinical levels of distress reported their abusers to use unpredictable emotional reward and punishment strategies and to provide the victim with gifts. This does not quite equate with the "asking" styles described by Nelson and Oliver but suggests that more manipulative or persuasive strategies by the perpetrator can be psychologically damaging.

However, as mentioned previously, the victim's initial interpretation of the abuse may not predict later psychological adjustment. Kelly et al. (2002) reported that, in their sample, men who experienced some initial positive feelings about the abuse reported more aggression, self-destructive behaviour and total symptoms than men who reported exclusively negative feelings. Furthermore, men who did not initially consider their experiences to be abusive reported more aggression, symptoms of PTSD and total symptoms than men who interpreted their experiences as abuse. The authors suggest their findings indicate that males who initially experience positive or mixed feelings about their abuse may be at heightened risk of psychological impairment in adulthood. As they note, however, this work is based on clinical samples and its generalisability is therefore limited. Similar findings may also exist in female victims, although, as some studies have suggested that more males than females report positive perceptions of their abuse (by women at least), this finding may be more immediately relevant to male victims.

## PERPETRATOR/VICTIM GENDER INTERACTION: AN ISSUE OF HOMOSEXUALITY?

Another potential influence on a victim's interpretation of the abuse is whether the perpetrator's gender is the same as their own. Nelson and Oliver (1998) reported that while most male victims reported sexual contact with women to be consensual and offering them a sexual experience, the majority of males abused by males reported the experience to be coercive. The trend is less clear for female victims as three-quarters of the females viewed their heterosexual experiences as coercive. There were only two cases of females abused by females but in both these cases the experiences were unambiguously described as abuse. Work with general population samples has revealed a similar trend for same-sex abuse scenarios to be viewed more seriously than heterosexual ones (Broussard et al., 1991; Maynard & Wiederman, 1997).

Duncan and Williams (1998) describe some possible consequences of homosexual abuse in males. Male victims of abuse by males may fear that they were abused because the perpetrator viewed them as homosexual and also fear that others view them in this way. Perhaps as a consequence of this, the authors suggest that some male victims adopt homophobic attitudes and behaviours and strongly subscribe to stereotypical male gender roles such as behaving dominantly and aggressively in heterosexual relationships. However, this could also be true of men abused by women; Denov (2004b) reported the case of one man abused by a woman who, in an effort to overcome feelings of unmanliness, became "hyper-masculine", playing aggressive sports and becoming involved in crime which, he stated, made him feel more like a man.

It is unclear whether there is a relationship between homosexual molestation in childhood and an adult homosexual sexual orientation. Kelly et al. (2002) report studies suggesting a link between male-on-male child sexual abuse and adult homosexual orientation. Tomeo, Templer, Anderson and Kotler (2001) studied childhood sexual abuse in both heterosexual and homosexual men and women. Their findings indicated that homosexual men and women were more likely to have been molested by a person of the same sex than the heterosexual participants. Forty-six per cent of homosexual men and 22 % of homosexual women reported having been abused by a person of the same gender compared with 7 % of heterosexual men and 1 % of heterosexual women. The authors further reported that 68 % of the homosexual men and 38 % of the homosexual women did not identify themselves as homosexual until after the abuse, which they state suggests that if homosexual molestation can lead to a homosexual orientation for the victims, this is more pronounced in males. However, the extent to which there is a direct causal relationship requires further examination.

## SEXUAL ABUSE BY MOTHERS: A SPECIAL CASE?

Finkelhor (1984) concluded his review of boys as victims of sexual abuse by stating that certain aspects "seem to set off abuse by mothers as quite distinct from abuse by fathers" (Finkelhor, 1984, p. 166). The lack of specific consideration of abuse by mothers in the literature is perhaps surprising given that women are reported primarily to abuse children who are known to them and often their own. Mars (1998) reported that while there are relatively few published cases of mother–child incest, studies have been divided as to whether this is harmful. Robertiello (1998, p. 238) commented that: "Society has laid a great deal of stress on the importance of fathers avoiding any suggestion of seductive behaviour with their daughters...There has not been the same degree of prohibition between mothers and sons." Some of these divergent views about harm caused may have arisen from the types of sexual acts committed by abusive mothers. Mothers may be more able to disguise abusive acts as child care, and Justice and Justice (1979) (cited in Mars, 1998) concluded that mothers are more likely to engage in acts that are less likely to be reported, including, "fondling, sleeping with a son, caressing him in a sexual way, exposing her body to him and keeping him tied to her emotionally with implied promises of sexual payoff" (Mars, 1998, p. 404). More recently, Kelly et al. (2002) similarly stated that mother–son incest was likely to be subtle and difficult to distinguish from routine caregiving practices. However, as Etherington (1997) notes, such statements downplay the physically violent sexual abuse perpetrated by some mothers and may perpetuate the idea that sexual abuse is simply an inappropriate expression of a mother's love.

The statements of survivors abused by their mothers clearly indicate the harm it can cause. Sgroi and Sargent (1993) report that victims describe abuse by a close female relative as the most shameful and damaging abuse they suffered. One survivor stated that the abuse by her mother was worse than that by her father: "There's something about a mother. When you're small, she should be the first person you go to if you're hurt; the first person to cuddle you...So when she's the one who abuses you, it leads to an even greater sense of despair than when your father abuses you" (Elliott, 1993b, p. 138).

Kelly et al. (2002) reported that despite the "less intrusive" nature of the sexual acts committed, men who had been abused by their mothers had more self-reported difficulties than men abused by other perpetrators. In therapy, "these men often expressed rage, shame and profound sadness that they were abused by the person who was supposed to teach them how to love, trust and feel safe in the world" (Kelly et al., 2002, p. 435). The primary theme emerging from these accounts, then, is one of betrayal in the maternal relationship.

Saradjian (1997) describes a cluster of symptoms that occur when the mother is the abuser, such as difficulties with sexuality and sexualising relationships, associating caregiving with sex, feelings of distrust and powerlessness and aggression towards the self or others. She further suggests that victims may become highly enmeshed with the mother and have difficulty in forming a separate identity. Ogilvie and Daniluk (1995) suggest that the consequences of sexual abuse by mothers include feelings of profound shame, stigmatisation and isolation, a strong sense of betrayal and victim self-blame. In her sample of male victims of maternal abuse, Etherington (1997) notes that a further type of abuse that is often not mentioned occurs when the mother humiliates her child sexually, either by rejecting, mocking or otherwise emasculating him. This, she states, can be particularly damaging to the adult male's self-esteem and relationships with women. However, these feelings may also be experienced by victims abused by other perpetrators.

There is insufficient research to compare the effects of maternal incest on sons and daughters. However, Ogilvie and Daniluk (1995) suggest two possible consequences that may be more specific to daughters abused by their mothers. The first relates to the development of one's own identity. These authors state that the mother–daughter relationship provides the context for the daughter's identity formation and disruptions in this relationship can leave daughters confused about their own identities, struggling to distance themselves from their mothers while also needing to connect with them to define their own identities. One survivor summarised this difficulty: "I still struggle with being as far away from my mother as possible identity-wise. I wanted to be as different as I could from my mother. I used to dress in men's clothes just so that I could be as different as I could from her" Ogilvie and Daniluk (1995, p. 600).

Denov (2004b) found that female victims of sexual abuse by women also struggled with their female identity, although this was not specific to abusing mothers. Saradjian (1997) also suggests that male victims of maternal abuse may have difficulty forming a separate identity. She describes one male victim who stated that he was not sure whether he was male or female, and another who said, "I constantly feel as if her body is engulfing mine. I never feel free of her, I have never felt free of her" (Saradjian, 1997, p. 8).

A second area that may have particular relevance for daughters abused by their mothers is the subsequent impact on their own ability to be mothers (Ogilvie & Daniluk, 1995). Survivors in their study expressed concern that they did not know how to mother and fears that they would become abusers themselves. As one survivor stated, "I have absolutely no concept of what the correct way to raise children is" (Ogilvie & Daniluk, 1995, p 600). The authors are not denying similar effects in male victims; there may indeed be impacts on the male victim's sense of identity and concerns about later parenting. However there may be qualitative differences in female victims; women sexually abused by their own mothers may have particular difficulties in dealing with societal expectations of women to be caregivers given that their own female carers were abusive.

Further work is needed to examine differential effects of maternal abuse on sons and daughters. A "homosexuality taboo", for example, may operate in mother–daughter abuse, which could impact on long-term effects. The other question requiring consideration is whether abuse by mothers differs from abuse by other women, particularly in its long term consequences and the treatment needs of its victims. Perhaps the most striking feature of this brief discussion has been the sense of betrayal that maternal sexual abuse produces.

## THE FEMALE ABUSER'S POTENTIAL FOR VIOLENCE AND PHYSICAL HARM

Toon[2] has suggested that women are less violent than men and less likely to inflict actual physical damage on their victims. Matthews (1998) stated that women offenders use force and violence far less often than men, threaten their victims less and if force is used it is of a lesser degree than males. Scavo (1989) reports that terms such as "threatening" or "forceful" are not generally accepted descriptions of feminine traits and this may lead to assumptions that women are less violent. Findings that females are less violent or cause less physical injury may also be influenced by the fact that survivors often fail to disclose abuse by a woman until much later. By the time they disclose and/or find someone who will believe them, all except the most severe and irreparable physical damage will often have healed. If victims of male abusers disclose earlier, more physical damage may be evident.

However, there are reports of women inflicting severe and long-lasting physical harm on victims. One survivor was told that she was unlikely to be able to have children owing to the severe internal damage sustained from sadistic abuse by her mother (Elliott, 1993b). Wolfers (1993) reported that 7 of the 10 female abusers in her sample used very high levels of violence, including kicking, beating and burning. Lewis and Stanley (2000) reported that a quarter of sexual assaults by females involved the use of weapons and victims were threatened with death in 3 cases, although as their small sample consisted of women sent for evaluation of competence to stand trial, this may not be representative of female abusers more generally. The Correctional Service of Canada (1995) reported that in 7 of the 10 cases in which information was available, female abusers used violence during their offences. However, the

---

[2] See note 1.

definition of violence is important; within these 7 cases, the violence ranged from "handling the victim roughly" to beating and actually killing a victim. The authors suggest violence is a common feature in their imprisoned sex offenders but the extent to which this can be generalised is questionable. Offences by women involving violence may be more likely to be reported and result in conviction than those without violence, thus inflating the level of violence amongst incarcerated samples. However, as McConaghy (1998) notes, there is considerable variation in reports of the use of force in sexual abuse of children generally, ranging from 0 % to 58 %. The studies from which these figures are drawn are likely to contain more male than female abusers and if this degree of variation is reported for male abusers it should be no surprise that there are similarly varying reports of force and violence in female offenders.

Physical harm may occur to victims if they offer resistance and the abuser uses force to gain compliance. Females are generally less physically imposing than men and, at least initially, victims could be less fearful of a female. For this reason some women might have to be equally or more forceful than men in order to commit their abusive acts. Kaufman, Wallace, Johnson and Reeder (1995) reported no difference between male and female abusers in their use of force to make children either watch or have sex. Only one perpetrator used a weapon to force a child into sexual activity and this was a woman. The Correctional Service of Canada (1995) reported one female who hit her daughter or took things away from her if she resisted the sexual assaults perpetrated by a male co-offender. In some cases, however, physical violence may be an inappropriate strategy. When women target adolescent boys, for example, the victim may be as strong as, if not stronger than, the abuser. This may link with Nelson and Oliver's (1998) report that most female abusers of boys "asked" for the child's participation, rather than just "taking" it. As most boys in their sample were aged 12 or more they may have been at an age when sheer physical force by the abuser would begin to be ineffective. Women targeting adolescents may also "romanticise" the abuse (Saradjian, 1996) and violence may therefore be incongruous. Manipulation or persuasion tactics may be more relevant for victims in this age group and this has similarities with female sexual coercion of adult males, as discussed in Chapter 5. Johnson and Shrier (1987) reported that female abusers relied on persuasion rather than physical force or threats although the content of this "persuasion" is not known and may have contained implicit threats. Whether such tactics are also adopted in female abuse of postpubescent girls is not known.

Violence may also be inappropriate in extrafamilial abuse by females, such as in the case of abusive teachers. Abusers must ensure they do not alert parents or others by obvious physical damage to the child, such as bruising. Children might also be more willing to disclose that a teacher hit them than that a teacher touched them sexually. In such instances, threats or other manipulative techniques may be more appropriate. Some reports of day care abuse suggest threats and verbal coercion to be particularly severe. Finkelhor et al. (1988), for example, reported that in day care abuse, perpetrators threatened harm to the child in 41 % of cases, harm to the child's family in 22 % of cases and threatened to kill a child's pet in 12 %. Kelley, Brant and Waterman (1993) added that threats in these cases were most likely to involve harm to the victim or their family. Faller (1990) notes that in addition to death threats against the victim or their family, a further frequent threat was to implicate the victim. The threats used in these cases often seem to go beyond what is necessary to ensure silence or compliance and may be made to inflict terror. Although these studies do not refer specifically to female abusers, as women are likely to be employed in child care, it seems acceptable to assume that some women would have made these threats. Such threats or manipulations are potentially more psychologically damaging. If a victim is forced into sexual activity, it may be easier to remove self-blame or feelings of responsibility. However, if victims are manipulated they may feel that they complied with the abuser and are therefore to blame. Such beliefs make it more difficult for victims to maintain a sense that they were treated badly and may lead them to believe that somehow they "deserved" the abuse (Cawson, Wattam, Brooker & Kelly, 2000).

In direct contrast, Krug (1989) reported no women using threats or bribery. However, these abusers were mothers and, given their position over their children, threats may have been unnecessary. As Ong (1985) stated, "although women may feel powerless outside the home, the structural powerlessness of women as mothers in the public sphere, turns into one of total power as a mother in the private sphere" (cited in Wolfers, 1993, p. 100). It would be interesting for researchers to investigate the tactics employed by women abusing within their family and whether these differ from women abusing extrafamilially.

## SEXUAL ABUSE BY WOMEN AND ITS ASSOCIATION WITH OTHER FORMS OF CHILD MALTREATMENT

As stated in the opening chapter of this book, there has been a contrast between our readiness to accept that women physically or emotionally abuse children and our unwillingness to acknowledge that they may also sexually abuse children. This may have further helped to disguise sexual abuse by women. In some cases, a woman prosecuted for physical abuse or neglect of a child could also have abused the child sexually, but this could have been ignored, perhaps because physical injury is more easily noticed or more easily disclosed by the victim. This is speculation only but may be an interesting avenue for further research.

By its very nature, sexual abuse could be said to be both physically and emotionally abusive. While the extent to which children are subjected to more than one type of abuse has not been studied in depth (Higgins & McCabe, 2001), some researchers have recorded other abusive behaviour by females, alongside the sexual abuse. This is perhaps not surprising, given that, as stated in Chapter 4, many factors associated with higher rates of child maltreatment have also been described in sexually abusive women. Finkelhor (1984) reported that over half of his cases of sexual abuse by mothers were combined with physical abuse. In Etherington's (1997) sample, 4 of the 7 men sexually abused by their mothers were also severely physically abused and one reported emotional abuse. Tardif, Auclair, Jacob and Carpentier (2005) reported that 31 % of sexually abusive women in their sample had also physically abused their victims, although such violence appeared more frequent in women who abused younger victims. Faller (1987) similarly reported that one-third of her sexually abusive women had also physically abused children, although physical neglect was more common, with over half the female perpetrators inflicting this type of maltreatment. Reporting on a larger sample, Faller (1995) again reported neglect to be the most common type of additional maltreatment committed by sexually abusive women. Emotional abuse as a separate category appeared relatively infrequently in these studies but this is at least partly likely to reflect the difficulty in separating the emotionally abusive aspects of sexual or physical abuse from other types of emotional maltreatment and of defining the particular behaviours constituting emotional abuse (Cawson, Wattam, Brooker & Kelly, 2000).

Some researchers have suggested that the emotionally abusive aspects of maltreatment have the most serious and far-reaching consequences for victims. Cawson et al. (2000) document several authors who suggest that the emotional trauma of any abuse is more lasting and harmful than actual physical injury. Evidence for the particularly damaging effects from the emotional aspects of maltreatment is provided by Hart, Binggeli and Brassard's (1998) literature review. They suggest that emotional maltreatment is associated with all types of child abuse and neglect and that when different types of abuse are separated out, emotional abuse is "equally or more strongly associated with negative effects, suggesting the possibility that it is the major underlying contributor to effects" (Hart et al., 1998, p. 48). They suggest that many negative developmental consequences arise from emotional maltreatment, including low self-esteem, negative life views, anxiety, depression, emotional instability and disruption to social functioning and emotional regulation, all of which can influence many aspects of an individual's life.

Cawson et al. (2000) studied emotional abuse in young adults by asking questions encompassing a number of dimensions of emotional maltreatment. These dimensions are shown in Table 7.1. Although only brief consideration can be made here, many of these dimensions seem applicable to sexual abuse, particularly in terms of power, control and the distortion of relationships, either with the abuser or others around the victim. These issues may be particularly significant when the abuser is female as many victims, like society

**Table 7.1**   Dimensions of emotional abuse (Cawson, Wattam, Brooker & Kelly, 2002)

| Dimension | Examples |
|---|---|
| Psychological control and domination | Attempting to control child's thinking. Isolating child from other sources of support and development |
| Psychological/physical control and domination | Physical acts that exert control/domination but cause distress rather than physical pain or injury |
| Humiliation/degradation | Verbal or non-verbal attacks on child's worth or self-esteem |
| Withdrawal | Withholding affection and care. Exclusion from family or from benefits given to other family members |
| Antipathy | Showing marked dislike of child, through words or actions |
| Terrorising | Threatening or frightening the child |
| Proxy attacks | Harming something or someone loved and valued by the child |
| Corrupting a child | Showing children pornography or using them to produce it |

Adapted from Cawson, P., Wattam, C., Brooker, S. & Kelly, G. (2000). *Child Maltreatment In The United Kingdom: A Study Of The Prevalence Of Child Abuse And Neglect.* London: NSPCC.

as a whole, will have internalised beliefs about women as caring and nurturing, rather than dominating and abusive, and yet their experiences will invalidate these beliefs. This may be particularly devastating in the context of a mother-child relationship (as shown in the feelings of betrayal noted earlier in this chapter), and may lead victims to believe that some negative aspect of themselves led to their abuse and view themselves as unloveable, bad, weak or blameworthy. These effects may be far longer-lasting than the physical discomfort or damage.

Research considering the overlap between sexual abuse and other types of maltreatment has largely focused on sexually abusive mothers, which may have skewed the findings. Nonetheless, Grayston and De Luca (1999) suggest that other types of child maltreatment may be most likely to accompany sexual abuse when the abuser has a major caregiving role. This is supported by Faller's (1987) work, which found that 9 of the 11 sexually abusive women who had not inflicted other types of maltreatment on their victims had no caretaking responsibilities for them. This also makes intuitive sense in light of the earlier discussion about female violence, which stated that physical aggression may be a less effective strategy in an extrafamilial setting.

The extent to which this association relates to the abusive mother's own history is uncertain. Morrel, Dubowitz, Kerr and Black (2003) summarise a number of studies that found that mothers with histories of childhood victimisation report greater parenting problems. Specifically, mothers who were physically abused as children demonstrated increased hostile-intrusive behaviour towards their children, whereas mothers with sexual abuse histories reported less knowledge of parenting skills and greater use of physical conflict strategies with their children. Hall, Sachs and Rayens (1998) reported that experiencing either sexual or physical abuse in childhood predicted a high potential for physically abusing children, although sexual abuse was the stronger predictor. Coohey (2004) found that mothers who physically abused their children were more likely to have been abused by their own mothers and to report difficult relationships with their mothers as adults.

Hall et al. (1998) also note that being in less supportive relationships is associated with a greater likelihood of abusing children. Coohey (2004) qualifies this, however, by suggesting that mothers who physically abuse children have difficulty in forming supportive friendships but there is little evidence to suggest they have less supportive family relationships. As has already been described, these findings are highly applicable to many sexually abusive women, who often report extensive victimisation, difficulties in peer relationships and negative relationships with parents. However, while sexually abusive mothers may share similarities with physically abusive mothers, this does not suggest that all sexually abusive mothers will maltreat their children in other ways. Further investigation of this area is important as, after reviewing the literature, Higgins and McCabe (2001) suggest that experiencing multiple types of victimisation may be associated with more negative outcomes for victims than a single type of maltreatment. Survivors reporting multi-type victimisation, they note, may therefore have particular needs that must be recognised and targeted by mental health services.

## DISCLOSING SEXUAL ABUSE

A further area with great potential for harm is the disclosure process. Victims must sufficiently overcome their fears of the perpetrator to relive the details of the abuse to someone who may not believe them, accuse them of lying or even blame them. Sinason (1994) notes that all victims of sexual abuse risk being disbelieved if they disclose. As she states, "their words puncture societal fantasies about community health and as a punishment their experiences are too often dismissed as fantasies" (Sinason, 1994, p. 156). If action is taken, the victim may have to repeatedly describe the abuse to a number of strangers and even to a court where attempts will be made to discredit them. After their disclosure, victims may also witness the break-up of family relationships. Browne and Finkelhor (1986) cite two studies demonstrating the harm that disclosure can produce. The Tufts Medical Centre (1984) found that when parents responded to disclosure with anger and punishment, children showed more behavioural disturbances, although the trauma was not lessened by more positive parental responses. The second study they describe (Anderson, 1981) reported that if parents reacted negatively, children showed two-and-a-half times more symptoms. Anderson (1999) reports work by Wyatt et al. (1990), which found that survivor self-blame increased in proportion to unsupportive and negative responses from others. This study considered victims of rape but there is no reason to suppose its findings could not also extend to victims of child sexual abuse. However, the particular impact of disclosing sexual abuse by a female remains an underresearched area (Denov, 2003b).

Disclosure of abuse by women might be particularly difficult and met with disbelief or denial. All participants in Denov's (2003b) study reported being fearful of disclosing their abuse as the perpetrator had been female. This may be even more difficult if the abuser is the mother. Ogilvie and Daniluk (1995, p. 600) cite one daughter abused by her mother: "I told one of my friend's mothers about my mother abusing me and she told me what a terrible kid I was for making up lies about my mother". FitzRoy (1998, p. 186) quotes another survivor of sexual abuse by her mother who also experienced disbelief from others: "I once tried to tell a school friend how I hated the things that my mother did to me, but when I started to describe some of the 'gentler' abuse, my friend looked totally horrified and said, 'she does WHAT?' I felt so ashamed, and never spoke about it again for over thirty years." Such denial or disbelief may reinforce or heighten the victim's sense of shame and mutes their objections and testimonies (Ogilvie & Daniluk, 1995).

Denov's (2003b) work categorised professional responses to disclosure of female sexual abuse into positive and negative responses. Of her sample of 14 participants, 43 % reported experiencing only positive professional responses whereas 14 % received only negative responses. The remaining 43 % reported both positive and negative responses. Positive professional responses were described as being supportive and understanding following the disclosure, taking the disclosure seriously and not doubting that females could be abusive. Negative responses, meanwhile, involved professionals being visibly uncomfortable in discussing abuse by females, expressing shock or disbelief at the perpetrator's gender or attempting to minimise the abusive experience. It is encouraging to note that the majority of victims in this study experienced at least some positive responses from professionals when they sought help. Perhaps this was influenced by the fact that these disclosures were primarily made between 1989 and 1998, which, as Denov (2003b, p. 52) states, was a time of "strong cultural awareness and sensitivity to child sexual abuse". Disclosures of female abuse before that time may have been more likely to meet with a negative reaction.

Although Denov's (2003b) study included both male and female victims, the relationship between victim gender and response to disclosure of female sexual abuse is under-explored and an area of conflicting views. Disclosure may be particularly difficult for boys abused by women, particularly in the light of the stereotypical beliefs already described. Bachmann, Moggi and Stirnemann-Lewis (1994, p. 723) describe a boy sexually abused by his mother from age five to eight. At the age of nine he was placed in foster care where "he related the sexual misconduct to his foster father (a minister) who, however, considered these revelations to be a product of the patient's imagination". As a consequence, the man did not make further spontaneous disclosures. The difficulty may be compounded if the boy has passed puberty. Even if he is believed he may be told that he should have enjoyed the experience and that if he did not there is something "wrong" with him. Alternatively he may be accused of initiating the activity. Sarrel and Masters (1982, p. 122) describe an 11-year-old boy's attempt at disclosure of abuse by a female:

> first his father whipped him severely, then he was taken to a priest and, in turn, to a psychiatrist. The priest and the psychiatrist saw him frequently over a 6 month period, repeatedly referring to his shameful conduct and his guilt in not reporting the sexual activity sooner . . . He was left with the feeling that sex was vile and that he could never be forgiven for the sins he had committed.

In this case, the boy had reported the abuse to be quite pleasurable and it was the disclosure that terrified him and left him with sexual difficulties.

Calder and Peake (2001a), meanwhile, suggest that although both boys and girls who disclose abuse by a female are often disbelieved, there may be a further disadvantage for female victims. They report that homosexual abuse of boys may actually increase the likelihood of these boys' disclosures being believed but that the same does not seem to hold true for girls abused by women. In such cases, they suggest, the homosexual nature of the abuse works in reverse and disbelief and denial are the most common responses.

Calder and Peake (2001a) state that the reaction of those to whom they first disclose determines whether the victim feels encouraged and able to seek or accept further help. Platts, Tyson and Mason (2002) highlight that a supportive relationship, potentially but not necessarily exclusively that with the therapist, is an important element in victims being willing or able to talk about the abuse they have experienced. Although their sample was small and comprised respondents who had experienced childhood abuse (but not necessarily sexual), Woodward and Joseph (2003) noted that almost half emphasised that personal growth and change for them had happened through experiencing genuine acceptance from others, from being listened to and being asked about their experiences. It is therefore important that professionals are able to take this stance. Denov (2003b) reported that victims who received positive professional responses to their disclosures felt relief and reassurance, which helped them to begin the process of healing. In contrast, negative reactions from professionals led to an increasing distrust of professionals, a heightened sense of anger and, in some cases, caused victims to question or deny their abuse experience. Denov (2001, p. 321) further reports that if the professional response denies or minimises the seriousness of their sexual abuse, victims of female offenders may feel revictimised: "professional denial of female sex offending, may, in some cases, increase and intensify the long-term effects of the sexual abuse on the victim".

As this chapter has highlighted, sexually abusive women harm their victims both physically and emotionally. The degree of psychological damage, however, may depend to some extent upon the victim's perception of the abuse and their experiences of disclosure. The research does not necessarily indicate that abuse by women is *more* harmful to victims and it may be minimising the experiences of victims of male offenders to suggest that it does. However, the evidence suggests that female abuse has the potential to cause as much harm and suffering to victims as abuse by males.

## SUMMARY OF MAIN POINTS

- In the earlier research particularly there were suggestions that sexual abuse by female perpetrators was less serious or harmful to victims.
- Some of the activities that have been described as characterising sexual offending by women have also been identified as causing greater psychological distress or difficulties for survivors.
- Victim reports suggest that sexual abuse by a female can be deeply traumatic, but the impact of the abuse may depend upon how it is perceived by the victim. However, the victim's perception at the time of the abuse does not necessarily predict the long-term psychological outcome.
- Research investigating possible differential effects of abuse for male and female victims has not always been consistent in its findings. However, factors other than gender may mediate the harm caused by sexual abuse, such as the age of the victim, the "style" of abusing used by the perpetrator and whether the perpetrator's gender is the same as the victim's.
- While it cannot be said that abuse by mothers is more damaging than abuse by other female perpetrators, victims abused by their mothers describe strong feelings of betrayal and there may be difficulties of enmeshment with the mother or in identity formation.
- Although reported rates of violence by female sexual abusers vary widely, some women are forceful and violent in their offending and may inflict serious physical damage. For some female abusers, however, violence may be a counterproductive strategy.
- Some research has found that other types of child maltreatment, particularly physical abuse or neglect, coexist with female sexual abuse. These other types of child maltreatment have most frequently been reported when the abuser is in a major caregiving role.

- Some researchers have suggested that emotional abuse is central to all child maltreatment and may have the most devastating and long-lasting effects. This may be of particular significance in cases of sexual abuse by women.
- The disclosure process may have a strong impact on victims and disclosing abuse by a female may reduce the likelihood of being believed. A supportive professional response is important in helping victims begin the process of healing.

# IV

# Furthering our Understanding and Developing Work in this Field

# 8

# ASPECTS OF FEMALE OFFENDING IN NEED OF FURTHER RESEARCH

As the previous chapters have demonstrated, researchers are now turning their attention to the issue of sexual abuse by women. However, our understanding of this behaviour in women lags behind the knowledge that we possess for male offenders and a number of issues remain underresearched. Some of these form the subject of this chapter.

## THE SEXUAL ASPECT OF FEMALE SEXUAL OFFENDING

More research needs to be conducted into the motives of female sexual offenders. Although a number of motivations have been suggested in previous chapters, consideration of sexual arousal or gratification as a motivating factor in female sexual abuse has frequently been missing from the research literature. Vandiver and Kercher (2004) for example, cite a number of motivations suggested by previous research and add others of their own. However, these do not include deviant sexual arousal. This omission may be related to our traditional "sexual scripts" regarding women. Byers and O'Sullivan (1998) suggest that, according to this script, men are highly motivated to engage in sexual activity whilst women are expected to be sexually reluctant and exchange sex for attention or commitment rather than engaging in sex for its own sake. Thus women are not seen as inherently sexual beings. Clearly much of the evidence already presented refutes this to some degree but such views may persist. Ng (2001), for example, states that the dominant male culture continues to suppress female sexuality, demonstrated by the lack of research in this area.

Matthews (1993) states that sexual abuse can be an expression of many different feelings – anger, disappointment, sadness or low self-esteem. However, there is no mention of it expressing sexual feelings. Allen and Pothast (1994) reported that female abusers had particularly high levels of sexual needs in their relationships, more so than male abusers. They also found that abusers were less fulfilled in their sexual relationships than nonabusers. Thus, if abusing women have high levels of sexual need yet these needs are not being met in adult relationships, could abuse of children fulfil sexual needs for some women? Anderson (1998) suggests that sexual arousal, in addition to other factors, contributes to female sexual aggression against adults. Why this factor remains relatively unconsidered in female offending against children is unclear, but perhaps it is more disturbing to think of women being sexually aroused by children.

O'Connor (1987) reported that sexual gratification was not a motivating factor for women committing sexual offences other than those of indecency. Maison and Larson (1995) also reported that women in their treatment programme did not have fantasies either about children or about the abuse. Mathews, Matthews and Speltz (1990) noted that whereas all the women in their sample who initiated at least some of the sexual activity acknowledged some arousal to or fantasies about their victims, the majority stated that sexual arousal was not a primary motivating factor. These women stated that the fantasies they did have resulted from them imagining that their victim was the perfect adult partner. Their later work (Matthews, Mathews & Speltz, 1991) additionally reported some female offenders as saying that arousal felt during the abuse linked with feelings of power.

Arguments against a role for sexual arousal in female offending come from findings that female abusers may experience sexual dysfunction. Wolfe (1985) (in Travin, Cullen & Protter, 1990) reported that half of a sample of 12 female abusers suffered general sexual dysfunction, although it is not clear whether this was during their offending or more generally. In Travin et al.'s own cases, only 1 offender of 9 reported having an orgasm during the abuse. This is similar to Howitt's (1995a) findings that few male child molesters reported an orgasm while offending. Clearly, however, these findings should be interpreted alongside information about these women's sexual functioning in their adult relationships. Furthermore, they should be compared with nonoffenders. Ng (2001) reports that, while estimates vary, rates of sexual dysfunction among women generally may be quite high, ranging from 19 % to 50 % in outpatient populations and from 68 % to 75 % if sexual dissatisfaction or other difficulties not traditionally defined as dysfunction are included. It is perhaps not surprising, then, that sexual dysfunction has been reported in some female sex offenders. Furthermore, as Ng mentions, the definition of "dysfunction" is important and different definitions may lead to different rates. Johnson and Shrier (1987) found abused male adolescents to be at increased risk for sexual dysfunction. As many female offenders report abuse experiences, this may be related to their sexual dysfunction, potentially inflating figures in the research. In contrast, while their sample was extremely small (N = 8), Kalders, Inkster and Britt (1997) reported only 1 of their female offenders to have a sexual dysfunction at the time of offending.

The intent here is not to imply that all women offend because they are sexually aroused by children. However, it is important that this area is not overlooked. Dandescu and Wolfe (2003) reported their findings to indicate that deviant fantasy is important in developing and maintaining most male sex offenders' behaviour. The majority of male child molesters in their sample reported deviant masturbatory fantasies both before and after their first offence, although they reported significantly more after their first offence which, the authors suggest, may imply that deviant fantasy is more important in the maintenance of sexual offending. Importantly, however, they note that a small proportion of offenders did not use deviant fantasy in their offending. Langevin, Lang and Curnoe (1998) found that although the sex offenders in their sample reported significantly more deviant sexual fantasies than controls, most sex offenders reported more nondeviant fantasies than deviant ones. The authors note that validity checks suggested the offenders' reports were credible. They conclude that while deviant sexual fantasy may be less central to offending than some have suggested, it may be important for a subgroup of offenders. It is important to consider these same issues with women offenders. The possibility that deviant sexual arousal or fantasy could motivate or maintain the behaviour of a subgroup of female perpetrators has been underresearched. Sexual arousal could be more important for women acting alone, for example, as they do not have others "encouraging" them to abuse. It could also be more important for women abusing certain age groups. Perhaps arousal has a greater role to play for women who abuse adolescents as such women may select victims according to their own sexual orientation (suggestive of some degree of arousal) or treat them as surrogate partners.

Finkelhor and Russell (1984) suggest that women are socialised to prefer male partners who are older, larger and more powerful than themselves. However, this does not preclude the possibility that some women may be genuinely attracted to children. Indeed, Nathan and Ward (2002) state that a diagnosis of "paedophilia" may be appropriate for some female offenders. Howitt (1995a) reported that negative sexual experiences in childhood (such as abuse) predicted sexual interest in children but whether this holds for females has yet to be established. Finkelhor, Williams and Burns (1988) found that in cases of day-care abuse, many of the victims were considered to be the attractive children. Some of the abusive women in these cases may have been aroused by these more attractive children, although attractiveness may not be a precondition for arousal.

Some researchers have considered the role of sexual arousal, however. Wolfers (1992) reported that half the women in her study were sexually aroused when they offended, although it is not clear whether this arousal was to the child, the acts committed, feelings of power or another aspect. The woman described by Cooper, Swaminath, Baxter and Poulin (1990) had violent sexual fantasies about children as well as other fantasies of violence or sadomasochism. Matthews (1993) and Scavo (1989) also report female offenders who had fantasies about sexual acts with children. Nathan and Ward (2002) cite work by Davin, Hislop and Dunbar (1999), which found sexual gratification to be a prominent motivator for a third of their self-initiated women offenders. Nathan and Ward's own work reported that nearly half their sample (5/12) admitted being motivated to offend partly by deviant sexual arousal. Women may have sexual fantasies about children, either while offending or between offending episodes. Saradjian (1996) found that women who initially abused young children admitted having repeated images and thoughts of sexual activity with children and many subsequently felt aroused. Only 35 % of the women said they masturbated to sexual fantasies when not engaging in sex with children, however. Women who abused adolescents reported sexual thoughts about their victims but these were of a romantic and idealised nature. Eighty per cent of these women admitted masturbating to fantasies involving their victims. Eldridge and Saradjian (2000), however, note that even if women were not masturbating to fantasies about abusing children, these fantasies formed part of their thinking and supported their offending. Many of the male-coerced abusers in Saradjian's sample also admitted sexual thoughts and images about children but, except in one case these thoughts only occurred after the women had been coerced into abusing. Many male-coerced women said that their arousal had become conditioned to sexual acts with children and eventually they came to feel more arousal in the abuse situation than in sexual activity with their partners. All but one of the women involved in ritual abuse had quite strong fantasies about children and these tended to focus on inflicting pain. Women not involved in ritualistic abuse may also become excited by the pain or distress of their victims. Margolin (1987) describes one mother (reported by Silber, 1979) who became increasingly excited as her son struggled to free himself from the discomfort she was causing him. Some women, then, do report sexual arousal to thoughts of children or thoughts of abusing them.

In addition to being aroused by the victims, arousal may be increased by particular aspects of the abuse. The offender described by Cooper et al. (1990) reported feeling angry at the time of the abuse and studies of her arousal patterns indicated that anger enhanced her sexual arousal. Thus offenders may not be aroused by the victims alone; the actual abuse situation and subsequent arousal may also be a motivating factor.

## Nonoffender's Sexual Arousal to Children

However, it is difficult to evaluate these findings without understanding the content and frequency of sexual fantasies in nonoffending women. The limited work in this area may be related to stereotypical views of women as sexually passive and uninterested, who have to be "encouraged" into sexual activity by males. Limited consideration has been given to the possibility of deviant sexual interests in females. Denov (2001) quotes from the DSM-IV, which states that "except for sexual masochism... paraphilias are almost never diagnosed in females".

Fantasies about children may not be restricted to male sex offenders; Briere and Runtz (1989) found that 21 % of the nonoffending male population self-reported an attraction to children. Langevin et al. (1998) cite several studies suggesting that nonoffenders report some deviant fantasies and their own study found that almost 16 % of their male controls (comprising both nonsex offenders and nonoffending controls) reported sexual fantasies of females in the 13–15 age range. While the percentages were not high, Fromuth and Conn (1997) reported that 6 % of a sample of college women indicated some sexual interest in children. This included fantasies about young boys or masturbating to such fantasies, in addition to being sexually attracted to or aroused by children. However, women who admitted to perpetrating abuse were more likely to report sexual interest in children than those reporting no perpetration behaviour. Clearly, however, there was little incentive for any of these women to report sexual interest in children. McConaghy (1998) cites 2 further studies (Malamuth, 1989; McConaghy et al., 1993) which found that 15 % of male and 2 % of female university students in the USA and Australia reported some likelihood of engaging in sexual activity with a prepubertal child if they believed they could do so with no risk to themselves. This is based on a hypothetical scenario and may not reflect what the students would actually do but if their only inhibitions are being caught the possibility remains that some might offend against children. However, stating that they might engage in such behaviour does not necessarily indicate sexual attraction to children. Saradjian (1996), meanwhile, reported that none of her comparison group of women admitted to sexual thoughts about children, although this was only a small sample (N = 36). It is of course possible that the percentage in the Briere and Runtz (1989) study was high because it sampled males who had abused children but had not been detected. In the Fromuth and Conn (1997) study, some of the women admitted to sexually abusing children.

## Measuring Sexual Arousal in Female Offenders

Assessment of sexual arousal in male sex offenders has typically been under-taken using plethysmography, a technique that measures penile responses to different stimuli. The underlying assumption of this procedure is that gen-ital response indicates sexual arousal and that consistent genital responses to particular stimuli suggest a sexual preference for those stimuli types (Kalmus & Beech, 2005). These authors report several studies that have been able to discriminate between sex offenders and nonsex offenders using

plethysmography but note that many participants have been wrongly classified and suggest that there are concerns about the validity and reliability of
the technique, particularly its low test-retest reliability.

A particular area of concern with plethysmography is the possibility of respondents suppressing or faking their responses. Kalmus and Beech (2005)
suggest that studies have indicated up to 80 % of participants to be able to suppress penile responses when asked and a smaller proportion are also able to
increase their response. These authors also cite a study by Freund, Watson and
Rienzo (1988) which found that men more experienced in plethysmographic
testing were able to fake their responses more effectively. Castonguay, Proulx,
Aubut, McKibben and Campbell (1993) found that offenders who had been
sentenced showed greater responses than those at the presentencing stage,
suggesting either that the latter group were able to control their responses or
that anxiety inhibited their response. These authors also reported that older
offenders showed less response. These findings all raise concerns about the
validity of the technique. Moreover, plethysmography remains an expensive
technique that requires a high level of skill in both administration and interpretation, and ethical issues have been raised in relation to developing sexually explicit stimulus materials involving children (Kalmus & Beech, 2005).

Nonetheless, assessment of female offenders with the vaginal photo-
plethysmograph is possible and measures vaginal blood volume, vaginal
pulse rate and amplitude and response duration to different sexual stimuli
(Cooper et al., 1990). In addition to providing treatment agencies with an indication of deviant arousal in offenders, the results could potentially be used
to challenge women who deny deviant arousal. However, many of the concerns discussed above are likely to apply to female offenders and Minasian
and Lewis (1999) warn that the use of this technique with women is controver-
sial. Additional ethical concerns have been raised, particularly with women
who have themselves been abused, as the technique could be deemed a form
of reabuse (Hilary Eldridge, 2003, personal communication). It is perhaps for
these reasons that Cooper et al. note that photoplethysmography techniques
have hardly been used with female offenders.

The Correctional Service of Canada (1995) suggests that monitoring fantasy
content and orgasmic reconditioning work could be useful with predisposed
female abusers (those predisposed towards offending as a result of their own
abuse). The success of such work, however, depends on greater awareness of
the role of sexual fantasy in female offending and a reliable means of measuring it. Using only the self-report of offenders may be problematic. Kalmus
and Beech (2005) describe several self-report measures of sexual interest, but
suggest that these are prone to denial and faking although the Multiphasic
Sex Inventory is able to identify denial and faking in respondents.

Studies using attentional and information-processing methodologies to
measure sexual interest are an important new development. Of these, Kalmus

and Beech (2005) believe that information-processing methods are the more promising. The theoretical basis of these methods is that sexual interest can be discriminated by attention being increased towards an attractive stimulus and thereby impairing a simple information-processing task, when compared with performance while viewing neutral or unattractive stimuli. As they note, however, more research must be directed towards these new techniques, as well as considering their applicability with female offenders.

## Female Offenders and Pornography

A related issue is the possible use of pornography by female abusers. Langevin and Curnoe (2004) state that there is little good evidence to suggest that pornography plays a major role in the commission of sex offences. However, consideration of this issue is important as these authors also note that offenders against children use pornography more than those offending against adults. It might be expected that, owing to the male-oriented nature of pornography, women would be less likely to use it. Studies with nonoffending women asking about their use of and/or reactions to pornography may therefore be illuminating but there is limited research in this area. Ferree (2003) discusses women's engagement in Internet sexual activity, noting that although women tend to prefer "interactional" activities such as participating in sexual chat rooms, a subgroup of women prefer solitary activities, including accessing pornography. Cooper, Demonico and Burg (2000) (cited in Ferree, 2003) found that women constituted only 14 % of a large group of Internet users and Ferree's work is therefore unlikely to represent women in general. However, it suggests that some nonoffending females access pornography and other sexual material. Whether this includes child pornography is not known.

Saradjian (1996) reported that women coerced into abuse by men were more likely to be involved with pornography, although this may result from the males' wishes rather than the females'. However, some women offenders may use pornography in their own right, perhaps including child pornography. While numbers were small and not significant, Kaufman, Wallace, Johnson and Reeder (1995) found that female offenders were twice as likely to use pornography as male offenders, although whether this was a direct part of the offending is unclear. Some females may also produce homemade pornography, as do some male offenders (Howitt, 1995b). Langevin and Curnoe (2004) note that offenders sometimes use heterosexual adult pornography to arouse the victim's curiosity as well as stimulate themselves. Females may similarly use pornography to "lure" their victims, particularly those abusing adolescent boys. Saradjian describes a case in which the female abuser hired pornographic films and then suggested to her victim that they acted out what they had seen, which perhaps suggests similar motivations.

## MALE COERCION OF FEMALES INTO OFFENDING

It is important to establish how many women are coerced into abuse by men. Grayston and De Luca (1999) state that research findings fairly consistently describe female offenders as most likely to abuse with another offender and less likely to abuse on their own. However, this is questionable and Johansson-Love and Fremouw (2006) note that, of the 13 studies they reviewed, only 3 reported most female sex offenders to have a co-offender, suggesting that many women offend on their own. Discussion of this area may be confused by lack of clarity about whether male co-offenders actually coerce women into abusing. Rudin, Zalewski and Bodmer-Turner (1995), for example, suggest that when female offenders are asked about male coercion, 50 % to 77 % report abusing with a male partner but this does not necessarily indicate that coercion was used. Victim studies may also produce different findings, either because victims are unwilling to report the female's involvement or because the abuse is assumed to be the responsibility of the male. Therefore the rates may additionally depend upon who is asked.

### Progression to Abusing Alone

A second question to be answered is how many women initially coerced by men go on to abuse independently. Matthews (1993) reported that 41 % of male-coerced women went on to abuse others. Again, however, the results may depend upon who is asked. Saradjian (1996) found that coerced women who went on to abuse alone usually abused the same victims as she had with her male coercer. This may lead to difficulties in distinguishing between episodes when both perpetrators abused and those when just the woman abused the child. The victim, too, may become confused, particularly if the woman tells the victim that the man has made her do it, even though he is not there; Saradjian identified some initially coerced women who used the male's power to silence their victims, even when they were abusing alone. Definitional differences may further confuse this issue; how many times must a woman abuse alone before it can be determined that she has progressed to abusing alone? Is once enough?

It is also important to consider how or if coerced women who go on to abuse alone differ from those who only abuse under coercion. There may, for example, be "protective factors" that lessen the likelihood of a coerced woman continuing to abuse independently. Matthews et al. (1991) found that in all but one case in which women abused first with male partners and then alone, the women admitted being sexually aroused during the abuse, a further reason for considering the role of arousal in female offending. Saradjian (1996) found that male-coerced women tended to rate their victims very negatively and this was most true of the women who went on to abuse alone. Three male-coerced women perceived the victims more positively and none of these went on to abuse alone. Coerced women who later abused alone also tended to see the victims as most similar to themselves, whereas women who did not abuse alone tended to see the children as different from themselves. Finkelhor et al. (1988) suggest that women who initiate abuse have more deviant histories than women who are coerced. By examining the characteristics of this group of women we can begin to understand their potentially different treatment needs.

A further area for research is women who co-offend with others, rather than being coerced by them. Societal expectations of women might lead us to assume that if a woman has abused a child, she must have done so under the coercion of a male. The research presented in Chapter 5, however, suggests that this is not necessarily the case and we must consider the alternatives of women abusing alone, as equal perpetrators with others or even coercing others. It is important to consider the needs met through co-offending and whether these might differ between those who abuse with other males or other females. It is also important to determine the ways in which such women rationalise and justify their behaviour, given that it is not the result of male coercion.

## (FEMALE) SEXUAL ABUSE IN DIFFERENT ETHNIC GROUPS AND CULTURES

Vandiver and Kercher (2002) state that, in research to date, female sexual offenders have typically been Caucasian. Therefore, further study of female sexual abuse in non-Caucasian samples is needed. Researchers have hypothesised different findings for other ethnic groups, although it is not always clear on what these hypotheses are based.

Finkelhor (1984), for example, stated that abusing mothers are primarily black. La Fontaine (1990), meanwhile, reported that while abusing mothers were more likely than fathers to be black, black women were still a minority among abusive females, which is more in keeping with Vandiver and Kercher's statement. These differences may result from differential reporting, possibly because families from other ethnic groups may be unwilling to talk about abuse, either for fear of shaming their family or community, or because they fear they will "feed" racism in others (Smith, 1989).

Further study of this issue would have to take into account cultural differences in child rearing. Some practices in other cultures might be considered as abusive in our society but are fully accepted within that particular culture. Lawson (1993), for example, cites work by Olson (1981) reporting that Turkish mothers kiss their children's genitals while changing nappies as an expression of their love and admiration for the children. Demause (1991) reports that some Japanese mothers masturbate their children in public in order to help them sleep and that many Japanese children sleep with their parents until they are 10 to 15 years old although the parents may still have intercourse while the child is in their bed. Thus, when examining sexual abuse in other cultures researchers must take account of cultural variation. In addition to variation in child rearing, different cultures have different views about the ages at which sexual activity is appropriate for children. Even within Europe, there is no overall consensus about the age at which young people are able to consent to sexual intercourse; the age of consent varies from 17 in Northern Ireland, to 14 in Austria and Italy and 13 in Spain (Ages Of Consent In Different Countries, 2005).

Equally important, further study of this area has to consider cultural variation in the "politics" of disclosing sexual abuse and the willingness of different groups to discuss these issues openly. Fontes, Cruz and Tabachnick (2001), for example, used focus groups to explore different community views and knowledge about child sexual abuse. Participants in their Latino groups sometimes spoke about sexual abuse within their families or communities and on these occasions group members generally acknowledged these stories and displayed empathy for the person revealing the abuse. In contrast, amongst African-American groups, almost no stories of abuse within the family were shared and on the few occasions they were, other group members largely ignored these disclosures. This is supported somewhat by Shumba (2004), who states that sexual abuse of male children is considered rare and a taboo subject in most African societies and, as a consequence, rarely reported or talked about publicly. This could obviously impact on responses to disclosure. Shalhoub-Kevorkian (1999) describes some of the responses to Palestinian girls' disclosures of sexual abuse: many girls were rebuffed by their community and family for bringing shame upon them, exiled from their homes or in some cases killed. In the face of such reaction there seems little incentive to disclose abuse. Furthermore, these reactions were all in response to abuse by males. In such a climate, abuse by women may not even be able to be conceptualised. Thus even for those living in the UK, cultural differences in attitudes towards disclosure or discussion of sexual abuse may impact on research in this area.

## ABUSE BY WOMEN IN THE HISTORIES OF ADULT RAPISTS

A number of studies have highlighted childhood sexual abuse by females in the backgrounds of men who later rape adult women. Burgess, Hazelwood, Rokous, Hartmen and Burgess (1987) (cited in Cavanagh-Johnson, 1989) reported that 56 % of a sample of rapists had been sexually abused as children and women were the perpetrators in almost 40 % of cases. Groth (1979) found that 38 % of rapists had been abused by adult females and 24 % by female peers. Eldridge[1] reported work by Rallings, Webster and Rudolph (2001) which examined the characteristics of childhood sexual abuse experiences in men undergoing the Sex Offender Treatment Programme in UK prisons. Thirty-nine per cent of offenders against adults reported being abused by a female perpetrator, although this was based on self-report. Denov (2001) cites work by Briere and Smiljanich (1993), which found that among sexually abused men who reported sexual aggression against women, 80% had been abused by a female during childhood. Duncan and Williams (1998) reported that males who had had coercive sexual experiences with females as children were more likely than comparison males to be sex offenders during their teens. They also found that coerced male victims of female abusers were more likely to commit sex offences as adults. It is not clear whether these two groups contained the same men or whether some offended only as teenagers or only as adults. Even if they had not committed sexual offences, however, male victims of coerced female abuse showed higher levels of violence in their adult intimate relationships.

Research has tended to emphasise the link between abuse by females and later sexual aggression against women; abuse by females in men who sexually abuse children has been less well documented. Crawford, Hueppelheuser and George (1996), however, indicated that male incest offenders were more likely to have been abused by a female, primarily an aunt or a sister. Allen (1991) found that just over one-third of male child sexual abusers in his study had been sexually abused as children and of those, 45% reported a female abuser. Rallings et al.'s (2001) study[1], meanwhile, found 19% of offenders against children to have been abused by female perpetrators, a lower proportion than for offenders against adults.

An association between abuse by women and later aggression towards them may be set up from an early age. Saradjian (1997) reported that many young male victims of female abuse in her study became physically aggressive towards mothers who had sexually abused them or very passive in relation to their mother and aggressive to others, particularly women. Kelly, Wood, Gonzalez, MacDonald and Waterman (2002) suggest that males find it particularly difficult to cope with abuse by a female as women are stereotypically seen as being weaker than they are. The feelings of shame and anger these men experience may then be directed towards women with whom they are intimately involved in adult relationships. In the case of rapists, perhaps this extends to women in general. Robinson (1998) states that the way children assimilate their abuse experience can act as a major deterrent to becoming offenders as adults. This raises the possibility that rapists assimilate their abuse experiences differently from male victims who do not go on to offend and perhaps also from male victims who later abuse children.

[1] Hilary Eldridge at the Tools to Take Home conference: "Treating Women Who Sexually Abuse Children". Birmingham, April 2003.

The self-report of sex offenders must be treated with caution. They may describe sexual abuse experiences to justify their own behaviour and excuse the harm they have caused their victims. If these accounts are fictitious, however, one wonders why offenders have disclosed abuse by females as, until recently, this might have made their accounts less believable. If sizeable proportions of sex offenders have been abused by females it may be important to address this in treatment, particularly if it impacts directly on their offending. However, we must be careful not to overemphasise this link, particularly as it has been suggested that the intergenerational transmission of sexual offending is not a satisfactory explanation for all sexual offending. Nor should we ignore offenders who have been abused by male perpetrators. Nonetheless, this demonstrates the importance of accepting abuse by females and the long-term harm it can produce.

Finally, it is important to consider whether there is a similar relationship with being abused by a woman as a child among sexually abusive women. Glasser et al. (2001) found no evidence of a link with earlier victimisation by a female in women abusers. Allen (1991) also found that only 6% of female offenders reported sexual abuse by a female perpetrator. However, it may be interesting to carry out further investigation with larger samples to examine whether there is any link between abuse by a female as a child and later female sexual aggression against adults.

## FEMALE OFFENDERS WITHIN THE CRIMINAL JUSTICE SYSTEM

Research needs to examine further the passage of female sex offenders through the CJS. Some researchers have suggested that female abusers tend not to be prosecuted unless their offending is very serious, in which case they may be treated more harshly than men. In following the legal consequences of abuse investigations, however, Allen (1991) reported that the outcomes tended to be similar for female and male offenders. More female than male offenders were imprisoned although, as the author notes, this may reflect the fact that part of the female offender sample was drawn from women in prison. Female offenders were also more likely to be placed on medication, perhaps suggesting a belief that for a woman to commit such an act she must be psychiatrically disordered. The sentencing of female abusers should also be further investigated. Are some types of offender more likely to be convicted than others and are there graduations in the severity of the sentence according to how far the woman is seen to deviate from social norms? Characteristics of the abuser and the victim may also influence the decisions made and offence characteristics might also be influential.

The experiences of female sexual offenders in prison could also be studied. Maison and Larson (1995) reported that female sex offenders are just as likely as male sex offenders to be victimised in prison but whether women suffer more victimisation because they are women who have committed such offences is unknown. As well as potentially impacting on their willingness to undergo treatment in prison, victimisation from other prisoners may serve to reinforce their previous experiences of victimisation, difficulties in forming relationships with others and low self-esteem. Whether this would lead to continued risk of offending upon release is unknown.

## FORMULATING APPROPRIATE RESPONSES TO PROTECT CHILDREN

There are perhaps three different levels at which we can attempt to protect children from sexual abuse by women. The primary and most important way we can protect children is to raise awareness that women do abuse and that the impact on victims can be as harmful as being abused by a male. Some research described in Chapter 2 indicated that sexual abuse by women is not well recognised by the general population and that harm to victims may be minimised, particularly, perhaps, if they are adolescent males. Allowing victims to feel safe and believed in when disclosing and taking appropriate action upon disclosure are important to ensure that abuse does not continue. This is perhaps particularly important in cases of abuse by women as they may be more likely to abuse victims for whom they have a caring role and from which it is therefore less easy for victims to escape. Mitchell and Morse (1998) emphasise this; of the female-abused women who responded to their survey, one-third reported that their abuse had occurred for between 11 and 20 years. While the authors note that their sample may not be representative of all victims of female abusers, Saradjian (1996) also noted that sexual abuse by women is likely to occur over a long period of time, particularly if the victims are biological children. If we are not open to the issue of sexual abuse by women, or the impact of their behaviour is minimised, offenders will not receive the help they need and their risk of offending continues (Denov, 2004b).

Of particular importance, perhaps, is the response of professionals to sexual abuse by women. Calvert and Munsie-Benson (1999) reported that participants in their general population survey said they would be most likely to report a child's disclosure of sexual abuse to either a doctor or the police, suggesting that awareness of female-perpetrated abuse is particularly important for these "first port of call" professionals. However, as Chapter 2 highlighted, these professionals may exhibit some gender bias in their thinking about sexual abuse, which it is important to address. This may be a question of simply drawing attention to these possible biases during training courses (Kite & Tyson, 2004) or a deeper consideration of how child sexual abuse is portrayed at the earliest stages of training; Denov's (2001) work found that, for the professionals in her study, sexual abuse had been described as a male-perpetrated crime committed against females. Therefore, there appears to be a strong argument for providing training on female sex offenders to a broad range of professionals, both those most likely to be working directly with female abusers and their victims and others such as solicitors, barristers and members of the judiciary (Bunting, 2005).

Professionals could routinely enquire about sexual abuse by females in the context of their daily practice (Denov, 2003b). This could help victims to make disclosures, by indicating that the professional is aware of and prepared to hear about such experiences. Clearly, however, the professional would have to ensure that they were genuinely open to discussing such issues. As Denov notes, there has been little research examining the impact on victims of an ambivalent professional response to their disclosures. Her own work, however, demonstrated the potentially damaging effects of negative professional responses. Mitchell and Morse (1998) asked female survivors of sexual abuse by women what clinicians should know. Being listened to and believed seemed of primary importance. As one survivor stated: "Be really, really gentle. Believe us. I've spent my life not being listened to . . . Validate our stories, validate our feelings" (Mitchell & Morse, 1998, p. 214). It is therefore important to ensure that adequate training and discussion of this issue is available, in order to help eliminate negative responding.

A secondary level of prevention suggested in some child maltreatment literature attempts to intervene before the onset of abuse, by identifying high-risk groups and offering them support. The research described in previous chapters has highlighted a number of characteristics of women who sexually abuse children but it is important to stress that not all female abusers have these characteristics and some women who do will not abuse children. There is not a "typical" female child abuser that we can identify and protect children from, any more than we can for male abusers. Hall, Sachs and Rayens (1998) suggest that low-income, single mothers with a history of abuse are particularly at risk for abusive parenting and that assisting such women to improve their social resources may reduce their potential for child abuse. While there may be truth in this, and while it may benefit these womens' lives in many ways to increase their resources, such focus on one group fails to recognise that other women may abuse and that their victims will remain unprotected.

Hall et al. (1998) were considering physical abuse of children but similar points have been raised in relation to sexual abuse by women. While stating that female abusers are a heterogeneous group, Grayston and De Luca (1999) nonetheless go on to describe the "typical" abusive female who comes from a dysfunctional family of origin, has experienced abuse, may be engaged in poorly paid and stereotypical female roles and is socially isolated. Elliott and Peterson (1993) similarly proffer a checklist of the typical characteristics of mothers at risk for sexually abusing their children including deprived backgrounds, a history of promiscuity or poor sexual relationships, being single parents with low incomes, substance abuse problems, emotional problems and personality disorders. Clearly many of these items are applicable to women who sexually abuse children but they are also relevant to other women from impoverished backgrounds who do not. These authors are not suggesting that only women with these characteristics abuse children but such lists may reduce recognition of the fact that female abusers come from a variety of backgrounds and may increase the probability that abuse by women with few or none of these characteristics will go undetected. Such work may be initially helpful if it raises awareness of women as abusers but may potentially contribute further to biased beliefs about offenders. It is also important to remember that rather than concentrating on risk factors alone, we should also consider the particular protective factors that an individual has or is able to develop (Hamilton & Browne, 2002). Research attention therefore needs to be directed towards identifying these factors in sexually abusive women.

The final level of support and protection we can offer to children is in intervening once abuse is known in order to prevent further victimisation. This does not prevent abuse from occurring in the first place but it may at least help victims to disclose sooner and receive supportive and appropriate responses from professionals. This remains dependent on the victim feeling able to disclose, however. Although the literature contains contradictory findings, certainly some women are sexually abusing young children. As Nagel, Putnam, Noll and Trickett (1997) note, younger children are less likely to disclose that they are being abused and it is therefore important to look for behavioural or medical indications of abuse in these younger victims. While there is little literature looking specifically at what such indications may be for children abused by women, the many behavioural similarities between abuse committed by male and female perpetrators suggests that some of these indicators could be the same as for abuse by men. As noted in Chapter 10, however, many signs of sexual abuse are unclear and easily attributable to other causes.

If victims do disclose to professionals it is important that they can be offered appropriate support. Although beyond the scope of this section, in offering therapeutic input to victims it is important to consider the particular needs of those sexually abused by females and the extent to which their needs may differ from those abused by males. Differing needs according to victim gender may also apply. Saradjian (1997, p. 7) reports the difficulties facing one survivor of female abuse: "I even felt stigmatised in a group for survivors of childhood sexual abuse as the others had all been sexually victimised by their fathers or other men, I felt so ashamed how could I tell them about my abuser." This victim was abused by her mother.

Another respondent in Mitchell and Morse's (1998) study said the following: "When I did briefly mention sexual abuse by my mother in a local support group, there was prolonged silence and discomfort, so I never mentioned it again. I got the feeling that it was a little too weird for people to deal with, so I dropped it" (Mitchell & Morse, 1998, p. 150).

Once abuse has taken place, the other avenue for protecting children is to increase understanding of the treatment needs of female abusers and develop appropriate treatment provision for them in order to reduce their risk of reoffending in the future. This issue forms the focus of the next chapter.

In summary, then, there is no easy answer to protecting children. Although inclusion of all the aspects described above may be important, perhaps our best overall response is to raise awareness and recognition of women as abusers among professionals, the general public and in education programmes in schools. In this way, we may at last move away from the idea that sexual abuse is something that only men do.

## SUMMARY OF MAIN POINTS

- Although increasing research attention is being paid to sexual abuse by women there are many areas that still require investigation.
- Researchers have appeared loath to consider the role of sexual arousal and fantasy in sexual offending by women. However, it remains possible that deviant arousal may motivate some female abusers to offend. Further consideration of this issue is important, alongside a greater understanding of how this could be measured and whether pornography may have any involvement in female offending.
- As well as establishing how many female offenders are coerced into abusing by men, it is important to consider women who may initially have been coerced but who have progressed to abusing alone. It may be possible to identify "protective factors" that lessen the likelihood of coerced women going on to abuse alone.
- The extant research has tended to study female abusers from Caucasian samples. We have less knowledge about female abusers from other ethnic groups. However, any research in this area would have to take account of cultural differences in childrearing as well as cultural variation in openness to discussing sexual abuse.
- A number of studies have reported a link between childhood sexual abuse of males by females and later sexual aggression against women. This link appears less strong in the histories of males sexually offending against children. It is important to examine whether a similar link exists for female offenders.
- It would be interesting to study sentencing patterns and whether there is a gender bias for female sex offenders. Female abusers' experiences of imprisonment should also be studied as these may impact on intervention programmes run in prison, or upon their risk when they are released.

- In order to protect children it is important to continue raising awareness of women as abusers, particularly among the professionals who may be sought initially when a victim discloses. Changes may need to be made to training courses and to the routine practice of professionals.
- Although it may be useful to summarise the "typical" characteristics of sexually abusive women we must be careful not to assume that women without these characteristics will not sexually abuse.

# 9

# INTERVENING WITH FEMALE ABUSERS: TREATMENT NEEDS, METHODS AND OUTCOMES

Hannah Ford and Hilary Eldridge

Ward and Stewart (2003) suggest that there are two main models of offender rehabilitation, which, while both aiming to change characteristics associated with offending, differ in their orientations. They term the first model "risk management" and suggest that the primary goal of this model is to reduce an offender's risk to the community rather than improve the offender's quality of life. In contrast, the second model focuses on enhancing offenders' capabilities in order to improve their quality of life and lessen the likelihood of them committing further offences. In this second model "the primary end or goal is not the reduction of crime, although it is argued that this will reliably follow from individual well-being" (Ward & Stewart, 2003, p. 126). They believe that the risk management model has been dominant and has focused primarily on needs that are linked to reducing reoffending. They argue, however, that addressing non-criminogenic needs is a necessary part of any intervention programme. This chapter will consider some of the needs that programmes for female offenders could address.

In addition to considering the specific needs to be addressed in treatment, researchers have also highlighted the importance of considering an individual's learning style and responsivity to the particular intervention being offered. Ward, Day, Howells and Birgden (2004), for example, report that when programmes are responsive to individual needs, greater reductions in recidivism have been found than in programmes based on risk-needs principles alone. They suggest that not only the individual's level of motivation but also the extent to which the programme takes account of individual characteristics such as cognitive ability, learning styles and values will influence the effect-iveness of the intervention. McGuire (2001) further notes that the most ef-fective interventions allocate an appropriate level of intervention according to the individual's level of risk, assess and target the criminogenic needs or dynamic risk factors associated with the offending behaviour and use appro-priate learning styles, which are adapted according to individual differences. He reports findings suggesting reductions in recidivism of greater than 50 % if these risk, needs and responsivity principles are incorporated into treatment programmes. The limited knowledge of risk factors for female sexual offend-ers makes applying these principles more difficult. However, responsivity should be addressed in working with female abusers. This will be discussed later in this chapter. This chapter also outlines the Lucy Faithfull Foundation's programme for female sex offenders as an example of work with this group of abusers.

## WHAT ARE THE TREATMENT NEEDS OF SEXUALLY ABUSIVE WOMEN?

It is difficult to answer this question in the sense of providing a definitive list of treatment targets. Intervention work should focus on each woman's indi-vidual, specific needs and, as awareness of the characteristics of these women grows, assessment of their treatment needs can more easily take place. To date, the small number of female sexual offenders in prison and initial lack of ac-knowledgement of the problem have meant that services for abusive women are limited and systematic individual or group intervention has not always been attempted. However, the difficulties in offering group interventions for sexually abusive women should, theoretically, facilitate a focus on individual needs.

While keeping in mind the need for an individual formulation of each offender's difficulties, the research presented throughout this book has high-lighted a number of potential areas for intervention. Eldridge and Saradjian (2000) comment that poor attachments and a history of meeting needs in de-structive ways are integral to the offending patterns of many of the women with whom they have worked. In many cases these needs were met through sexual offending. Haley (1990) suggests that any symptom, such as sexual offending, begins as a "personal solution" to an area of difficulty within an individual's life. An analysis of the women's lives led Eldridge and Saradjian to hypothesise that the women in their sample had not learned or been able to meet their needs, resulting in negative emotional states that they tried to reduce to avoid becoming anxious and depressed. They had learned that their needs for power, control or affiliation, for example, could be met through sexually abusing children. Therefore, it is important that interventions identify the specific internal and external obstacles that prevent women from meeting their fundamental needs (Sorbello, Eccleston, Ward & Jones, 2002) and find ways of overcoming these to meet needs in nonabusive ways. Consequently, in their work with female offenders, Eldridge and Saradjian integrated relapse prevention throughout treatment as a New Life Plan in which the women could learn new skills and find alternative, nonabusive means of meeting their needs.

Clark and Howden-Windall (2000) examined factors relating to reconviction rates in 195 female nonsexual offenders who left prison in 1995. The women were representative of the female prisoner population with regards to age and offence type but the sample was weighted in favour of longer sentences. They concluded that the best predictors of reconviction in female nonsexual offenders were those predictive for the male offender population. Specifically, criminal history variables such as previous offence history, early onset of offending or previous sentence were significantly related to reconviction. However, familial factors such as a problematic home life when growing up and lack of continuity of care were highly predictive of reconviction. Such factors were often exacerbated by being combined with few educational qualifications and substance abuse, which were also highly related to reconviction. This supported Eldridge and Saradjian's (2000) contention that to reduce reoffending, treatment for female sex offenders should address the women's background experiences and the effects on their attitudes, beliefs and perceptions of how to meet their goals.

While historical factors such as past experiences are fixed, they are linked to factors more amenable to change such as pro-offending attitudes, emotional loneliness, self-esteem and interpersonal skills deficits, which can be targeted in treatment. The women participating in the pilot of the Lucy Faithfull Foundation's programme had preprogramme test results indicating low self-esteem, high underassertiveness, high emotional loneliness, external locus of control and an inability to cope with distress in others. These are common features of high deviance male sexual offenders (Beckett, Beech, Fisher and Scott-Fordham, 1994). Eldridge and Saradjian (2000) therefore felt that it would be appropriate for intervention to address dynamic risk factors identified for male sexual offenders. Therefore, some treatment targets may be similar to those of male offenders and include work on denial and minimisation, offence-supportive beliefs and attitudes, victim empathy, socioaffective difficulties and relapse prevention (Beech & Fisher, 2004), or poor self-management and interpersonal skills, fragile commitment to prevention of reoffending and specific problems such as deviant arousal (Correctional Services Accreditation Panel, 2002).

Some particular areas of treatment need are suggested by the different female offender typologies. Women who initiate abuse independently, for example, may have different needs from women coerced into abuse. Women coerced into abuse may require techniques such as assertiveness training or improvements in social skills to help them develop new relationships. Matthews (1993) suggests similar treatment goals in working with male-coerced offenders, proposing that a major aim is to reduce dependency on males. However, she feels that it is also important to redevelop feelings of empathy, which have often been suppressed as a means of coping with witnessing and participating in the abuse of children. Women abusing alone, however, may require more work on their core beliefs about children and their motivations for abusing. Matthews suggests that "predisposed" offenders need primarily to address their own traumatic past but that deviant sexual fantasy may also be relevant to this group. In therapeutic work with "teacher/lover" offenders, meanwhile, Matthews states that the primary goal is to increase awareness of the abusive nature of their behaviour and to address the cognitions and feelings associated with that.

Eldridge and Saradjian (2000) suggest that Ward and Hudson's concept of approach and avoidant pathways to offending applies to female as well as male sexual offenders. This "pathway" concept suggests that offenders follow different "pathways" to an offence according to how they regulate their behaviour (either actively or passively) and the goals they are striving to achieve (whether or not they are aiming to sexually offend). Thus, offenders who are aiming to avoid offending may either underregulate their behaviour and not employ strategies to prevent it from happening, or may try to avoid offending but use ineffective or counterproductive strategies. Offenders whose goal is to commit a sexual offence, meanwhile, may either underregulate their behaviour and follow overlearned scripts in committing their offence, or may regulate their behaviour effectively and plan carefully how to achieve their goal (Ward & Hudson, 2000). Bickley and Beech (2002) suggest that offenders following these different pathways have different treatment needs. Those aiming to offend, for example, will require interventions focusing on their beliefs about the appropriateness of sexually assaultive behaviour and the harm caused to victims. Offenders aiming to avoid offending, however, are less likely to need work in this area and may instead require help in building strategies to cope with threats to their avoidance goal. Similarly, the treatment needs of offenders with difficulties in their self-regulation may include impulse control, mood management and dealing with high-risk situations, areas that seem less relevant to offenders with effective self-regulation skills (Ward & Hudson, 2000). If, as Eldridge and Saradjian suggest, these pathways are also followed by female sexual abusers, then a different intervention focus according to pathway type may be relevant.

However, Ward and Stewart (2003) argue that while targets such as these constitute criminogenic needs that, if changed during treatment, are associated with reduced recidivism rates, other individual needs may be comparatively neglected within treatment programmes. Instead, Sorbello et al.

(2002) suggest that rehabilitation programmes should focus on identifying the particular internal and external obstacles that prevent women from obtaining their fundamental needs and then help them to find ways of overcoming these to meet their basic needs. This is not a complete departure from the treatment targets outlined above; interpersonal difficulties or maladaptive attitudes and beliefs, for example, could act as obstacles to women meeting their needs and therefore would be considered in treatment. It is the underlying objective that, they argue, should be different.

Further consideration must be given to how we can assess the treatment needs of female sexual abusers. Many psychometric tools have been developed for male abusers and have been used by researchers such as Eldridge and Saradjian (2000) and Ring (2005) but their validity and reliability with female sex offenders has not been adequately tested. Thus, as Saradjian (1996) notes, we have to rely more heavily on the self-reports of female abusers and be wary of their inherent drawbacks. Using tools developed for males may be better than nothing but we need to develop tools that are appropriate for women. In the UK, The Lucy Faithfull Foundation is working with Richard Beckett of Oxford Forensic Services to establish a battery of normed psychometric tests. This kind of work is all the more important as our awareness of and receptivity to sexual abuse by women increases.

Different types of offender may require differing amounts of time in treatment. Matthews (1998) suggests that "teacher-lover" offenders are relatively easy to work with therapeutically once they cease to question their need for treatment. Initially, they may not identify themselves with other child abusers, however, and express disgust at the thought of sexual contact with a young child (Matthews, 1998). Similarly, Saradjian (1996) notes that women who abuse adolescents are the most difficult to engage in therapy because their own denial of their behaviour as abusive may be reinforced by societal beliefs. Once they have engaged, however, she suggests that their progress is likely to be good. "Predisposed" offenders, meanwhile, tend to have particularly difficult or traumatic backgrounds and therefore have a lot of damage to repair (Matthews, 1998). She suggests that it is important to deal with offenders' experiences of abuse as:

> They are probably unable to develop genuine empathy for their victims and truly to understand the impact of their behaviour until they have received empathic support for their own pain . . . To force them into mechanical statements of remorse is to teach them that they must once again comply with empty commands and compromise their own reality (Matthews, 1998, pp. 262–263)

However, incorporating female offenders' own victimisation into treatment programmes and addressing this without allowing it to excuse their perpetrating behaviour, may be a challenge to treatment providers. This issue is discussed again later.

## COULD MALE TREATMENT MODELS BE APPLIED
## TO FEMALES?

Several authors have suggested that it may not be appropriate to apply male models of offending and treatment to females as we do not know enough about female offenders and how they compare with males (Adshead, Howett & Mason, 1994; Nathan & Ward, 2002; Saradjian, 1996). As Chapter 3 discussed, there are a number of overt similarities in the offending behaviours of male and female abusers but it is important to think beyond these behavioural similarities and more fully consider the underlying dynamics.

The lack of data about abusing women's psychometric profiles, how they differ from male offenders, other female offenders and nonoffending women, what factors link to reoffending, treatment outcome and reconviction data creates obvious difficulties for planning programmes. Treatment programmes for female offenders have been set up in the USA. Matthews (1993) discusses the Genesis II programme, which has many of the same treatment targets as work with male offenders but also offers more gender-specific elements such as sexuality issues or addressing dependency on males (Correctional Service of Canada, 1995). In the UK, the Lucy Faithfull Foundation was commissioned by the Prison Service to develop an assessment and treatment programme and provide associated staff training. The programme draws on clinical practice with both male and female offenders. In designing their programme, Eldridge and Saradjian (2000) considered what clinical practice and research, especially that of Matthews, Mathews and Speltz (1991), and Saradjian (1996) indicate about the motivation of female sex offenders, the range of their abusive behaviours, the techniques they use to gain victim compliance and prevent disclosure and their patterns of offending.

However, as mentioned previously, although some treatment targets may be similar to those identified in programmes for male offenders there may need to be differences in how programmes are delivered when working with women. One of the effective practice principles in rehabilitation programmes is that of responsivity, which requires us to consider whether male and female offenders should be treated in the same way (Sorbello et al., 2002). These authors note that not only may programme content require adaptation to meet the differing needs of women but so too may the therapeutic process. Without specifically discussing sex offenders, Bouffard and Taxman (2000) report that many male treatment models include confrontational techniques to tackle resistance to change and challenge beliefs and attitudes thought relevant to the behaviour the programme is aiming to change. However, they question the extent to which this is appropriate in programmes for women, who may have experienced victimisation and abuse. Marshall and Serran (2000) note that while the denial and distorted thinking displayed by many sex offenders (including women) may need to be challenged, there are a variety of ways of doing this ranging from aggressive confrontation to supportive challenging. Some therapists have suggested the need for therapist control and confrontation when working with this client group but they feel such a therapeutic style has disadvantages. It may, for example, further reduce client self-confidence and it fails to model empathy. Although these authors were not considering treatment programmes for women it is likely that these issues may be even more relevant for women, many of whom already feel powerless, have experienced aggression or victimisation from others and have very low self-esteem. A more supportive, although not collusive, therapeutic stance may be important in engaging women in therapy and beginning to promote change.

## OTHER ISSUES IN TREATING FEMALE SEXUAL ABUSERS

As mentioned previously, addressing female offenders' own experiences of abuse without allowing this to dominate treatment or excuse their offending behaviour is a difficult balance to achieve. However, such work may be important in helping women to develop empathy for their victims. In addition, women abused as children and female sexual offenders often rate themselves as being powerless and Saradjian (1996) notes that therapy itself can be a relationship in which the woman may feel that the therapist holds the power. Thus, she states, as sex offenders often find that they are required to undertake therapy rather than choosing to do so, this power imbalance could exacerbate other feelings of powerlessness and increase the risk of triggering further sexual abuse of a child. It is perhaps in acknowledgement of these difficulties that Saradjian states the most effective therapy to be that which involves "walking the tight-rope" of the victim-perpetrator boundary.

However, previous abuse experiences and other early difficulties may also have direct effects on therapeutic engagement. Craissati (2003) (cited in Beech & Ward, 2004) noted that experiencing two or more childhood difficulties and never having cohabited correctly identified 87 % of offenders who were poor treatment attenders. Childhood difficulties and contact with adult mental health services correctly identified 83 % of offenders who were noncompliant with intervention programmes. This work was not specifically examining female offenders and "childhood difficulties" were not limited to abuse experiences, but it highlights the need to consider past experiences in sex-offender treatment programmes.

Some studies have suggested that some women abusers have high levels of denial. This has implications for their progress in treatment. Denial is not a predictor of recidivism (Beech & Fisher, 2004) but it must be addressed as it limits the extent to which offenders can work on their offence-related problems. By reducing denial, offenders may talk more openly about themselves and their thoughts, feelings and behaviours. When individuals can accept some responsibility for the offence, it helps them to examine the choices and decisions they made (Beech & Fisher, 2004). Levels of denial may differ both individually and according to offender type; Saradjian (1996) states, for example, that women coerced into offending by male partners tend to attribute responsibility to him and, particularly if they are no longer involved with those partners, may not see themselves as needing treatment.

Sgroi and Sargent (1993) report that female offenders may be more sceptical than males that sex offenders can change. Allen (1991) also reported this to be the case but found that scepticism was greatest in women who had not undergone treatment. This, too, has ramifications for treatment; beliefs in one's self-efficacy and ability to deal with high-risk situations without resorting to the problematic behaviour has been found to be an important variable in the outcome and future success of attempts to change behaviours (Casey, Day & Howells, 2005). Negative beliefs such as these may lower motivation, which may be further reduced by the poor access to resources and supportive social networks that has been reported for many female sex offenders. Thus, while some female offenders may be aware that the costs of offending outweigh the benefits, they may feel that they lack the opportunity or power to respond differently (Kemshall, 2004). Maison and Larson (1995) suggest that many female offenders lack motivation for therapy, partly because they may have numbed the pain of their own abuse. This further emphasises the importance of addressing previous experiences of abuse and suggests that work to build self-belief and motivation for treatment will be important treatment precursors for some women.

Travin, Cullen and Protter (1990) suggest that there may be a high dropout rate among female abusers, particularly when they accept responsibility for their offences and are overwhelmed by shame and guilt. Males, they say, are more likely to stay in denial and so are less likely to be affected. To some extent, this is supported by Matthews (1993), who reports that men move out of guilt and shame more quickly than do women. Saradjian (1996) states that therapy raises many emotional difficulties for female offenders, including shame and guilt. Women will need support in dealing with these. However, as the social supports and networks of female abusers are often very limited, Saradjian suggests that it may be helpful to ensure that support is available to women before they commence a treatment programme and that this is maintained until the women are able to begin building their own social networks. This may also avoid the potential exacerbation of feelings of powerlessness and isolation that were discussed previously. In this respect, an avenue for further consideration is the Circles of Support initiative, which is rooted in faith-based communities in Canada and the USA (Kemshall & McIvor, 2004). In recognition of the fact that many sex offenders have social and interpersonal difficulties, this initiative aims to provide the Core Member (the offender) with a "circle" of trained volunteers from the community who meet regularly with the offender on an individual and group basis and assist him or her in safe and supportive reintegration into the community. This scheme has been piloted with male offenders in the UK and although there has not been any long-term evaluation of outcome, the Thames Valley scheme reports that expected rates of recidivism have been reduced, that only 3 of 20 men have been recalled on licence and that none have actually committed a further sexual offence. This is reported to be similar to the recidivism rates of the circles operating in Canada (Circles of Support and Accountability in the Thames Valley, 2005).

## WHAT ARE THE OPTIONS FOR GROUP TREATMENT?

Given the comparatively small numbers of female sexual abusers in prison, at least, and the difficulties in forming groups of such women, one question for consideration is whether females are best served by treatment in groups containing only other female abusers, or whether including them in groups of male sex offenders is a possibility. Welldon (1988) suggests that in mixed groups, owing to popular stereotypes that women do not abuse or do not cause harm, female abusers may not be viewed seriously by other group members, which would be antitherapeutic. The other, equally nontherapeutic extreme, is that female abusers could be viewed as more "deviant" than their male counterparts simply because they are women. The appropriateness of mixed-sex groups depends to some degree on the extent to which male and female offending is similar, particularly in its underlying dynamics. However, Welldon believes there is much to be gained from having mixed groups of males and females. Perpetrators of both genders, she states, are able to highlight their different attitudes, leading to "unexpected qualities of confinement and insight ... which are virtually impossible in a one-to-one situation" (Welldon, 1996, p. 46). However, this option raises a number of issues, including the female abuser's own history of victimisation, particularly if she was abused by a man. Being in a group with other abusive men could prove cathartic but runs the risk of being intimidating and antitherapeutic. This situation could be equally difficult for males who have been abused by females, which, as Chapter 8 highlighted, seems quite prevalent among some male sex offenders, particularly if female abusers are not viewed seriously by the group as a whole. Similarly female abusers who have been victimised or coerced by males may find it difficult to speak out in groups, particularly if they are in the minority. Careful consideration would also need to be given to the leadership of mixed gender groups and, in such cases, having therapists of both genders in every session may be particularly important.

The reality remains, however, that given the small number of women convicted of sexual offences, forming groups is a difficult prospect for treatment providers, either in prison or in the community. The Correctional Service

of Canada (1995) noted that of the 11 women for whom it had information, 6 (55%) had not undertaken any specific sex-offender programmes,
in some cases because there were simply none available. Some women instead received individual counselling sessions with psychologists. It therefore seems, as Eldridge and Saradjian (2000) state, that "women in treatment
for sex offending are in a minority and are often worked with individually
rather than in groups". The downside of such individual work, they report,
is that women can feel isolated and "bizarre", both of which could impact
on intervention work. This may be particularly difficult in a prison setting;
Saradjian (1996) describes how female abusers attending a prison-based programme became isolated from other prisoners on account of attending the
group and being identified as sex offenders. As a consequence, the women
became unhealthily supportive of and collusive with one another and began
to excuse and explain away each other's offending. Bouffard and Taxman
(2000) further suggest that low self-esteem and feeling socially stigmatised
may impact negatively on intervention work. Eldridge and Saradjian's solution to this has been the development of the New Life Manual (Eldridge &
Saradjian, in press a), which helps female offenders to realise they are not alone
and that other women have been able to go on to lead abuse-free lives. This
manual can be used for individual work or in association with a groupwork
programme.

   An interesting suggestion has been made by the Office of Juvenile Justice
and Delinquency Prevention (2001). Given limited resources and reported
similarities between adolescent sex offenders and other adolescent non-sex
offenders, they question whether the needs of adolescent sex offenders could
be met through interventions that are effective with adolescents who have
committed other types of offences. Clearly this would help to overcome difficulties of numbers and would also bypass some possible pitfalls of mixed-
sex groups. This question has not been satisfactorily answered in relation to
adolescent offenders but is mentioned here as a further possible option in
the treatment of adult female sex offenders. However, the suggestion rests
on an assumption of similarities in the needs of these different types of female offenders and, although Chapter 4 outlined some areas of similarity
between female sex offenders and non-sex offenders, further consideration
must be given as to whether this is sufficient to argue similarity in their
needs. Clearly, discussion of their offending in the group could present major difficulties. As female sexual offending challenges general beliefs about
women's behaviour, female sexual offenders in a group of general offenders
could be subjected to extreme hostility, or their behaviour may be reframed
in more gender-consistent terms as other group members seek to make sense
of it, in much the same way as some professionals were shown to in Chapter 2. This has obvious implications for the therapeutic environment of such
groups.

## THE LUCY FAITHFULL FOUNDATION ASSESSMENT AND INTERVENTION PROGRAMME – A CASE EXAMPLE

This manualised programme was piloted in a female-only prison during 2000/2001 as a combined individual and groupwork programme and in community-based individual work by the Lucy Faithfull Foundation. The programme comprises an individual assessment phase, which includes psychometric testing, followed by three intervention blocks, which can be run as group or individual work. There is optional additional individual work focusing on fantasy management, personal abuse-related issues and individual/family life plan development. In the prison pilot the intervention blocks were run as groupwork. The rationale for the different programme elements is drawn from research and clinical practice and the structure and content are summarised in Figure 9.1.

Intervention One begins with motivational work on overcoming obstacles to change as well as gaining offence descriptions and identifying offending patterns, including pro-offending thinking and arousal patterns and helping women to challenge and modify these. During Intervention One there is opportunity for the women to learn new ways of thinking and coping with difficult feelings, which they are encouraged to practise throughout the programme. Intervention Two contains an extensive module dealing with sexual and nonsexual relationships, which have often been poor in female offenders. There is also a victim empathy module. The final intervention block draws together work done throughout the programme in formulating the New Life Plan. It concentrates on desirable and achievable goals toward an abuse-free future and further develops problem-focused coping skills. The programme does not have a specific assertiveness module but aims to develop these and other interpersonal skills throughout. There is an integral theme of applying skills learned in the programme to everyday life experiences and revisiting real life practice in group. Many women need considerable work on emotion regulation and the programme is being revised to include additional sessions on this in Intervention Two.

From the beginning of the programme women work on their "New Life Manual" (Eldridge & Saradjian, in press a). This can be processed in individual or groupwork and links to the sessions in the intervention blocks. The manual includes anonymised stories that typify different kinds of female offender and indicates different patterns of offending. It helps women to identify their individual offence patterns and devise strategies for managing their moods, feelings, thoughts and relationships. It also helps them to understand that other women have behaved in ways similar to themselves and have changed, giving the message that an abuse-free life *is* possible.

At the end of the programme the psychometric tests administered initially are repeated. Given the small number of participants to date it is too early

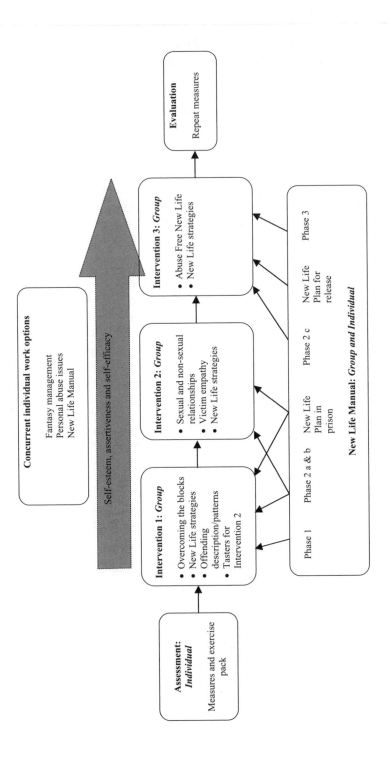

**Figure 9.1** Structure of the Lucy Faithfull Foundation's Assessment and Intervention Programme for female sexual abusers

to provide programme outcome data. However, comparison of pretreatment and posttreatment psychometric scores has indicated significant improvements in key target areas (Hilary Eldridge, personal communication).

## HOW EFFECTIVE ARE TREATMENT PROGRAMMES FOR FEMALE OFFENDERS?

There are difficulties in determining the effectiveness of interventions with female offenders, particularly given the very small numbers of women completing such programmes. It is also important to consider what is meant by a programme being "effective". While the previous discussion indicated that women undertaking the Lucy Faithfull Foundation programme demonstrated improvement in key target areas, these do not necessarily translate into reduced rates of recidivism/reconviction. However, the study of reconviction rates is also plagued by methodological difficulties. Firstly, reconviction rates for male sex offenders are typically low; Hanson et al. (2002) conducted a meta-analytic review of 43 studies and reported that on average, only 10 % to 15 % of sex offenders were detected for having committed a new offence, even after four or five years. However, a low official rate of reconviction does not necessarily mean that an individual has not offended; Falshaw, Friendship and Bates (2003) calculated the rate of sexual recidivism (defined as offence-related behaviour, whether illegal or not, which had a clear sexual motivation) to be more than 5 times greater than the official reconviction rate. Reconviction studies also rely on official records of criminal convictions and are therefore dependent on the accuracy of their recording and input by the appropriate authorities (Friendship, Falshaw & Beech, 2003).

These points are based on work with male sex offenders and we do not know whether they are equally applicable to women. It could be suggested that, given the potentially lesser acknowledgement of female sexual abuse within the CJS and the "paternalistic" attitudes described in Chapter 2, women may be less likely to be reconvicted of a sexual offence than men, although whether having previously been convicted may count more against a female offender is beyond the scope of this chapter. It is perhaps on account of difficulties such as these that Johansson-Love and Fremouw (2006) note that there is a lack of information about the treatment and potential recidivism of female abusers. Kemshall (2004) states that evaluations of programmes for female offenders have generally been limited to self-report type evaluations. The short programme described by Barnett, Corder and Jehu (1990), for example, noted that upon completion of the group women reported fewer cognitive distortions and stated that they felt more assertive, more able to talk about their offences and accept responsibility for them and had a greater understanding of abuse. These women also stated that the group had helped them to make sure that they would not offend again although, as the authors note, there was no means of testing the long-term accuracy of these claims. Where there are attempts to evaluate the impact of treatment on recidivism, insufficient detail is often given. For example, Matthews (1998) stated that only one of the 40 women undertaking her treatment programme had committed a new sexual offence at the time of writing, but gives no indication of the timescale of this evaluation. Beech, Erikson, Friendship and Ditchfield (2001) stated that reconviction rates have traditionally been calculated over a two-year period but Hedderman and Sugg (1996) suggested that in the case of sex offenders, two years may be insufficient. Without an indication of the timescale involved in Matthew's work her reported outcomes cannot be properly evaluated.

The introduction to this chapter described how the most effective interventions determine the level of intervention according to the individual's level of risk, assess and target the criminogenic needs associated with the offending behaviour and respond to individual differences. This chapter has suggested how programmes could be responsive to the needs of women and has pointed out the difficulty in measuring criminogenic needs in females using psychometric test batteries largely constructed for male offenders. There are similar difficulties in assessing the risk of reoffending in female offenders. This has important implications; responses from multi-agency public protection arrangements across England, Wales and Northern Ireland emphasised that the lack of risk assessment tools for female abusers created difficulties in forming management plans for these offenders and sometimes resulted in a downgrading of their risk (Bunting, 2005). Beech, Fisher and Thornton (2003) review the many different risk assessment tools developed for male offenders and question their applicability to other sex-offender populations. However, as Aylward, Christopher, Newell and Gordon (2002) state, "actuarial risk assessment tools not validated on women are being used to assess risk". Beech et al. (2003) describe work by Williams and Nicholaichuk (2001), which used an actuarial risk assessment tool (the RRASOR) with female sexual offenders, but note that this was based on a very small sample (N = 11) and that it is therefore difficult to draw firm conclusions from it. The items in the RRASOR tool thought to be related to sexual reconviction are past sexual offences, age at commencement of risk, extrafamilial victims and male victims. Whether these or factors identified by other risk assessment tools are equally relevant to female sexual offenders is an avenue for further research. Equally, other tools that do not rely solely on fixed, historical factors to determine risk use a number of psychometric measures. As stated previously, although some work is under way to adapt such measures for females, this is not at a stage where it can be used reliably and validly. Furthermore, as discussed in Chapter 5, at least some female offenders will have been coerced into sexual abuse by others or co-offended with others. As Beech et al. note, it is therefore important to assess the extent to which these women are able to resist such pressure from others in the future as part of a risk assessment. In addition, they state, as female offenders may be the primary caregivers to children, this also requires careful assessment.

It is currently difficult to allocate female offenders to a level of service or intervention based on their risk and needs as not only are programmes in limited supply but transferring male risk/needs models to females may not be appropriate. A fundamental question that remains to be answered is whether the differences between male and female sex offenders create differences in the relative importance of currently identified static and dynamic risk factors and whether there are specific risk factors for women. There is much work to be done in this area and, until this is underway, the outcomes and effectiveness of intervening with female offenders will not be easy to evaluate.

## SUMMARY OF MAIN POINTS

- Treatment provisions for female offenders are hampered by the small numbers of such women, particularly within the prison system.
- There are a number of possible areas for intervention when working with female offenders, some of which may be quite similar to the treatment targets of programmes for men. There may also be different types of needs according to the different offender typologies.
- However, there may be other more gender-specific needs. It seems important to address female offenders' histories of abuse without allowing this to excuse their offending behaviour.
- The feelings of low self-efficacy reported by many female offenders may affect their belief that they can change their offending, which may reduce motivation for treatment.
- It is important to develop means by which we can assess the needs of female offenders. Some of the psychometric measures used with male sex offenders may not be appropriate for females.
- The style and method of programme delivery should be responsive to the needs of females. The confrontational styles adopted in some male programmes may not be appropriate for women.
- It is difficult to evaluate the effectiveness of programmes for female offenders given the limited provision and small numbers. In addition to carrying out further research in this area it is important to develop risk and needs assessments specifically for women, otherwise the interventions we can offer them may not be based on the best practice principles of risks, needs and responsivity.

# V

# Widening Our Focus

# 10

# MOTHERS WHO ARE PARTNERS OF MALE OFFENDERS: ARE THEY COLLUSIVE AND THEREFORE ABUSIVE?

The term "collusive mother" has been widely used in relation to a number of different ideas about the mother in cases of father–child incest, particularly sexual abuse by a father against his daughter. This mother-blaming attitude rests on an assumption that although the mother may not actually touch her child sexually, she allows the child to be abused by others, either by ignoring signs of abuse, by proactively assisting the abuse to take place (Green, 1996), or by failing to act when the child discloses. McCarty (1986, p. 451) describes one such "collusive mother": "Mrs. C had known about the abuse since its beginning and took no actions to prevent it. She even took her 15-year old daughter to get an abortion". The image of the "collusive mother" is perhaps congruent to some degree with our schema of women; the women do not actually abuse their children but they are also passive and do not attempt to stand up to their male partners. Furthermore, as Jacobs (1990, p. 502) suggests, this blaming of mothers is consistent with "cultural norms that justify male violence by blaming the female victim for the actions of the aggressor".

In considering the "collusive mother", however, it is important to be clear about what is meant by collusion. For the purposes of this chapter, it is suggested that in order to be truly collusive both the abuser and the "collusive" mother must know that the abuse is occurring and, secondly, that both parties are willing for it to occur – that is, the mother is in agreement and is happy for her child to be abused. A mother cannot collude with the sexual activity if she is unaware of its occurrence.

## THEORIES AROUND COLLUSION

The origins of the belief in the "collusive mother" may be grounded in a number of theoretical approaches. Green (1996) reports that the family systems approach involves substantial blaming of the mother, viewing the abuse as occurring within specific family dynamics in which the mother plays a central role. The mother has been blamed for being too submissive or dependent on her male partner, too domineering in the relationship or for "reversing" roles with her daughter, including her sexual role. Thus as Birns and Meyer (1993, p. 129) state, "within this framework, incest is almost always viewed as a three person crime: the victim, the perpetrator and the mother".

Mother-blaming may also stem from theories of incest suggesting that fathers engage in sexual relations with their daughters because their wives sexually desert them (Bolen, 2003) or withdraw from their husbands (Gelinas, 1983). The mother "colludes" with the abuse so that she does not have to have sex with her partner. Such beliefs may have underpinned some early treatment models, which counselled mothers on ways to improve their sexual relationships with the offenders and required that mothers apologise to their daughters for the mother's role in the sexual abuse (Bolen, 2003).

Mother-blaming theories ascribe a particular set of personality characteristics to the mothers in incestuous families. They typically suggest these women to be passive, immature and overly dependent on their male partners (Green, 1996) or weak, irresponsible and subtly hostile to their victimised daughters (Smith & Saunders, 1995). The male partners, meanwhile, are described as overcontrolling, emotionally cold and physically abusive (Green, 1996) or being passive and dependent or having both passive and oppressive traits (Smith & Saunders, 1995). Interestingly, Smith and Saunders' own research did not find evidence of such traits in parents in incestuous families, suggesting instead that mothers and father/perpetrators were more likely to associate with partners having the same kind of personality characteristics as themselves. Perhaps findings such as these add weight to the statement by Tamraz (1996) (in Elliott & Carnes, 2001) that "much of this [mother-blaming] literature was based on theory and opinion rather than on research".

Nonetheless, Calder and Peake (2001b) state that, even today, some material continues to indicate the mother to be at least partly responsible for the abuse. Research published by Glasser et al. (2001, p. 492) states that, "incest often involves the collusion of the non-perpetrating parent or siblings and, in this sense, occurs in an inclusive system". Furthermore, Barrett (1993, p. 141) reports that in her experience some antipathy continues to be expressed towards mothers: "The struggle I currently hear in the field with respect to mothers is . . . 'I believe that they didn't know it was happening but now that they know, how can they stay with the offender?' or 'How can she ask her child to forgive the offender' ".

Bell (2002, p. 347) takes this further, stating that in her 11 years of working in this area, "it was striking that frequently more anger was expressed at a mother's 'not knowing' than at a father's active abuse of a child". Clearly in some cases, the mother may know of the abuse. However, it is all too easy to apportion blame to the mother without giving thorough consideration to the issues involved. The following discussion highlights some of these issues.

## DO MOTHERS KNOW ABOUT THE ABUSE
## BEFORE IT IS DISCLOSED?

This is an important question to consider in discussing collusion in mothers. As the definition presented at the beginning of this chapter stated, a mother cannot be collusive if she is unaware that the abuse is taking place. Examination of the literature indicates that some have found it impossible to accept that most mothers do not know about the abuse. Finkelhor and Russell (1984, p. 173), in discussing how these women are often included as perpetrators in incidence figures, state that, "it is true that, in many cases of intrafamilial sexual abuse, mothers (or other female caretakers) know that abuse is occurring and fail to stop it". Bolen (2003, p. 1343), however, notes that some earlier writers on the subject concluded that even though many mothers denied any knowledge of the abuse, this denial "was simply an unconscious method of allowing the incest to continue". In the past, at least, the assumption that mothers know of the abuse at some level appears also to have applied to professionals working in the field. Birns and Meyer (1993) cite a study by Dietz and Craft (1980), which found that while most social workers believed the mothers to also be victims of abuse by the fathers, almost all the workers still believed that the mothers gave their unconscious consent to the abuse, and 65 % believed the mother to be as guilty as the father. While this study is over 20 years old, the extent to which attitudes have changed is perhaps debatable. Calder and Peake (2001b) cite a later study by Breckenbridge and Berreen (1992), which found that between 40 % and 60 % of workers believed that mothers know about the abuse. A more detailed breakdown indicated that only 10 % of workers felt a mother would know in most cases, while 61 % felt that a mother would know in some cases. However, as the authors state, this means that, "overall 71 % of workers would have in their minds when dealing with a disclosure of sexual abuse within the family that mothers know: at least in some if not all cases" (p. 122). It is perhaps in the light of such findings that Calder and Peake (2001a, p. 61) fear that some professionals: "approach mothers suspiciously, rather than with an open mind, until the extent of their involvement can be ascertained. Such an approach is one of seeing them as guilty until proven otherwise". Interestingly, this readiness to accept mothers as having some responsibility for the abuse stands in contrast to the more general reluctance to recognise women as abusers.

Margolin (1991) suggested that many male abusers are "protected" by females who often have close relationships with them. Crawford, Hueppelheuser and George (1996) reported that 40 % of the spouses of incest offenders in their sample were aware of the abuse before a disclosure was made and that 80 % thought there were problems in the relationship before the abuse was known. These authors go on to state that, "even those who express surprise when the offence is revealed often have been doing an elaborate job of denying the reality of the abusive situation" (Crawford et al., 1996, p. 305). However, their study was based on the self-reports of women who had been in treatment for at least 2 years. The reason for treatment is not explicitly stated but it is assumed to be related to the incest and so these women may not be representative of nonoffending mothers generally and their recall of whether they knew about the abuse may have become less clear with time and perhaps from considering the incestuous situation in their therapy.

Even if sexual abuse was not actually taking place, some mothers have been described as indirectly collusive for placing their child in the care of known sexual offenders. That is, they knowingly placed their child into a situation in which sexual abuse was a possibility. Margolin (1991, p. 216) offers examples of this kind: "in nine cases parents knew that the man they were leaving their child with had a history of child molestation and/or other assaultive acts. One youth even told his mother that the caregiver had made sexual advances to him. However, the mother still left him with her."

Belief in the "collusive mother" may not be restricted to professionals. Although not asking specifically about incest, Calvert and Munsie-Benson (1999) reported that when their general population sample was asked whether parents of a sexually abused child would know that the child had been abused, 71 % of respondents said the parents would most likely know and a smaller proportion (29 %) said that parents would most likely never know. In the light of such findings it is perhaps easy to see why mothers have been implicated in incest and, assuming that the mothers in these situations also share such beliefs, it is equally easy to see why they often feel such guilt (discussed later in this chapter) when the abuse is finally revealed.

In addition to the possible professional and societal belief that the mother must know of the abuse, some research suggests that a proportion of victims too may believe their mothers were aware of the abuse and failed to prevent it from reoccurring. Calder and Peake (2001b) cite work by Scott and Flowers (1988), which asked female victims of abuse by their fathers about their mother's responses. Twenty-nine per cent of the adolescent victims and half of the adult victims believed their mothers had known about the abuse but did nothing to protect them, although this still suggests that at least half did not believe their mothers knew. Calder and Peake (2001a) suggest that mothers are viewed as caring, all-knowing, loving and responsible for their children. Thus when a child is abused, that child believes the mother must have known and feels betrayed by her inaction. This belief may be assisted by findings that mothers are frequently in the home when the abuse occurs (Sirles & Franke, 1989). Thus if their mothers were in the home when the abuse occurred, victims may misinterpret this as a sign that their mother was aware of the abuse and condoned it. One survivor illustrates this: "She just knew. I know she knew. How could she not know? We were doing it right outside the trailer and she was right inside" (Jacobs, 1990, p. 509). This strong sense of betrayal may be similar to that reported by victims who were actually abused by their mothers.

Other researchers, however, have found less evidence of collusion in mothers of abused children. Lukianowicz (1972) reported that 16 out of 26 mothers did not know about the abuse until their daughters disclosed it. Jacobs (1993) (in Freel, 1995) undertook in-depth interviews with 50 survivors of incest and found that 84 % believed their mothers were unaware of the abuse, or that they took action when a disclosure was made. Clearly, however, this reflects the victim's perception rather than the reality for the mother. Calder and Peake (2001b) cite a number of studies suggesting that most mothers had been unaware of the abuse before disclosure. Hooper (1992), they report, found that when the perpetrator lived in the home, 66 % of women did not know about the abuse for a substantial period of time and nearly two-thirds found out in a sudden, clearly identifiable incident. Calder and Peake (2001a) suggest that research generally indicates that nonabusing mothers are unaware of the sexual abuse and, although samples are often small and may be affected by mothers' unwillingness to admit to a researcher that they knew of the abuse, the studies described here suggest that between about 60 % and 84 % of mothers did not know about the abuse prior to disclosure.

However, it is perhaps too simplistic to ask whether mothers know about the abuse before disclosure and expect a "yes or no" answer. There may well be different levels of "knowing". Calder and Peake (2001a), for example, state that many mothers may be aware of problems in their families but are not aware of the sexual abuse. They suggest that mothers may attribute the problems they are aware of to other family difficulties such as alcoholism. Mothers may also be aware of the shortcomings of their partners; McCallum (2001) describes one mother who was aware that her husband was "not a good father" but had no idea that he was sexually abusing her children. In Bell's (2002) sample of mothers, even those women who themselves suffered violence and abuse from their partners did not initially think that the partner would pose a sexual risk to their children. Hooper and Humphreys (1998) suggest that a range of levels of knowledge exist in mothers, from those who are totally unaware, to those who had concerns but were not sure about what, to those who suspected sexual abuse but were unable to confirm their suspicions. Some mothers had found out about the abuse and believed they had acted protectively but later found out that the abuse had reoccurred, whereas other mothers denied the abuse for some time before accepting that it had occurred and taking action. It is also worth remembering the point made by Smith

(1989) that mothers are a convenient scapegoat. If the mother knows about the abuse, she says, it is likely that other family members will also know. Yet if they do not take action either, it is still the mother who is blamed.

## WHY DO WE EXPECT MOTHERS TO KNOW ABOUT THE ABUSE?

This is likely to be related to idealistic beliefs that, as mothers are the primary carers and protectors of their children, they should therefore be omniscient in all matters concerning their children. As Bell (2002) states, it is felt that a "good" mother would have recognised the abuse. However, sexual abuse is a secretive activity and many factors are working against the mother being aware. Foremost of these is probably the perpetrator himself who will groom the environment and perhaps also the mother to ensure the greatest likelihood of remaining undetected. Victims may have been groomed to keep the abuse secret and may wish to protect the mother from learning the truth, or may be acting on ingrained beliefs of the need to "keep up appearances" (Bell, 2002), or may have had their belief in their mother's ability to help them undermined by the perpetrator (Lovett, 1995).

Calder and Peake (2001b) present a comprehensive list of reasons as to why mothers are *not* likely to know that abuse is occurring. These include a general lack of knowledge about sexual abuse, inaccurate media portrayals of sexual offenders, grooming by the perpetrator and possible attempts to separate the mother and child, or the perpetrator offering a reasonable explanation for changes in the child's behaviour. Furthermore, these authors state, the "warning signs" of sexual abuse are often not very specific and could be explained by other things or may not elicit any particular concerns.

Kelly (1996) further states that mothers may be blamed for having chosen to form a relationship with an abuser. As she points out, however, women are usually unlikely to know that their partner has abused or will abuse children. If any choice is operating at all, she suggests, it is likely to be by the male who has selected the woman because she is vulnerable in some way and therefore more manipulable.

## THE MOTHER'S RESPONSE TO DISCLOSURE

Leifer et al. (2001) state that recent research has indicated the mother's belief of her abused child and her ability to act supportively to play a key role in the child's ability to resolve their abuse experiences. For this reason it is important to consider the various responses by mothers following disclosure and the factors that influence these responses. A further reason to consider the factors affecting a mother's response is that, as Calder and Peake (2001a) state, the mother's behaviour following disclosure is often used to judge her ability to protect and support the victim. A number of authors have noted that out-of-home placement decisions by professionals are based largely on the level of the mother's belief about the abuse and her subsequent protective action (Pintello & Zuravin, 2001) and partial support or ambivalence on the part of the nonoffending partner currently appears to be viewed by professionals as an inadequate level of support (Bolen & Lamb, 2004).

Research in this area has considered two key questions: does the mother believe her child's disclosure and, if so, does she respond in a supportive manner? These are important when considering the concept of collusion. As the earlier definition indicates, to be collusive, a mother must know that the abuse is occurring (or believe it when it is disclosed) and then indicate that she is willing for it to continue. This second aspect is particularly problematic, however, and as discussed later in this chapter, a mother's inaction does not necessarily indicate that she is willing for the abuse to occur.

## DO MOTHERS BELIEVE THEIR CHILDREN'S DISCLOSURE?

Research attempting to answer this question is divided. Elliott and Carnes (2001) suggest that it was primarily the earlier literature that reported that many mothers disbelieve their child's disclosure and that this disbelief or de-nial was seen as collusion on their part. Nonetheless, De Jong (1988) reported that about one-third of mothers in his sample were "nonsupportive", that is they thought the abuse disclosure a lie, a misunderstanding or primarily the child's fault. The majority of the nonsupportive mothers fell into the first two categories. Sirles and Franke (1989) reported that 78 % of mothers believed their children. However, this leaves over 20 % who did not. More recently, Pintello and Zuravin (2001) reported that 31 % of mothers in their sample neither believed nor protected their sexually abused child although this find-ing may be influenced by the fact that over half the mothers in the sample were currently in a sexual relationship with the offender, which, as discussed later, may impact on her level of belief. Overall, however, Hiebert-Murphy (2000) suggests that most studies report the majority of mothers to believe their child's disclosure.

Research has highlighted factors that may influence the extent to which a mother believes her child. Elliott and Carnes (2001) report several stud-ies suggesting that mothers are more likely to believe and support younger children. This is supported by Sirle and Franke's (1989) findings that 95 % of mothers of preschool-aged victims believed their child, compared with 82 % of mothers of victims aged 6 to 11. There was a particularly large decrease for older victims, with only 63 % of mothers believing their teenage children. However, some studies fail to find such effects; De Jong (1988), for example, reported no differences in maternal response according to the victim's age.

Victim gender may also be influential, with a suggestion that mothers may be more likely to believe and help sons rather than daughters (Elliott & Carnes, 2001). In support of this, Pintello and Zuravin (2001) found that male victims were more than twice as likely to be believed and protected by their mothers as female victims. Belief may also be influenced by the type of abuse suffered by the child. Sirles and Franke (1989) found that the majority of mothers believed their child's report when it described digital or oral contact with genitals but were less likely to believe reports of genital–genital contact. Pintello and Zuravin (2001) also found that mothers were less likely to believe and protect their child if the victim displayed sexualised behaviours, perhaps, they suggest, because the presence of such behaviours may lead the mother to assume that the child encouraged or initiated the abuse. Sirles and Franke (1989) further report that the whereabouts of the mother at the time of the abuse influenced her belief. Mothers were much more likely to believe a child who stated that the mother was not in the home at the time the abuse occurred, while Pintello and Zuravin (2001) noted that mothers were less likely to believe the abuse the longer it had been occurring.

This brief discussion of the literature cannot hope to be fully comprehensive but it clearly indicates that different factors may affect whether the mother believes her child. Further work needs to consider additional factors that may be influential, as well as examining possible interactions between factors.

It is interesting that so many studies suggest that most mothers believe their children's report. We might expect that an initial and natural response to such distressing news would be one of disbelief or denial, and indeed Hill (2001) states that the first reaction of many of the mothers in his sample was one of incredulity. Of course, we do not know if the studies described above relate to the mother's response in the immediate aftermath of disclosure or when she has had time to assimilate the information. However, Calder and Peake (2001a) emphasise that denial by the mother is a normal, healthy reaction as it gives her time to absorb the shock of the news and to prepare herself to deal with it. The difficulty, they state, occurs if the mother is unable to move on to the next stage of the reactive process. This is an important point; denial is not a static factor and a mother experiencing initial denial may go on to believe fully and support her child. Indeed fluctuations may exist in both directions and denial could coexist with some level of belief. This is neatly summarised by a mother in Hooper and Humphreys' (1998) study who was clearly attempting cognitively to deny the abuse while experiencing emotions congruent with belief: "In my head I just didn't want to believe, I was saying "No it's not possible". At the same time, inside me there was an anger. Such anger that I had never experienced before" (Hooper & Humphreys, 1988, p. 569).

Calder and Peake (2001a) describe a study by Johnson (1992) which found a similar mixture of belief and disbelief. These mothers, however, all believed cognitively that the abuse had occurred but were denying it on an emotional level. In time, however, this turned into acceptance. It is for such reasons that these authors again stress that a mother's initial response should not be accepted as her only and final one. Rather, mothers' responses should, "be understood as normative responses in a sequence of both cognitive and emotional reactions".

## IF THEY BELIEVE THE CHILD, HOW DO MOTHERS REACT?

Demause (1991, p. 126) reported that "sexual abuse usually involves a parent or guardian who, if not the direct perpetrator, covertly brings about the incident in order to satisfy their own incestuous wishes", which concurs with the definition of collusion involving willingness for the abuse to take place. Thus, if nonabusing mothers are collusive, we might expect them to show little negative emotional response to the disclosure of sexual abuse. In fact, the literature tends to describe the opposite response. Many researchers have reported mothers facing enormous emotional turmoil when the sexual abuse is disclosed. Elliott and Carnes (2001) state that many experience significant psychological distress following disclosure and a variety of psychological symptoms. Lewin and Bergin (2001) found that compared with mothers of nonabused children, the mothers of sexual abuse victims had higher levels of both depression and anxiety and that these mothers also engaged in less optimal attachment behaviours (less sensitivity, cooperation, acceptance and accessibility) in interactions with their children. De Jong (1988) suggests that reactions such as denial, guilt, anxiety, fear of repercussions or depression may all lower the likelihood of the mother responding in an appropriate and supportive manner. McCallum (2001) adds that the strong sense of shame experienced by some mothers can prevent them seeking help or support, further reducing their capacity to protect their children.

McCallum (2001) also suggests that disclosure can up-end a mother's whole sense of self-esteem and self-image. By accepting that her partner has committed the abuse she calls into question her own actions in choosing that partner and allowing him access to the children. In essence, McCallum states, these women have to re-evaluate their roles as both wives and mothers. Calder and Peake (2001a) cite work by Hooper (1989) which suggested that the mother's sexuality and sense of femininity is also threatened as she may view the abuse as a mixture of betrayal of trust, infidelity and rejection by the partner and the child, as well as being actual abuse. Such psychological distress would perhaps not be expected in a mother who is willing for the sexual abuse of her child to continue.

Freel (1995) cites work by Deblinger, Hathaway, Lippman and Stear (1993) which found that a significant proportion of nonabusing mothers tried to protect the child when they become aware of the abuse. While believing the child's report is clearly an important first step in responding supportively, some studies suggest that a protective response does not automatically follow, however. Calder and Peake (2001) describe work by Lyon and Kouloumpos-Lenares (1987) which reported that although 70 % of the mothers believed the child, only 50 % responded with protective action, emotional support and cooperation with relevant agencies. More recently, Heriot (1996) (in Elliott & Carnes, 2001) found that 20 % of mothers who believed their child failed to take protective action. Although a fairly small percentage, Pintello and Zuravin's (2001) study also reported that 13 % of mothers believed their children but did not protect them. Thus, the process between believing and taking action must be mediated by additional factors.

However, this may still not indicate collusion according to the initial definition. It is probable that a mother's response cannot always simply be categorised as supportive or nonsupportive. Elliott and Carnes (2001), for example, suggest that although a mother's response may be supportive in some ways, such as meeting physical and safety needs, it may be generally unsupportive in other ways, such as withholding emotional support. Thus, as these authors state, consideration of this issue will be muddied by different definitions of behaviour constituting support and protection. Differences in reports of supportive action may arise depending on whether the mother, the victim or relevant professionals are asked. Furthermore, victims and professionals may have difficulty in understanding the mother's motivation behind particular courses of action. If a mother does not take any action against an offender, this does not necessarily mean she is colluding with him. Calder and Peake (2001b) suggest several reasons for delays in the mother's response. She may be confused over the correct action to take in the light of her own and others' conflicting needs, or her lack of self-confidence and belief in her own judgement may inhibit action. Her own history may have made her vulnerable and unable to consider action to protect her own child. A mother may remain inactive not because she is unconcerned about the abusive situation but because she does not know how to act, particularly if she herself was abused and no one intervened. She may feel powerless against the abuser or afraid of him. She may also feel that too much will be lost by taking action, particularly if the family is dependent on the male financially, for example. None of these, however, suggest that she is colluding in the sense that she *wants* the abuse to continue.

It seems important also to distinguish between a mother taking no action and taking ineffective action. The mother may act in a way that is either inappropriate or ineffective. Calder and Peake (2001b) report the case of one mother who knew about the abuse but was unable to stop it and therefore tried alternative means to protect her child. She slept with the child in an effort to protect her and placed crackly paper under the bedroom door so that she would wake when the perpetrator opened it.

Alternatively, if the male abuses while intoxicated, for example, the mother may remove alcohol from the home or stop the abuser from going out drinking. Or, mothers might try to speak to the abuser, perhaps making ultimatums that anger him to the extent that the abuse worsens for both the child and the mother. Strategies such as these may not be known to the children so that when the children later describe the actions of the parents, they report the mother doing nothing. The mother may be blamed or become the focus of the victim's anger if she is perceived to take no action. Leifer, Kilbane and Grossman (2001) reported that children of nonsupportive mothers more often blamed their mothers for the abuse. Calder and Peake (2001b, p. 118) describe the relationship between one mother and daughter: "She still hits and kicks me, and blames me. She said, 'You were cooking his dinner and let him come up and do the naughty things'. She didn't realise that I didn't know".

Calder and Peake (2001b) suggest that if the mother's response does not meet the child's current psychological needs, the child is likely to view the response as being nonsupportive. Elliott and Carnes (2001) add that often a parent's perception of what constitutes supportive behaviour is not sufficient to meet the child's needs and this is likely to affect how the parental response is reported by the child. However, Hooper and Humphreys (1998) suggest that even when mothers do respond supportively, child victims frequently have complex feelings towards their mothers, which may involve anger and a sense of betrayal by their mothers for not protecting them sooner. Furthermore, Green (1996) suggests that nonabused siblings may also sometimes direct their anger towards the mother.

If we ask mothers about their responses to disclosure, meanwhile, some may be more willing to say they did nothing than to admit an attempt at intervention actually made things worse. As Bolen and Lamb (2004) note, operationalising the term "guardian support" may not be consistent and may tend to be most frequently indicated by believing the victim, emotional or meaningful support or taking action against the perpetrator. Such indicators, these authors note, however, may primarily reflect the norms and expectations of child protection services and other professionals as to how nonoffending partners should act following disclosure of sexual abuse. They may not take full account of the many different factors impinging on the nonoffending partner in this situation. Thus, the motives underlying the behaviour of the so-called collusive mothers need more detailed study. While some mothers may fail to protect their children in abusive situations, it is not always through choice and may not be indicative of collusion.

## OTHER FACTORS AFFECTING THE MOTHER'S RESPONSE TO DISCLOSURE

It seems we place a heavy load on mothers. As Green (1996, p. 340) states, mothers are: "expected to take action swiftly, rationally, and decisively in areas that may bring about wrenching, long-term upheaval not only in her own life but the life of her family, [and] her culpability is confirmed if she does not".

However, a number of factors may influence the ease with which mothers can take such action. Perhaps the most frequently cited of these is the mother's own experience of childhood abuse. Some studies indicate high levels of abuse in these mothers' backgrounds. Hiebert-Murphy (2000) reported that 74 % of mothers in her sample disclosed at least one experience of contact sexual abuse during childhood or adolescence and 41 % of these reported incidents in both childhood and adolescence. Of course, these findings can only be properly evaluated when compared with general population rates of sexual abuse. Nonetheless, Kelly (1996) states that these mothers' experiences of abuse are presumed to make them less able to protect their own abused children.

Jacobs (1990) suggests that a mother's failure to intervene in father–child abuse may be partly a denial of her own childhood abuse. Calder and Peake (2001c) further suggest that when abused mothers learn of the abuse of their children, the subsequent trauma may lead to them reexperiencing their own abuse. They suggest that many mothers have responded to their own abuse by minimising, denying or forgetting the experience and thus when they discover the abuse of their own children, they face a huge dilemma and may ultimately choose not to pursue this information. Therefore, they suggest, these women are still using the coping strategies they developed to deal with their own abuse and, drawing on work by Hooper (1989), they suggest that this lack of action should be viewed as coping rather than collusion. Calder and Peake (2001c) go on to describe work by Ovaris (1991) who noted that suffering sexual abuse as a child can impact on the mother's self-esteem, her view of the world and expectations of herself, of others and of life in general. Most common, they state, is a belief that she cannot protect herself from adversity, which may extend to a belief that she is not able to protect her children. Some responses may go to the other extreme, however. Kreklewetz and Piotrowski (1998) (in Ruscio, 2001) stated that incestuously abused mothers were often fearful and overprotective, heavily supervising and monitoring their daughters' activities both at home and beyond, in an effort to protect them from victimisation.

Whether or not mothers have experienced past sexual abuse, some may be subjected to physical abuse by their sexually abusive male partners. Sirles and Franke (1989) reported that physical abuse of the spouse occurred in 44 % of cases of abuse of the child. Birns and Meyer (1993) cite Truesdell, McNeil and Deschner (1986) who found that 73 % of mothers of incest victims were physically abused by the perpetrator. De Young (1994) (in Freel, 1995) reported that in incestuous families, 85 % of abusing men also abused their wives physically, sexually or emotionally, while only 1 of the 11 mothers in Bell's (2002) sample reported never having experienced any physical violence from her partner. However, as Bell notes, mothers who have experienced domestic violence may find it easier to believe that their partners could be abusive in other ways, which could inflate the level of domestic violence reported by mothers who have identified sexual abuse of their children. Nonetheless, as

Birns and Meyer (1993) state, when mothers are labelled as passive, weak or collusive, their behaviour may result from the abuse they are suffering from the perpetrator rather than inherent personality traits. They may be subjected to the same threats as the abused child and reveal nothing to others for the same reasons. Calder and Peake (2001b) state that women living in violent situations can be immobilised through shock or fear. Moreover, they note, children may be frightened to tell possible protectors about the abuse for fear of repercussions, either for themselves or their mother. Furthermore, if they have witnessed domestic violence, they may perceive the mother as a "victim" and believe that she is unlikely to be able to protect them. Domestic violence can further hide sexual abuse by leading the child sexual abuse victim to accept that violence is a regular occurrence in their home, or by leading mothers to believe that disturbed behaviour in their children is a consequence of their witnessing the parental violence (Bell, 2002).

It must be difficult for a mother to comprehend that someone she knows and possibly loves and trusts could have sexually abused her child. A number of studies have suggested that the nature of the mother's relationship with the perpetrator can influence her responses after disclosure. Leifer et al. (2001) reported that when the mother was not supportive of the child, the perpetrator was more likely to be a biological father, stepfather or the mother's boyfriend and to be living in the home. Sirles and Franke (1989) found that most mothers believed their child if the perpetrator was an extended family member, were a little less likely to believe if the perpetrator was a biological father (86 % believed) and somewhat less likely to believe if the perpetrator was a stepfather or live-in partner (only 56 % believed). This largely accords with studies reported by Elliott and Carnes (2001) and Pintello and Zuravin's (2001) work, which suggest that the mother is less supportive and protective when the offender is a current partner. Faller (1988) reports broadly similar findings but states that mothers whose children are abused by biological fathers are the most "collusive", followed by mothers whose children were abused by stepfathers or live-in partners. The least "collusive" women were those who were relatively independent of the male perpetrator. However, it should be noted that some studies have failed to find a relationship between the mother's level of support for the child and her relationship with the perpetrator (e.g. De Jong, 1988).

The self-perceived quality of the relationship may also be important. Two mothers interviewed by McCallum (2001) believed they had strong marriages and thus were extremely shocked by the disclosure. Another mother, however, had experienced many forms of violence from her husband and so was more readily able to accept that he had also abused the children. Calder and Peake (2001a) similarly report that if the sexual relationship between the mother and perpetrator is good, this can act as an obstacle to her believing that the sexual abuse occurred. Elliott and Carnes (2001) further suggest that the mother may be less protective of her child when her relationship with the offender is more dependent or intimate.

The mother's general relationship history may also be pertinent. Leifer et al. (2001) state that unsupportive mothers have more troubled histories of attachment relationships and more problematic current relationships. The findings that mothers may be less supportive if the offender is a stepfather or live-in partner may be partly explained by the fact that a woman who has previously experienced relationship breakup or divorce may be more reluctant to end another relationship. Relationships with parents may also be important. Leifer et al. (2001) reported that the childhoods of unsupportive mothers were characterised by separations from their biological parents and less continuity of care. The mothers of these unsupportive mothers described their relationship with their daughters more negatively, reported less contact with their grandchildren (the victims), and also took significantly less protective action on their behalf. Calder and Peake (2001a) describe work by Salt, Myers, Coleman and Sauzier (1990) which found that mothers reporting a poor relationship with either parent seemed less able to be concerned about their sexually abused children. Furthermore, unsupportive mothers had either experienced poor relationships with the maternal grandmothers, or, as children, had had absent mothers. Noll (2005) takes this one stage further, hypothesising that perhaps mothers who were themselves abused have disrupted working models of attachment, perhaps leading to them experiencing difficulties in forming appropriate relationships with adults and, consequently, perhaps unintentionally selecting potentially abusive partners.

## WHAT DO MOTHERS STAND TO LOSE FOLLOWING DISCLOSURE?

Research suggests that mothers in incestuous families have often been criticised for their responses (or lack of) to the situation and this criticism and blame may mirror the mother's own self-blame (Kelly, 1996). However, it is important to consider this from the mother's perspective as she stands to lose a number of things she may have come to rely on in her life. Bolen and Lamb (2004) suggest that the higher the costs and stressors of disclosure, and the less resources are available to them, the more likely it is that nonoffending partners will respond to the disclosure with ambivalence. The foremost of these costs, perhaps, is the loss of the partner himself. Indeed the mother may find herself in the unenviable position of having to choose between her partner or her child and such "torn loyalties" may be difficult to bear. This is described by a mother in McCallum's (2001) study: "you have the offender to whom you are married and obviously love... and you've got your daughter who you love, and there's a lot of tugging that goes on in the beginning" (McCallum, 2001, p. 322). The situation may be compounded if the mother has been groomed by the offender or if he denies the abuse and continues to groom her. Hooper and Humphreys (1998) report the feelings of another mother: "It's so hard to confront him when I still love him . . . he makes me feel as though I am the guilty one for thinking such things about him . . . it's very confusing" (Hooper & Humphreys, 1998, p. 570). Mothers may be further blamed if they decide to stay with their children but also profess some support for the offender. Calder and Peake (2001a) state that this choice is not generally understood by professionals who may try to force the mother to choose between her child and the offender. Even if they separate from their partner, mothers still risk losing their children. Calder and Peake (2001a) state that the evidence suggests between 40 % and 73 % of sexually abused children are removed from their homes after disclosure.

The number of mothers who choose to stay with their partners rather than their children is not known. Crawford et al. (1996) reported that in their study, over 90 % of spouses never leave the offender, although further reading of their paper indicates that the majority left upon disclosure, but that 81 % were eventually reunited. There may be a number of practical reasons for this, not least the financial losses involved if the offender has been primarily responsible for providing the family income. Certainly, Leifer et al. (2001) report that mothers who were not supportive were more financially dependent on the perpetrator than supportive mothers. In addition, they may value the support and companionship of the male partner and be loath to lose that, particularly if, as Smith and Saunders (1995) suggest, some mothers have difficulties with social relationships. If they leave their partner, they may face many additional responsibilities and new practical tasks. One mother in McCallum's (2001) study stated: "I didn't know how to make the furnace work when it stopped one night and I was worried about the pipes freezing. I didn't even know who to call up to help me" (McCallum, 2001, p. 325).

Attempting to relieve financial difficulties by returning to work may be problematic. Calder and Peake (2001a) indicate that this may involve potential retraining and the need to find safe childcare to facilitate this. As they state, "her ability to trust anyone will clearly be at an all time low given the recent events" (Calder & Peake, 2001a, p. 110). In addition to a general loss of trust, the mother may find that she has lost support from others if, for example, she chooses to stay with or support the offender. In addition she may find herself pressured not to press charges by the perpetrators' friends or relatives (De Jong, 1988) and may lose their support if she does. As McCallum (2001, p. 328) states: "this potentially places extra pressure on mothers as they now cope with the loss of support as well as finding explanations to offer children for the absence of relatives from their lives".

Mothers may also find themselves caught in a double bind with the supporting agencies. Calder and Peake (2001b) state that mothers are generally represented either as collusive, in which case they are offered no support, or as good and protective mothers, who are then largely left to cope alone. This denies both "types" of mother the support they need and leads women in this situation to frequently report a lack of understanding and support from professionals (Hill, 2001). In short, mothers may be in a situation in which they view themselves as having much to lose but less to gain in their response to disclosure. Above all, it seems that mothers are expected to focus not on their own needs but on those of their children. As McCallum (2001, p. 329) states: "while women are coming to terms with the knowledge that their marriages were fundamentally flawed and the grief and loss associated with that, they also have to put their own needs aside to care for their children".

## WHAT ABOUT THE "COLLUSIVE FATHER"?

As sexual abuse by women has until recently been minimised or ignored, it is not surprising that little consideration has been given to the possibility of a reversal in the situation should the mother be the abuser. Mayer (1992) cites one victim who believes that her father knew about the abuse by her mother but did nothing to prevent it. Faller (1995) also provides examples of apparently collusive fathers who "seemed to minimise the mothers' deficits and, in two cases, not protect their children from the mothers" (Faller, 1995, p. 21). Crawford et al. (1996) describe a case of mother–daughter abuse in which the father was aware but did not intervene. Mars (1998) describes a case of mother–son incest in which the father knew of the sexual activity and yet when the mother chose to prepare a bath for her son (a major part of the abuse) "father would leave the house and visit the maternal grandparents, returning home later" (Mars, 1998, p. 407). Of course, all the points made in relation to collusive mothers may be applicable to these fathers. However, this is an interesting area for further investigation.

Ogilvie and Daniluk (1995) reiterate that victims of father–child incest often feel anger towards or blame their mother for "letting" the abuse happen. Interestingly, however, these authors state that in their cases of mother–daughter abuse, none of the victims expressed hostility or rage towards their fathers for not protecting them. Instead, these women believed it was a mother's role to protect and care for her children rather than the father. Saradjian (1997) reports a similar finding stating that when a child is sexually abused by a woman, even if there is a nonprotecting male parent, then anger is not projected onto him in the way that hostility is expressed towards nonabusing mothers.

## THE CONSEQUENCES OF MOTHER-BLAMING

At this point, it is important to reiterate that there will be some mothers who are aware of the sexual abuse of their children, have colluded with it or have even been active participants. However, it seems unhelpful to level this belief at all mothers in abusive families. By blaming the mother, we absolve the perpetrator of responsibility for the offence and appear not to have moved all that far on from the early treatment models described at the start of this chapter. Furthermore, by placing responsibility for the abuse with the mother we reduce our ability to explain child sexual abuse, given the multiple contexts in which it occurs (Conte, 1982, in Faller, 1988).

Strong feelings of guilt appear common in these mothers. Hill (2001), for example, stated that in his sample of mothers, after the initial shock of the abuse, the universal feeling was one of guilt. This guilt appeared to centre around the women having failed to recognise the abuse was occurring, from having failed to protect their children and, consequently, feeling that they had "failed" as mothers. As one woman in this sample said, "I couldn't bear to look at women with children. I used to not like these other mothers who I thought wouldn't let their children down" (Hill, 2001, p. 388).

Bell (2003) notes that some mothers felt tremendous guilt for having encouraged their partners and children to spend more time together. It was only later that it became clear that this was time in which the sexual abuse was taking place. McCallum (2001) reports that the mothers she interviewed already felt guilty and they found it difficult to cope with the feeling that others blamed them too. Being blamed by others only served to increase their feelings of victimisation. Mary Faux[1] notes that nonoffending partners often feel that they are stigmatised for being "an offender's partner" and are labelled either as this or as "the victim's mother", rather than as a person in their own right with their own particular needs. Calder and Peake (2001a) point out that if the mother senses blame, she may well deflect her energies from supporting the child to defending herself. This may lead to antagonism towards the agencies attempting to offer support; Jackson and Mannix (2004) reported that in all but one case of six mothers who sought counselling, feelings of being blamed led these women to stop using these services. Their own sense of guilt or a fear of being blamed may also result in mothers feeling unable to turn to their usual support networks of family or friends (Hill, 2001; Jackson & Mannix, 2004). Feelings of being blamed may result in further loss of self-esteem and an enhanced sense of isolation, again reducing the mother's ability to act in a protective capacity. It is therefore important to consider the extent to which blaming mothers may inhibit both their own attempts and the relevant agencies' attempts to protect the victims, particularly as a warm relationship between mother and victim may aid the victim's recovery (Lovett, 1995).

Green (1996) reports that mother-blaming is less prevalent now than in the past, although whether it has completely disappeared is less easy to say. Certainly, as Bolen (2003) points out, greater clarity about what child protection workers are being taught with regard to nonoffending mothers is important. Mothers in incest families continue to find themselves in an extraordinarily

---

[1] Mary Faux at NOTA conference: "Standing by your man? Working with partners in an accredited sex offender treatment programme". Edinburgh, September 24, 2003.

difficult and potentially isolating position and agencies need to further develop ways of working with and helping these women. This is unlikely to be simple. As stated previously, feelings of guilt or fears of being blamed may hinder mothers in seeking out services or accepting help. Mothers may also be expecting blame from professionals and are likely to be aware of and sensitive to this, whether or not they have actually been confronted with such blame (Bell, 2003). Therefore, irrespective of the attitude of the worker, the woman's own feelings about herself could influence her interaction with professionals. This is summed up by one woman in Hill's (2001) research: "in my case it was just because I felt so bad about myself that I thought they must be thinking the same things about me even if they were smiling nicely" (Hill, 2001, p. 390).

Given the many and varied needs of such mothers, specialist intervention programmes may be important, helping these women to understand and deal with what has happened and giving them skills and support to protect their children and themselves. Forbes, Duffy, Mok and Lemvig (2003) describe an early intervention service for the nonabusing parents of sexual abuse victims. This service offers empathy and education to parents about child sexual abuse and helps and advises them in reinforcing their parenting skills and managing potential difficulties for the victim, but is more child-focused and perhaps deals less with the emotional consequences for the parents themselves. Nonetheless, the authors found that following the intervention there was a decrease in parental distress and psychopathology, suggesting that the input is still beneficial to parents. Perhaps this results from them understanding the consequences for the victim better and feeling more skilled as parents. More qualitative research with the parents would be useful in this respect. The Thames Valley Sex Offender Groupwork Programme, meanwhile, was developed with a Partner's Groupwork Programme to address the needs of women whose partners are attending the treatment programme (Still, Faux & Wilson, 2001). However, Hill's (2001) work indicates that the importance of peer support should not be underestimated, as mothers may remain wary of child-protection agencies or feel inhibited from turning to friends or family. His research highlighted the huge relief felt by mothers in the group of having all had the same experience and of the group being non-judgemental and safe. This was summarised by one mother who stated: "you could talk about feeling like a failure as a mother and be totally safe because all those other people had felt exactly the same" (Hill, 2001, p. 392).

However, having briefly considered whether in the case of sexual abuse by women there might be nonoffending fathers in the same position, it is important to consider what help they might need and whether these services would also be available to them. Although their data were not separated out by gender, the service described by Forbes et al. (2003) did include some males. However, whether men would easily be able to fit into some of the other groups described remains an area for further research.

## SUMMARY OF MAIN POINTS

● Particularly in the early literature concerning incest, there was a tendency to blame mothers and to view them as "colluding" in the abuse. More recent research has suggested that this attitude is now less prevalent but it is unclear whether it has disappeared entirely.

● Although there are some discrepancies, the literature suggests that only a minority of mothers know about the sexual abuse before disclosure and it is likely that an even smaller percentage actively collude with the abuse.

● Responses by those mothers who do know of the abuse may not reflect collusion so much as ineffectual responses or uncertainty about what to do.

● A number of different factors may influence whether a mother believes her child's disclosure of abuse, including the child's age and gender and the type of sexual acts reported by the child. The mother's subsequent response to this information may also be affected by her own experiences of abuse, abuse within the current relationship or the nature and self-perceived quality of the relationship with the perpetrator.

● The mothers of abused children often stand to lose many things once the disclosure is made, both in practical or financial terms and emotionally. It seems that we may often expect mothers to disregard their own losses and needs to focus on the needs of the victim.

● By blaming mothers or viewing them as having colluded in the abuse we are removing blame from the perpetrator and further fuelling the mother's own feelings of guilt and failure. This potentially reduces the likelihood of her seeking help and support from the appropriate agencies which, in turn, may reduce her ability to help and support the victim. In this respect, access to peer support groups for mothers of abused children may be of major importance.

# 11

# FEMALE ADOLESCENTS AND CHILDREN WHO SEXUALLY ABUSE

The main focus of this book has been to examine our current knowledge in relation to sexual abuse by women. However, a level of denial similar to that initially surrounding women abusers exists around the notion that female adolescents or children can be sexually abusive. Indeed, Minasian and Lewis (1999) state that information about this group of offenders is even more limited than that concerning adult women abusers. The National Clearing House on Family Violence (1990) found that of the 349 reports of sexual offences by adolescents received in Toronto between 1984 and 1986, 98 % of the alleged offenders were male and only 2 % female. Långström (2001) cites a number of studies which consistently report that adolescents account for about one-third of sexual offences against children, but states that, "girls constitute at most 5 % of identified young persons committing sex offences" (Långström, 2001, p. 8). As with their adult counterparts, then, official statistics may downplay abuse by young females. Righthand and Welch (2001) cite similar figures for studies conducted during the 1980s, but suggest that more recently a higher incidence of sexual offending by young girls has been reported. Hickman, Jaycox and Aronoff (2004) cite a number of studies that vary in estimating sexual violence perpetration in girls to range from 2 % to 24 %, compared with ranges of 3 % to 37 % in boys. It should be noted, however, that these figures relate to studies of sexual aggression within the context of dating relationships. However, irrespective of whether these figures are accurate or the result of denial and underreporting, it is clear that some female adolescents and children are sexually aggressive towards other children. This final chapter considers this issue more fully and, although it does not offer a fully comprehensive review of the literature, relevant findings and pertinent issues are highlighted.

## WHY IS SEXUALLY ABUSIVE BEHAVIOUR BY FEMALE ADOLESCENTS AND CHILDREN NOT FULLY RECOGNISED?

The first possible reason for the lack of recognition is the apparently low rates of perpetration by young females, as described above. However, these figures may represent a reframing of the behaviour by others or underreporting by victims and indeed many of the issues described in relation to abuse by adult females may be equally applicable here.

Professionals may have had little experience with this group of perpetrators (Scavo, 1989) and may therefore have difficulty in knowing how to respond when presented with such cases. Indeed, their response may be to deny. Burton, Nesmith and Badten (1997, p. 157) state that historically "clinicians and researchers have denied or ignored the capability of youth and children to be sexually abusive". Ironically, this may be one reason why professionals come across few cases. Buist and Fuller (1996) suggest that professionals have been too ready to explain sexual behaviour in children as "normal sexual experimentation", which has served to deny and minimise the seriousness of the behaviour. Blues, Moffat and Telford (1999), meanwhile, cite Ryan and Lane's (1991) suggestion that when girls behave in sexually abusive ways they are often seen as "acting out" their own abuse, rather than actually abusing other children. Blues et al. (1999) further suggest that the age at which sexually abusive behaviour is deemed worrying enough for intervention is slightly later for girls than boys and they state that, in their experience, many girls have only been offered help for their own experiences of abuse, even when their abusing behaviour was known. This suggests that, as with adult women abusers, young females are often seen as victims, not victimisers, their own sexually aggressive behaviour is deemed less serious than that of males and this "explaining away" of their behaviour may result in fewer cases reaching professionals.

Such views may be propagated within the CJS. Scott and Telford[1] report that out of 16 girls they have worked with, 11 were of an age to be convicted but none were interviewed by the police. Hirshberg and Riskin (1994) reported that 65 % of the adolescent females in their sample had no court involvement at all following their sexually abusive behaviour. This may reflect the judicial "paternalism" sometimes displayed towards females, which could be compounded in the case of younger females. Scavo (1989) suggests that professionals may be unwilling to stigmatise young offenders and the National Clearing House on Family Violence (1990) suggests that there is often a desire to protect adolescents from harmful "labels", resulting in plea bargaining to

---

[1] Jane Scott and Paula Telford at NOTA conference: "Working with girls". Edinburgh, September 26, 2003.

avoid conviction for a sexual offence. There is evidence of this in Australia, where young women who have engaged in sexually aggressive behaviour have instead been charged with common assault (Harris, 2001). As with some adult female offenders, then, young women may be treated more leniently by the courts. Roy (2001) states that courts often perceive young female abusers as: "victims of their past, where they are given more chances . . . receive lighter sentences and . . . tend to be referred more to mental health services than do similar young men" (personal communication to Harris, 2001).

Kubik, Hecker and Righthand (2002), however, report somewhat contradictory evidence, stating that arrest rates for sexual offences and rapes committed by adolescent females appear to be increasing more rapidly than those for adolescent males. They suggest, however, that these increasing rates may reflect growing awareness of female offending and a greater willingness to hold girls accountable for their actions, rather than an increase in sexual offending by adolescent females per se. Even if the situation is now changing, factors such as these are likely to have contributed to the collection of relatively few data on young female sexual abusers (Hunter, Lexier, Goodwin, Browne & Dennis, 1993; Becker, Johnson & Hunter, 1996) and even where females are included in research findings, their results often are not reported separately from those of males (Fromuth & Conn, 1997). This is also likely to be partly responsible for the lack of services we have to offer these young people (Blues et al., 1999).

## THE RESEARCH SO FAR: COMPARING SEXUALLY ABUSIVE MALE AND FEMALE ADOLESCENTS

Most research to date has been descriptive, comparing sexually abusive male and female adolescents on a number of variables. Harris (2001) organised her review of the literature around factors such as family environment and abuse history, psychological predisposition and modus operandi, and suggested that overall there were more similarities than differences between male and female adolescents. She reported that both male and female adolescent abusers are often raised in chaotic and abusive home environments and may be indirectly victimised through exposure to domestic violence. This is supported by Blues et al. (1999) who noted domestic violence to be a significant feature in the lives of many adolescent abusers with whom they have worked. These authors also report physical and emotional abuse to be common experiences for girls and boys who are sexually aggressive and, perhaps as a consequence, for them to have formed unstable attachment relationships with their caregivers. Kubik et al. (2002) found similar proportions of male and female adolescent abusers to have a history of child protection issues. In terms of other potentially predisposing difficulties, Blues et al. noted many male and female adolescent abusers to have poor self-esteem and difficulties at school. Similar suggestions were made by Kubik et al., who found comparable proportions of males and females to have problems at school and to exhibit behaviours such as running away, difficulties with anger and problematic relationships with peers. Finally, Harris (2001) notes that male and female adolescent abusers are similar in the types of sexual acts they commit, an assertion supported by Kubik et al. who suggest that females commit the full range of sexually abusive acts and that there are "no obvious differences between the groups' sexual offence characteristics" (Kubik et al., 2002, p. 77).

Nonetheless, some differences have been reported. Fehrenbach and Monastersky (1988) suggested that girls tend only to abuse other children, whereas over one-third of the boys in their sample abused victims of their own age, or older. Harris (2001) cites a number of studies suggesting that sexually aggressive female adolescents are most likely to abuse within the family and are much more likely than males to know their victims. The studies reported by Hickman et al. (2004), however, clearly indicate that some girls are using sexual aggression in dating relationships, that is with victims outside of the family and who are presumably of a similar age to the perpetrators themselves. Righthand and Welch (2001) describe work by Ray and English (1995) which found that sexually abusive girls tended to be younger than their male counterparts and also had more extensive histories of abusive experiences. Kubik et al. (2002) reported that sexually aggressive adolescent females in their sample were more likely to have been maltreated in a variety of ways than a sample of sexually aggressive adolescent males, including being abused by a larger number of perpetrators, being abused by someone they knew and to have been penetrated during sexual abuse. However, both their samples were very small and such differences could also reflect greater reluctance to disclose abuse experiences amongst male victims.

Blues et al. (1999) report some evidence that girls are less likely to use force and rely more on coercion to prevent the abuse being disclosed. These authors further state that even when girls have used aggression or coercion, there is a difference between the sexes; for some boys the aggression has become part of the sexual gratification but this has not been identified in girls.

Harris (2001) states that the biggest difference between male and female referrals to the Children's Protection Society in Victoria, Australia, was their motivation for the offence. Boys were seen as offending for reasons of power and control while girls were described as abusing within the context of a "nurturing" relationship (albeit a distorted one) and for reasons of emotional connection. While the context of sexual aggression used within peer dating relationships may be slightly different, Hickman et al. (2004) cite work by O'Keefe (1997), which found that violence perpetrated by girls was related to a belief that female-to-male violence was justified whereas male-to-female violence was not. It should be noted that this work was not specific to sexual violence but it raises an interesting question about how sexually abusive girls justify their behaviours. Such justification could also be related to Hilton,

Harris and Rice's (2003) findings that in a sample of 16 year olds, male-to-female sexual aggression was rated as more serious than female-to-male sexual aggression. Thus, this latter type of behaviour may partly be viewed as more justifiable as it is generally viewed as being less serious. Whatever the different motivations may be, however, Blues et al. (1999) suggest that the biggest difference between sexually abusive males and females lies in how society and professionals perceive and respond to them.

Research has also compared the extent to which males and females begin their sexual aggression in childhood or adolescence and continue into adulthood. Many studies with adult male offenders have reported that a large proportion began offending during their teenage years (Kendrick, 2004). Benoit and Kennedy (1992) report several studies demonstrating that sexually abusive male adolescents often go on to become adult offenders. They cite findings by Groth, Longo and McFadin (1982) that half of a sample of adult sex offenders reported committing their first offence as teenagers. Interestingly, retrospective studies with adult female abusers have not generally reported sexually abusive behaviour in adolescence. None of the women in McCarty's (1986) work reported sexually aggressive behaviour during adolescence. The women in Saradjian's (1996) study said they had not abused in adolescence and Matthews (1993) reported that only 2 of 36 women had sexually abused others as teenagers. Little work has studied the continuation of sex offending in adulthood in sexually abusive adolescent females. However, Fromuth and Conn's (1997) study with college women suggested that, in contrast to college men, women stop their offending by mid-adolescence.

This has led to some speculation that female offending is more likely to be "one-off" behaviour that does not continue in later life. Fehrenbach and Monastersky (1988), for example, reported that only 4 of their 28 offenders had committed more than 1 sex offence and only 2 appeared to be involved in repetitive patterns of sexually abusing. Harris (2001) documents some researchers' beliefs that girls are more likely than boys to "grow out" of their offending and Hunter et al. (1993) emphasise that no progression has been established between adolescent and adult sex offending in females. These apparent differences between males and females may result from women denying that they have committed sexual offences earlier in life; as described previously, some research has suggested women to be more likely to deny their offences than males. More generally held beliefs that abusive acts by children are "sexual experimentation" may also have been adopted by these women so that they believe that previous acts were not abuse, or at least use such beliefs to excuse their behaviour. However, it is also possible that the progression from adolescent to adult offending found in many males does not exist in females.

Not all researchers are in agreement, however. Scavo (1989) states there is no reason to believe that untreated sexually abusive females are less likely than males to carry on abusing into adulthood. Blues et al. (1999) indicate that for all the girls they have treated, there was evidence that without interven-tion their sexually abusive behaviour would have continued into adulthood. Hirschberg and Riskin (1994) note that although some subjects appeared to have engaged in isolated incidents of abuse, the greater proportion had repet-itive patterns of sexually abusive behaviour. Ninety per cent of their subjects had two or more reported victims. These authors suggest that different treat-ment needs might exist for adolescents displaying repetitive, compared with isolated, abusive behaviours.

The reason for these divergent findings is not immediately apparent. How-ever, in addition to the suggestions already made, sampling differences may also contribute. Fehrenbach and Monastersky (1988), for example, studied an outpatient population while Hirschberg and Riskin's (1994) sample was drawn from a residential treatment programme which, as the authors state, received adolescents referred "due to the dangerous and chronic nature of their maladaptive behaviours" (Hirschberg & Riskin, 1994, p. 4).

In summary, then, research has suggested a number of similarities between sexually abusive male and female adolescents, although important distinc-tions have also been highlighted. What has been less thoroughly considered in this comparative research are the similarities and differences between adult and adolescent female offenders. The discussion in this section has raised the possibility that there could be different groups – females who are sexually abusive only as adolescents and females who abuse only as adults, as well as those who may begin such behaviour in adolescence and continue into adult-hood. If this is so, the discontinuation of some offending in adulthood requires explanation and we need to consider why some women only start abusing as adults. This is an interesting area for study but these age groups need to be compared on a number of other dimensions.

## ADOLESCENT AND ADULT FEMALE SEXUAL ABUSERS: A COMPARISON

As discussed earlier, sexually abusive behaviour by adult and adolescent females has been minimised by society and professionals for perhaps quite similar reasons. A brief review of the literature reveals other areas of similarity between female offenders in these two age groups.

### Similarities between Adult and Adolescent Female Sexual Abusers

Both adolescent and adult female offenders appear to have chaotic family backgrounds and upbringings. Hirschberg and Riskin (1994) report that none of the 20 girls in their sample came from an intact family and many of the families had multiple problems. Seventy per cent of the girls had at least one parent with a serious substance abuse problem and 45 % had at least one parent who had been hospitalised due to mental illness or terminal disease. Blues et al. (1999) state that for most of the young people they have encountered, domestic violence has been or is commonplace in their lives. Mathews, Hunter and Vuz (1997) further suggest that there are high levels of trauma in the childhoods of sexually abusive adolescent girls, that they have been exposed to models of interpersonal violence and aggression and that such environments are not conducive to forming healthy attachments or a positive sense of self.

Such a lack of attachments may be displayed in these adolescents' peer relationships. Like many adult female offenders, there is a suggestion that adolescents' relationships with others tend to be quite poor and that they are socially isolated (Office of Juvenile Justice and Delinquency Prevention [OJJDP], 2001). Tardif, Auclair, Jacob and Carpentier (2005) noted that the majority of sexually abusive young females in their sample were not undertaking any occupational or recreational activities and that they showed poor social adaptation. Blues et al. (1999) cite work suggesting that many young sexually abusive females have few or no peer-aged friends. However, Mathews et al. (1997) reported that while few of the adolescents in their sample admitted sexual involvement with peers, most possessed adequate social skills. The OJJDP (2001) also reported that relative to male adolescents, females appeared to have more adequate social skills. Perhaps, then, they lack motivation, rather than the actual skills, to form appropriate relationships. The extent to which adult and adolescent females similarly lack appropriate peer relationships or the abilities to form them requires further examination.

These two groups appear very similar in their own experiences of abuse; Tardif et al. (2005), for example, reported that 61.5 % of adult female abusers and 60 % of adolescent female abusers had been sexually abused and 46.2 % and 40 % respectively reported physical abuse. These abusive backgrounds appear to be fairly unanimously agreed upon within the literature. Hunter et al. (1993) for example found that all 10 adolescents in their sample had been sexually abused and 80 % had been physically abused. The authors state that the girls were typically quite young when they were first abused, that the abuse occurred over a long period of time and that there were multiple perpetrators. The abuse was also quite invasive, with 90 % experiencing actual or attempted vaginal intercourse and 60 % actual or attempted anal intercourse. Force was reported in the experiences of 90 % of the subjects. Similar findings were reported in their work with a larger sample (Mathews et al., 1997). Blues et al. (1999) further report that physical and emotional abuse is a common experience for adolescent female abusers. Scott and Telford[2] report that all but one of the girls they have worked with were victims of both sexual and other emotional harm and almost two-thirds were also victims of physical abuse.

[2] See note 1.

Following on from the discussion in Chapter 8 about female sexual abuse appearing in the histories of many male sex offenders, it is interesting that Mathews et al. (1997) report many sexually abusive female adolescents in their sample to have been sexually abused by a female. In fact, over three times as many females as males reported the presence of a female perpetrator. Scott and Telford stated that 25 % of the girls they have worked with were sexually abused by another female. Hirschberg and Riskin (1994) meanwhile, reported that the adolescents in their sample were abused primarily by males; only two subjects (11 %) reported abuse by a female. This could, of course, reflect underreporting of abuse by women.

The American Academy of Child and Adolescent Psychiatry (AACAP) (1999) suggest that while both boys and girls who have been sexually abused may experience their first sexual arousal during their victimisation, there is some evidence that boys are more likely than girls to be sexually aroused at such times. Higgs, Canavan and Mayer (1992) suggest that if victims respond sexually to their abuse, there is often overwhelming trauma, guilt, confusion and feelings of responsibility. Hunter et al. (1993) reported that 80 % of the sexually abusive female adolescents in their sample reported sexual arousal or excitement during one or more of their victimisation experiences. All reported arousal to one or more experiences with a male perpetrator and four out of six reported arousal to abuse by a female. Interestingly, the authors note, arousal seemed to be stronger when it involved a perpetrator of their own gender but was also more disturbing to the victims. All the adolescents reporting arousal to abuse by a female described the arousal as making them very much or somewhat upset. In contrast, only 29 % of those abused by a male reported feeling upset by the arousal they experienced. This may be a further example of the "homosexuality taboo" discussed previously.

In the light of such chaotic and abusive backgrounds it is perhaps not surprising that some studies have reported high levels of substance abuse or psychiatric disorder in adolescent female abusers. As is perhaps the case with adult females, however, such findings may also be used to "explain" their offending and thereby minimise the fact that females can be inherently sexually aggressive. The OJJDP (2001) cite work by Bumby and Bumby (1997) suggesting that young female abusers experience a number of psychological symptoms and difficulties, particularly in terms of anxiety and depression, but that they do not differ from sexually abusive male adolescents in this respect. Other studies of abusive adolescent females have shown multiple behavioural problems (James & Neil, 1996, cited in Harris, 2001). Mathews et al. (1997) reported that over half of their female adolescent sample had histories of mood disturbances such as anxiety or depression, and nearly half met the diagnostic criteria for posttraumatic stress disorder. Tardif et al. (2005) found that nearly half of the adolescent females in their sample had a history of both violence against others and drug consumption.

The Bumby and Bumby (1997) study also reported high levels of substance abuse; 75 % of the girls had abused alcohol and 58 % had abused drugs (cited in OJJDP, 2001). However, these figures can only be properly interpreted if compared with rates of substance misuse among nonabusive adolescent females. Blues et al. (1999) meanwhile, stated that substance abuse had not been a feature of any of the girls they had treated. Harris (2001) reports that whereas substance abuse is reportedly common among sexually abusive young females, it is usually linked to their response to their own abuse experiences and is considered a product of that victimisation.

There are further similarities in aspects of the actual offence process. Like adult women, adolescent females are reported to engage in acts covering the full spectrum of sexual offending. Hirschberg and Riskin (1994), for example, reported that whereas the most common behaviours engaged in by their sample were fondling and genital contact without penetration, cases of oral sex, digital penetration and intercourse were also reported. Mathews et al. (1997) reported that their adolescent female abusers engaged in behaviours comparable in frequency and magnitude to their male counterparts.

The possibility of force should not be underestimated with young female abusers. Hunter et al. (1993) reported that 4 of the 10 adolescents in their sample admitted to using force in at least one instance and several indicated that they had threatened the use of force. Mathews, Matthews and Speltz (1990) suggest that in intergenerationally predisposed adolescents (those with a history of severe abuse who show similarities between the abuse they suffered and that they perpetrate), it is fairly common for the acts they commit to be more aggressive than those they suffered. They suggest this may reflect unresolved feelings about their own victimisation. Hirschberg and Riskin (1994) stated that 30 % of their sample reported using physical force or coercion. This rose to 40 % if threats of force were included. However, these high figures may be an effect both of small sample sizes and sample composition. Hirshberg and Riskin drew their sample from a residential treatment programme whereas Hunter et al. described their sample as consisting of "more severely disturbed juvenile female sexual offenders". Mathews et al. (1997) who studied a larger sample of female adolescents from both residential and community-based programmes found only 13 % admitted to using force, although this lower figure could result from underreporting of their true actions. Tardif et al. (2005) also reported that "seduction, blackmail and game playing" were the most commonly used means for their adolescent females to perpetrate abuse, although they note that two used force and threats. Nonetheless, some adolescent females appear to use force in their abuse and a subsample of these may include physical force or coercion. How these girls view their abuse is an interesting question for further research. Hilton et al. (2003) noted that adolescents who reported perpetrating physical or sexual aggression rated such scenarios as being less serious than adolescents who did not admit to such behaviour. Use of force may also be present in younger children. Cavanagh-Johnson (1989) reported that female children who sexually abused others used excessive physical force in almost one-quarter of cases. Less excessive physical coercion was used in a further 15 % of cases. Thus some of the children were using more physical force than they had to.

As with abusive women, it is not altogether clear whether boys or girls are more likely to be the victims of adolescent female abusers. Margolin (1991) reported that female babysitters directed more than half of their abuse towards male children. Mathews et al. (1997) found that young female abusers showed some preference for victims of the opposite gender and Tardif et al. (2005) reported that the majority of their adolescent female sample abused male victims only (60 %) or victims of both sexes (26.7 %). Only 13 % offended solely against females, an interesting contrast to the adult female abusers in their sample who primarily offended against female victims. Blues et al. (1999) state that, in their own experience, the younger the children are at the age of onset of their sexually abusive behaviour, the less likely they are to be gender specific in their victim selection. Research suggests that victims of female adolescent abusers are often young (Fehrenbach & Monastersky, 1988; Hirschberg & Riskin, 1994) and related or known to the perpetrators in most cases (Fehrenbach & Monastersky, 1988; Mathews et al., 1997), a similar finding to some studies of child sexual abuse by adult women which were described in Chapter 3. In contrast, Hunter et al. (1993) reported that 39 % of their adolescent sample had abused a stranger. However this may again reflect the sample composition as other studies do not report such high rates of stranger abuse.

It has been suggested that sexually abusive female adolescents may often abuse in the context of babysitting (Scavo, 1989), a task particularly likely to be undertaken by girls in this age group. Hirschberg and Riskin (1994), meanwhile, reported that only two of their subjects abused while babysitting. They state, however, that many of the girls in their sample had "parentified" roles and extensive caregiving responsibilities for other children in their family. Thus, as these authors state: "these girls not only have the opportunity to molest younger children, but other factors including their own abuse history, inadequate parenting and resentment towards the children they must care for, may combine to form a witches' brew that can boil over to aggressive sexual misbehaviour" (Hirschberg & Riskin, 1994, p. 5).

## Differences between Sexually Abusive Adult and Adolescent Females

Despite areas of similarity between adult and adolescent female abusers, some differences have also been suggested. The first of these is that adolescents appear more likely to abuse alone (Fehrenbach & Monastersky, 1988; Hunter et al., 1993; Tardif et al. 2005). Hirschberg and Riskin (1994) report only one girl in their sample to have abused with a male. This girl made obscene telephone calls and propositioned an unknown boy while her boyfriend was present. However, the extent that this could truly be described as offending "with" a male is unclear. Cavanagh-Johnson (1989) reported a case of four girls abusing together, although the girls were below the age of 13. Scott and Telford[3] report that the majority of the girls they have worked with acted alone but in 25 % of cases there was a strong suspicion that the girls had been coerced, primarily by older young people. Although some adult women abuse alone they appear more likely to abuse in conjunction with another individual than adolescent abusers. Of course, this difference could reflect the fact that many of these adolescent girls are too young to have formed relationships in which others are likely to be influential as coperpetrators, particularly given previous findings that many female adolescent abusers have had few peer sexual relationships. If some of these adolescents go on to abuse in adulthood, it would be interesting to discover whether they continue abusing alone or began to perpetrate their abuse with others and, if so, the reasons why.

A second difference is that more attention has been given to the issue of deviant sexual arousal in adolescent female abusers, an area neglected in studies with adult females. This is not to say that there is an actual difference in the importance of sexual arousal for adult and adolescent females but more research attention has so far been given to this in relation to adolescents. Tardif et al. (2005) found that 60 % of their adolescent female sample reported sexual arousal and deviant sexual fantasies about the victim before carrying out the abuse. Hunter et al. (1993) also suggested that sexual fantasy is important for adolescent abusers and that they may develop deviant sexual arousal. They reported that 80 % of their adolescents fantasised about the behaviour they engaged in and 60 % fantasised prior to their first perpetration. Given the reportedly high levels of past victimisation in sexually abusive adolescent females, deviant arousal may not be surprising. AACAP (1999) report work by Becker et al. (1989, 1992) which found that a history of sexual and physical abuse in juvenile sex offenders is associated with higher phallometrically measured arousal to both deviant and nondeviant stimuli. If this holds true for females, it is all the more surprising that this issue has not been fully considered with adult female abusers, given their documented history of victimisation.

The possible importance of sexual motivations in adolescent sexual aggression is demonstrated by Faller's (1987) finding that sexual abuse by adolescents aimed primarily to gratify the offender. This may relate to Faller's (1995) suggestion that adolescents abuse because they lack access to or are unappealing to their peers. Limited support for this proposal has been found with males. O'Callaghan and Print (1994) reported that fewer sexually abusive

[3] See note 1.

male adolescents had had a number of girlfriends compared with non-sex offenders and the sexual abusers also felt themselves to be less successful with girls than their peers. Only 26 % of the sexual abusers had experienced nonabusive regular sex with a peer compared with 59 % of the non-sex offenders, although this means that one quarter of the abusive adolescents had some sexual success with peers. Given that Mathews et al. (1997) reported adolescent female abusers to have had few peer sexual relationships, some of these girls may seek sexual gratification through abuse. This view is not universal, however. Thomas (1999) states that adolescent female abusers: "do not appear to be sexually motivated, do not fantasise about abuse and do not receive sexual pleasure from the commission of abusive acts" (cited in Harris, 2001 p. 29).

It is important to stress that sexual abuse by adolescents is unlikely to be driven solely by the desire for sexual gratification. Indeed, sexual abuse may meet a number of needs. Righthand and Welch (2001) describe a study of juvenile sex offenders conducted by Ryan et al. (1996). Only about one-third of the juveniles perceived sex as a way to demonstrate love or caring for another person. Just under one quarter perceived sex as a way to feel power and control others, 9 % viewed it as a means of dissipating anger and 8 % believed it was a way to hurt, degrade, or punish. It would be interesting to examine the extent to which these views are shared by sexually abusive adolescent females, particularly given their own histories of abuse.

A related issue is the use of pornography. Hunter et al. (1993) found that 40 % of adolescent female abusers had viewed pornography, although whether this was through choice or part of their own abuse by others is not reported. Later work by Mathews et al. (1997) reported that 34 % of abusive female adolescents had viewed pornography compared with none of the adolescent male abusers. Again, however, the context is not clear. Tardif et al. (2005) further noted that 47 % of the adolescent females in their sample had made "regular and excessive use" of pornographic material. As with adult female offenders and nonoffenders, however, there is little understanding of adolescent females' possible use of pornography. Studies of adolescent sex offender pornography use have focused on males, finding that a sizeable proportion have been exposed to hardcore pornography or use sexually explicit materials (see Righthand & Welch, 2001, for a summary). However, even studies with sexually aggressive male adolescents are limited and this is a relevant area for future research.

## TREATMENT NEEDS OF ADOLESCENT FEMALE ABUSERS

Higgs et al. (1992) argue that sexually abusive girls and women are often overlooked by the treatment community. Whether this is related to some professionals' beliefs that offending by young females is "one-off" behaviour is not clear. However, many of the same difficulties reported in relation to the treatment of adult females are equally applicable to adolescents. This includes the relevance of applying male models of treatment to females. Pepi (1998) notes that programmes and services for adolescent females are generally replications of those designed around a male model and therefore may not meet the gender-specific needs of young females. Other pertinent issues are whether treatment groups could contain both males and females or, indeed, both sexual and nonsexual offenders.

Hirschberg and Riskin (1996) describe the components of their residential treatment programme for adolescent female abusers. They argue that the many similarities in behaviour between males and females mean that similar treatment approaches to those used with males are justified. Many of the modules in their programme mirror those undertaken with male abusers, including components to recognise thinking errors, understand the sexual offence cycle, recognise the impact of the offence on the victim and to increase victim empathy. Further important elements in adolescent programmes are work on self-esteem, social skills and peer relationships, work to increase assertiveness skills and anger management where appropriate, general sexual education and a relapse prevention component (Harris, 2001).

However, although such elements are likely to be relevant to many child sexual abusers of both genders and all ages, certain additional aspects may be particularly important in the treatment of adolescents. The first of these is inclusion of the adolescent's family in any work undertaken. This is particularly important as a major obstacle to treatment is likely to be the denial and minimisation encountered from both the adolescents and their families (Becker et al., 1996). AACAP (1999) cite a study by Sefarbi (1990) which found that half of the sexually abusive adolescents initially denied the abuse and this denial was usually supported by their family. The family response may influence that of the adolescent; if the family denies the allegations this may act as a barrier to the young person taking responsibility. Rejecting responses from the families, meanwhile, may impinge on the adolescents' ability to talk about their abusive behaviour (Blues et al., 1999). If the family is not supportive and encouraging of the treatment process, the young person may be less likely to engage fully (Scavo, 1989).

There are additional reasons to include families in the assessment and treatment of adolescents. One of these is their ability to provide information. Indeed, Scavo (1989) suggests that families are usually the best source of information regarding adolescents' early development and their current level of social and emotional functioning. An examination of family history may help to understand how adolescents began abusing, perhaps through their own victimisation, as a consequence of modelling or having access to sexually explicit materials (DiGiorgio-Miller, 1998). The families of sexually aggressive adolescents can themselves be chaotic or dysfunctional and the disclosure of the sexual offence can increase feelings of anxiety, guilt, fear or sadness (Scavo, 1989). Incorporating families into the treatment process can help to support, reassure and educate the family, helping to reduce denial, victim blaming, or rejection of the adolescent. This creates a safer environment for both the offender and any victims within the family (Scavo, 1989). Unless the family openly acknowledge the abuse and comes to understand its development, the abuse is more likely to reoccur and any family victims will be at greater risk as they will be less likely to disclose (DiGiorgio-Miller, 1998).

The above comments apply both to male and female adolescents. The OJJDP (2001), however, suggest that the maintenance of key family relationships is especially important for girls (cited in Harris, 2001). Whether family work is of greater importance for sexually abusive female adolescents is yet to be determined. Nonetheless, including the family in treatment is widely recommended in the literature. Harris (2001) reports suggestions that work could go beyond just that with the family, so that therapists could "work closely with the family, the school and any other significant social system that the young person is a part of" (Harris, 2001, p. 56). This is advocated by Veneziano and Veneziano (2002), who state that multisystemic therapy is one of the most promising approaches in the treatment of adolescent sexual abusers.

In view of the extensive victimisation suffered by many adolescent female abusers, researchers have stressed the importance of addressing their own abuse experiences during treatment. This may also be relevant to boys who have been victimised but may be particularly relevant to girls as figures generally suggest they are more likely to be abuse victims. Graham (1996) appears unwilling to over-focus on young people's own abuse experiences in case they become an easy explanation for their offending; he is reluctant to "take the victimisation of the offender too seriously [as it might] provide the offender with an excuse" (cited in Harris, 2001, p. 20). Many disagree with this sentiment, however. Hirschberg and Riskin (1994) state that it is important for abused offenders to explore the trauma, their feelings and thoughts about it and to develop better ways of coping. Addressing this issue may also benefit the treatment process. Scavo (1989) states that recalling her own feelings of being victimised helps the adolescent to develop empathy for her victim(s). Discussion of the issue also assists her understanding of the relationship between her own abuse experiences and those that she has committed. Blues et al. (1999) further add that girls' sexually abusive behaviour may be most readily accessed in settings where their feelings and emotions are discussed in relation to their own abuse experiences.

One further element that may be important for some adolescent female abusers is their own deviant sexual arousal and the role this plays in their offending. AACAP (1999) state that phallometric assessment has generally been used cautiously with adolescents as there is a reluctance to further expose them to sexual stimulation through the portrayal of deviant sexual activities. Nonetheless, some research has indicated arousal to have a potential role in adolescent offending and so provision should be made to address this when appropriate. Consideration should be given to how this can be assessed and incorporated into the treatment programme.

Långström (2001) reports evidence that younger sexually abusive people are more likely than adults to admit to their offences once confronted with them. Whether or not adolescents are more likely to accept responsibility for their offending is not certain, however, and whether there are differences between males and females is also unclear. Blues et al. (1999) attribute previous suggestions that females may be more likely to take responsibility for their aggression to societal expectations of women's roles. They cite other evidence indicating that there are few gender differences in terms of accepting responsibility and state that denial and minimisation are features of both boys and girls in treatment.

Harris (2001) notes that stereotypical assumptions suggest that girls are socially more likely than boys to engage in group discussion and are therefore more amenable to group treatment. Returning to the issue of the extent to which male programmes can be applied to females, Mathews et al. (1997) question whether the approaches used with males, which they describe as confrontational in nature and focusing primarily on accountability and behavioural changes, are adequate or sufficient for adolescent females. Blues et al. (1999) cite work by Matthews (1993) which suggests that girls are more easily able to access their feelings than boys, including their feelings about their own abusive experiences. This can then be used in addressing their offending behaviour.

What may be most important, however, is the development of an appropriate, individualised assessment of need and formulation of the problem behaviour. In the case of sexually abusive young males and females, workers need to remember that they are young people at various stages of development. Each young person may be better served by receiving a dual assessment which considers them both as a perpetrator of abusive sexual acts *and* as a young person with their own child protection needs. Analysis of their needs in both these areas is likely to result in more relevant and effective intervention and allows us to think in terms beyond just their similarities to or differences from adults.

## FEMALE CHILDREN WHO SEXUALLY ABUSE – A BRIEF NOTE

Although the need for brevity prevents this subject being covered in depth, research indicates that prepubescent children also engage in sexually abusive behaviours. Cavanagh-Johnson (1989) contends that this is a problem still largely ignored or denied and that the "social service and criminal justice system have no protocols with which to guide their actions when they come into contact with these children" (Cavanagh-Johnson, 1989, p. 572). Minasian and Lewis (1999) further state that this group of young abusers is "underserved and understudied". Yet this is not an entirely new phenomenon; Burton et al. (1997, p. 158) note that descriptions of sexual offences by children "appeared sporadically in professional literature as early as the 1940s".

In studies of children engaging in sexually abusive behaviours, girls have featured strongly in the statistics (OJJDP, 2001). Silovsky and Niec (2002) studied preschool children with sexual behaviour problems and found a higher proportion of girls (65 %) than boys (35 %). This, however, may result from the greater likelihood of female children being abused; researchers have postulated a relationship between childhood sexual abuse and inappropriate sexual behaviours in children (Holmes & Slap, 1998, cited in AACAP, 1999; Silovsky & Niec, 2002). These sexually abusive children are reported to share many characteristics of their older counterparts, including chaotic, abusive and traumatic backgrounds (Silovsky & Niec, 2002) and poor relationships with peers, inadequate parenting and suffering anxiety and depression (Cavanagh-Johnson, 1989). These children commit a wide range of sexually abusive behaviours and generally know their victims (Cavanagh-Johnson, 1989), although this latter finding may reflect the limited opportunity for younger children to offend against victims unknown to them. However, this author also reports some differences in sexually abusive female children. She describes some specificity in victim selection in that, more than half of the time, the girls in her sample abused their own siblings who had not previously been abused and were therefore suggested to be objects of the abuser's jealousy and anger. She further notes that few, if any, of the girls were committing such acts to achieve their own sexual satisfaction. This may of course be a function of their younger age.

Whether sexually abusive female children differ significantly from males is also uncertain. Burton et al. (1997) found that female children were younger than males at the time they were seen and also younger when their first sexually abusive behaviour was discovered. However, they question whether this is an actual gender difference or whether sexual behaviour in female children is viewed differently, or whether these differences result from females being more closely monitored, for example. Their findings differ from those of Blues et al. (1999), who noted that the age at which sexually abusive behaviour was deemed sufficiently concerning to require intervention was slightly later for girls than boys. Assessment of potential gender differences is therefore important.

A further question that cannot yet be satisfactorily answered is the extent to which childhood sexual aggression continues into adolescence and then into adulthood. In other words, does sexual abuse perpetration in childhood predict a lifetime of sexually aggressive activity? There is currently no clear answer to this question. Hunter et al. (1993) report that the sexually abusive adolescents in their sample typically began their behaviour prior to adolescence and that it continued as they grew older. Silovsky and Niec (2002) further report that any treatment offered to such children is usually given in the hope that it will prevent the development of a pattern of sexually abusive behaviours that would continue later in life. This implies that if such behaviour is not addressed there is believed to be a strong possibility of its continuation. However, only further research, particularly longitudinal studies, may eventually provide some answers.

## SUMMARY OF MAIN POINTS

- While the reported figures of sexual abuse by adolescent females are fairly low, some adolescent females and children are sexually abusive towards others.
- However, these low figures may reflect underreporting of sexual abuse by female adolescents or the explaining of abusive behaviours perpetrated by adolescents or children as a form of experimentation. The denial that initially surrounded sexual abuse by women may also exist for abuse committed by females in this age group.
- Research has identified a number of similarities between adolescent males and females who sexually abuse. However, there are also some areas of difference.
- There are also a number of similarities between sexually abusive adolescents and adult females. However, important differences have also been found between these two groups, particularly in terms of abusing with others and the attention given to the contribution of deviant sexual arousal to offending.
- The treatment needs of adolescent female abusers may be broadly similar to that of their adult counterparts. However, including the family in the treatment process and addressing their own experiences of abuse may also be important in any intervention for this group.
- Younger female children may also be sexually abusive to others. Further research with this group is important, particularly in determining whether sexual abuse perpetration at an early age continues in later life.

# CONCLUDING THOUGHTS

Forbes (1993) was sceptical of the construction of the new category of "female sexual abuser", arguing that research based on such small samples was flawed, that female abusers were few in number and that focusing on this group distracted attention away from the primary problem of sexual abuse by men. In the early 1990s her arguments perhaps seemed justified; official statistics certainly supported the view that women were rarely sexual abusers of children and this filtered through to the CJS and child protection-related agencies, as well as the general population. Even today, the number of women imprisoned for sexual offences is tiny compared with the number of men incarcerated for similar offences. However, this book has demonstrated some of the cautions with which both official statistics and victim self-reports of abuse by women should be viewed and expanded on some reasons why such behaviour by women was not readily accepted. Forbes was probably quite accurate when she said that this consideration of this topic was "made more chilling and freakish since it is women's sexual deviance" (Forbes, 1993, p. 102).

Now, when female sexual abusers have at last attracted research interest, fears that this would draw attention away from abuse perpetrated by males do not seem to have come to pass. There continues to be a large gap between our knowledge of male sexual offending and our knowledge of similar behaviour in females and treatment provision for females remains small-scale and limited compared with the options available for men. Many of the research, theory and practice developments in the field of sexual offending use male child sexual abusers as "templates" (Polaschek & Hudson, 2004) and the resulting theories or treatment approaches are often transferred onto other groups of sex offenders without sufficient consideration of whether this is appropriate. This may make methodological sense in terms of the larger sample sizes available but it raises the question of whether work with other groups of sex offenders (including women) is guided by best theory and practice. Clearly this has implications for treatment outcomes and recidivism rates. Therefore, while research is increasing our understanding of sexually abusive behaviour in women, even an in-depth review of the evidence base indicates that many more questions remain to be asked than have currently been answered.

Forbes (1993, p. 108) suggested that the identification of women as sexual abusers represented a contemporary "search for equivalence", an attempt to equate abuse by men with abuse by women, leading to a "gender-free analysis of child sexual abuse". As the earlier chapters of this book describe, in overt behavioural terms at least, the abuse committed by male and female offenders shares many similarities. Recognising this may be of particular importance to victims of sexual abuse by females. Failure to equate the severity of abuse committed by women with that committed by men may, in the past, have led to victims of abuse by women receiving less support and the harm caused to them going unrecognised. Saradjian (1996, p. 6), for example, reports one survivor's anger at reading in a book about sexual abuse that not only was sexual abuse by women rare, but that it appeared to be less serious and traumatic than that perpetrated by males.

However, Forbes may be right in suggesting that the study of sexual abuse should not disregard gender and that "any discussion of women as sexual abusers must also include the woman's particular history and the general social conditions in which female sexuality develops and is expressed" (Forbes, 1993, p. 107). The pertinence of this is apparent from the often highly abusive, difficult backgrounds of sexually abusive women, as well as the general position of women in society. There may still be reluctance to consider women and their sexual desires, as evidenced when examining what little is known about the sexual interests and pornography usage of nonoffending women.

Behavioural similarities between male and female offenders are not sufficient to justify the same treatment needs and approaches and it is important to consider the precursors and underlying dynamics of sexual abuse by women. As has been discussed, reliance on male treatment models, assessment tools and therapeutic styles may not be appropriate for female offenders and so, in this sense, a gendered analysis of sexual abuse seems relevant. However, while sexual abuse by women is now acknowledged, and it is recognised that the low numbers of such women reported in official data may be an underestimate, the small number of women convicted for sexual offences makes it difficult to divert resources to this group. Grubin (1998, p. 1) summarises this problem: "From criminal justice and public health perspectives, male abusers represent a much larger problem and it is argued that, at present, it is hard to justify a shift in emphasis and resources towards female sex offenders".

While there are clearly genuine practical and financial limitations which must be considered, such a policy leaves a group of victims and offenders unsupported and their needs unrecognised. While this book has never intended to incite "fresh moral panic" (Forbes, 1993, p. 102) by suggesting that women are abusing in the same numbers as men, it does assert the need to continue developing our knowledge and understanding of these women so that we can offer them appropriate possibilities for treatment and intervene effectively when abuse is alleged to have occurred.

This book has sought to outline what the research base tells us about women who sexually abuse, to link this with literature from other relevant areas of study and to highlight some of the questions that still remain to be both asked and answered. In this way, it is hoped that it offers a contribution to the growing body of work in this area and provides food for thought to practitioners and researchers. Knowledge is, of course, essential, but in and of itself it is not sufficient to increase treatment resources either for victims or offenders. Therefore, it is also hoped that this work has demonstrated the importance of progress and development in this respect and that others can use this to take things forward. Unless we are able to do this, it is ultimately the past, present and future victims of female sexual abusers who are cheated.

# REFERENCES

Abel, G. G. & Rouleau, J. L. (1995). Sexual abuses. *The Psychiatric Clinics of North America, 18*(1), 139–153.

Adshead, G., Howett, M. & Mason, F. (1994). Women who sexually abuse children: the undiscovered country. *The Journal of Sexual Aggression, 1,* 45–56.

Ages of consent in different countries (2005). Retrieved November 24, 2005 from Web site: http://www.measuroo.com/Leg-A/Age_of_consent.phf

Allen, C. M. (1990). Women as perpetrators of child sexual abuse: recognition barriers. In A. L. Horton, B. L. Johnson, L. M. Roundy & D. Williams (Eds). *The incest perpetrator: A Family Member No One Wants to Treat* (pp. 108–125). Newbury Park: Sage.

Allen, C. M. (1991). *Women and Men Who Sexually Abuse Children: A Comparative Analysis.* Orwell: The Safer Society Press.

Allen, C. M. & Pothast, H. L. (1994). Distinguishing characteristics of male and female child sex abusers. *Journal of Offender Rehabilitation, 21*(1–2), 73–88.

American Academy of Child and Adolescent Psychiatry (AACAP) (1999). Practice parameters for the assessment and treatment of children and adolescents who are sexually abusive of others. *Journal of the American Academy of Child and Adolescent Psychiatry, 38*(12) (suppl.), 55–76.

Anderson, I. (1999). Characterological and behavioural blame in conversations about female and male rape. *Journal of Language and Social Psychology, 18*(4), 377–394.

Anderson, P. B. (1998). Women's motives for sexual initiation and aggression. In P. B. Anderson & C. Struckman-Johnson (Eds). *Sexually Aggressive Women: Current Perspectives and Controversies* (pp. 79–93). New York: The Guilford Press.

Anderson, P. B. & Melson, D. T. (2002). From deviancy to normalcy: women as sexual aggressors. *Electronic Journal of Human Sexuality, volume 5,* October 23, 2002. Retrieved January 24, 2005, from the Web site: http://www.ejhs.org

Anderson, S. C., Bach, C. M. & Griffith, S. (1981). *Psychosocial Sequelae In Intrafamilial Victims Of Sexual Assault And Abuse.* Paper presented at the 3rd International Conference on Child Abuse and Neglect. Amsterdam.

Atlas, J. (2000). Pederasty, blood shedding and blood smearing: men in search of Mommy's feared powers. *Journal of Psychohistory, 28*(2), 116–149.

Aylward, A., Christopher, M., Newell, R. M. & Gordon, A. (2002). *What about Women Who Commit Sex Offences?* Notes From ATSA conference, 2002.

Bachmann, K. M., Moggi, F. & Stirnemann-Lewis, F. (1994). Mother–son incest and its long-term consequences: a neglected phenomenon in psychiatric practice. *Journal of Nervous and Mental Disease, 182*(12), 723–725.

Banning, A. (1989). Mother–son incest: confronting a prejudice. *Child Abuse and Neglect,* *13*, 563–570.

Barnett, S., Corder, F. & Jehu, D. (1990). Group treatment for women sex offenders against children. *Groupwork, 3*(2), 191–203.

Barrett, M. J. (1993). Mothers' role in incest: neither dysfunctional women nor dysfunctional theories when both are explored in their entirety. *Journal of Child Sexual Abuse, 2*(3), 141–143.

Becker, J. V., Hunter, J. A., Stein, R. M. & Kaplan, M. S. (1989). Factors associated with erection in adolescent sex offenders. *Journal of Psychopathology and Behavioural Assessment, 11*, 353–362.

Becker, J. V., Kaplan, M. S. & Tenke, C. E. (1992). The relationship of abuse history, denial and erectile response profiles of adolescent sexual perpetrators. *Behaviour Therapy, 23*, 87–98.

Becker, J. V., Johnson, B. R. & Hunter, J. A. (1996). Adolescent sex offenders. In C. R. Hollin & K. Howells (Eds). *Clinical Approaches to Working with Young Offenders* (pp. 183–195). Chichester: John Wiley & Sons.

Beckett, R. C., Beech, A. R., Fisher, D. & Fordham, A. S. (1994). *Community-based treatment for sex offenders: an evaluation of seven treatment programmes.* Home Office Occasional Report. Available from Home Office Publications Unit, 50 Queen Anne's Gate, London SW1 9AT.

Beech, A., Erikson, M., Friendship, C. & Ditchfield, J. (2001). *A Six-Year Follow-Up of Men Going through Probation-Based Sex Offender Treatment Programmes.* Research Findings no. 144. London: Home Office Research, Development and Statistics Directorate.

Beech, A. R. & Fisher, D. D. (2004). Treatment of sex offenders in the UK in prison and probation settings. In Kemshall, H. & McIvor, G. (Eds). *Managing Sex Offender Risk.* (pp. 137–163). London: Jessica Kingsley.

Beech, A. R., Fisher, D. D. & Thornton, D. (2003). Risk assessment of sex offenders. *Professional Psychology: Research and Practice, 34*, 339–352.

Beech, A. R. & Ward, T. (2004). The integration of etiology and risk in sexual offenders: a theoretical framework. *Aggression and Violent Behavior, 10*(1), 31–63.

Bell, P. (2002). Factors contributing to a mother's ability to recognise incestuous abuse of her child. *Women's Studies International Forum, 25*(3), 347–357.

Bell, P. (2003). 'I'm a good mother really!' Gendered parenting roles and responses to the disclosure of incest. *Children and Society, 17*, 126–136.

Benoit, J. L. & Kennedy, W. A. (1992). The abuse history of male adolescent sex offenders. *Journal of Interpersonal Violence, 7*(4), 543–548.

Bickley, J. A. & Beech, A. R. (2002). An investigation of the Ward and Hudson pathways model of the sexual offence process with child abusers. *Journal of Interpersonal Violence, 17*(4), 371–393.

Birns, B. & Meyer, S. (1993). Mothers' role in incest: dysfunctional women or dysfunctional theories? *Journal of Child Sexual Abuse, 2*(3), 127–135.

Blues, A., Moffat, C. & Telford, P. (1999). Work with adolescent females who sexually offend. In M. Erooga & H. Masson (Eds). *Children and Young People Who Sexually Abuse Others* (pp. 168–182). London: Routledge.

Bolen, R. M. (2003). Nonoffending mothers of sexually abused children: a case of institutionalised sexism? *Violence against Women, 9*(11), 1336–1366.

Bolen, R. M. & Lamb, J. L. (2004). Ambivalence of non-offending guardians after child sexual abuse disclosure. *Journal of Interpersonal Violence, 19*(2), 185–211.

Bouffard, J. A. & Taxman, F. S. (2000). Client gender and the implementation of jail based therapeutic community programs. *Journal of Drug Issues, 30*(4), 881–900.

Breckenbridge, J. & Berreen, R. (1992). Dealing with mother blame: workers' responses to incest and child sexual abuse. In J. Breckenbridge & M. Carmody (Eds). *Crimes Of*

*Violence: Australian Responses To Rape And Child Sexual Assault* (pp. 97–108). Sydney: Allen & Unwin.

Briere, J. (1988). The long-term clinical correlates of childhood sexual victimisation. *Annals of the New York Academy of Sciences, 528*, 327–334.

Briere, J. & Runtz, M. (1989). University males' sexual interest in children: predicting potential indices of 'pedophilia' in a nonforensic sample. *Child Abuse and Neglect, 13*, 65–75.

Briere, J. & Smiljanich, K. (1993). *Childhood Sexual Abuse And Subsequent Sexual Aggression Against Adult Women.* Paper presented at the 101st annual convention of the American Psychological Association. Toronto, Ontario.

Briggs, F. & Hawkins, R. M. F. (1996). A comparison of the childhood experiences of convicted male child molesters and men who were sexually abused in childhood and claimed to be non-offenders. *Child Abuse and Neglect, 20*(3), 221–233.

Broussard, S., Wagner, W. G. & Kazelskis, R. (1991). Undergraduate students' perceptions of child sexual abuse: the impact of victim sex, perpetrator sex, respondent sex and victim response. *Journal of Family Violence, 6*(3), 267–278.

Browne, A. & Finkelhor, D. (1986). Impact of child sexual abuse: a review of the research. *Psychological Bulletin, 99*(1), 66–77.

Browne, K. (1989). The health visitor's role in screening for child abuse. *Health Visitor, 62*, 275–277.

Buchanan, A. (1996). *Cycles of Child Maltreatment: Facts, Fallacies and Interventions.* Chichester: John Wiley & Sons.

Buist, M. & Fuller, R. (1996). *Working with Young People Who Have Sexually Abused Others.* University of Stirling: Social Work Research Centre.

Bumby, K. M. & Bumby, N. H. (1997). Adolescent female sexual offenders. In B. K. Schwartz & H. R. Cellini (Eds). *The Sex Offender: Volume 2. New Insights, Treatment Innovations And Legal Developments* (pp. 10.1–10.16). Kingston, NJ: Civic Research Institute.

Bunting, L. (2005). *Executive Summary: Females Who Sexually Offend against Children: Responses of the Child Protection and Criminal Justice Systems.* Retrieved January 3, 2006 from the Web site: http://www.nspcc.org.uk/Inform/Research/Findings/Females WhoSexuallyOffend_ifega27751.html

Burgess, A., Hazelwood, R., Rokous, F., Hartmen, C. & Burgess, A. (1987). *Serial Rapists And Their Victims: Re-Enactment And Repetition.* Paper presented at the New York Academy of Sciences Conference on Human Sexual Aggression: Current Perspectives. New York City.

Burnam, M. A., Stein, J. A., Golding, J. M., Siegel, J. M., Sorenson, S. B., Forsythe, A. B. & Telles, C. A. (1988). Sexual assault and mental disorders in a community population. *Journal of Consulting and Clinical Psychology, 56*(6), 843–850.

Burton, D. L., Nesmith, A. A. & Badten, L. (1997). Clinician's views on sexually aggressive children and their families; a theoretical exploration. *Child Abuse and Neglect, 21*(2), 157–170.

Bybee, D. & Mowbray, C. T. (1993). Community response to child sexual abuse in day-care settings. *Families in Society, 74*, 268–281.

Byers, E. S. & O'Sullivan, L. F. (1998). Similar but different: men's and women's experiences of sexual coercion. In Anderson, P. B. & Struckman-Johnson, C. (Eds). *Sexually Aggressive Women: Current Perspectives and Controversies* (pp. 144–168). New York: The Guilford Press.

Calder, M. C. & Peake, A. (2001a). Reactions to the discovery that her child has been sexually abused. In M. C. Calder, A. Peake & K. Rose (Eds), *Mothers of Sexually Abused Children: A Framework for Assessment, Understanding and Support* (pp. 58–114). Lyme Regis: Russell House Publishing.

Calder, M. C. & Peake, A. (2001b). Links with the perpetrator. In M. C. Calder, A. Peake & K. Rose (Eds). *Mothers of Sexually Abused Children: A Framework for Assessment, Understanding and Support* (pp. 115–156). Lyme Regis: Russell House Publishing.

Calder, M. C. & Peake, A. (2001c). Personal qualities, resources and networks. In M. C. Calder, A. Peake & K. Rose, (Eds), *Mothers of Sexually Abused Children: A Framework for Assessment, Understanding and Support* (pp. 157–179). Lyme Regis: Russell House Publishing.

Calvert, J. F. & Munsie-Benson, M. (1999). Public opinion and knowledge about childhood sexual abuse in a rural community. *Child Abuse and Neglect, 23*(7), 671–682.

Casey, S., Day, A. & Howells, K. (2005). The application of the transtheoretical model to offender populations: some critical issues. *Legal and Criminological Psychology, 10*, 157–171.

Castonguay, L. G., Proulx, J., Aubut, J., McKibben, A. & Campbell, M. (1993). Sexual preference assessment of sexual aggressors: predictors of penile response magnitude. *Archives of Sexual Behaviour, 22*, 325–334.

Cavanagh-Johnson, T. (1989). Female child perpetrators: children who molest other children. *Child Abuse and Neglect, 13*, 571–585.

Cawson, P., Wattam, C., Brooker, S. & Kelly, G. (2000). *Child maltreatment in the United Kingdom: A Study of the Prevalence of Child Abuse and Neglect*. London: NSPCC.

Chandler, S. M. (1982). Knowns and unknowns in sexual abuse of children. *Journal of Social Work and Human Sexuality, 1*, 51–68.

Chasnoff, J., Burns, W. J., Schnoll, S. H., Burns, K., Chisum, G. & Kyle-Spore, L. (1986). Maternal – neonatal incest. *American Journal of Orthopsychiatry, 56*(4), 577–580.

Circles of Support and Accountability in the Thames Valley (2005). London: Quaker Communications. Retrieved January 3, 2006 from Web site: http://www.quaker.org .uk/shared_asp_files/uploadedfiles/82F718A7-9344-4A5C-A4A7-4BO53FF22239_circlesofsupport-first3yrs.pdf

Clark, D. & Howden-Windall, J. (2000). *A Retrospective Study of Criminogenic Factors in the Female Prison Population*. London: Her Majesty's Prison Service.

Condy, S., Templer, D. I., Brown, R. & Veaco, L. (1987). Parameters of sexual contact of boys with women. *Archives of Sexual Behaviour, 16*(5), 379–394.

Conte, J. (1982). Sexual abuse of children: enduring issues for social work. In J. Conte & D. Shore (Eds). *Social Work And Sexual Abuse* (pp. 1–20). New York: Haworth.

Coohey, C. (2004). Battered mothers who physically abuse their children. *Journal of Interpersonal Violence, 19*(8), 943–952.

Cooper, A., Delmonico, D. & Burg, R. (2000). Cybersex users, abusers and compulsives: new findings and implications. *Sexual Addiction and Compulsivity, 7*, 5–30.

Cooper, A. J., Swaminath, S., Baxter, D. & Poulin, C. (1990). A female sex offender with multiple paraphilias: a psychologic, physiologic (laboratory sexual arousal) and endocrine case study. *Canadian Journal of Psychiatry, 35*, 334–337.

Correctional Service of Canada. (1995). *Case Studies of Female Sex Offenders in the Correctional Service of Canada*. Retrieved October 18, 2002 from Web site: http://www.csc-scc.gc. ca/text/pblct/sexoffender/female/toc_e.shtml

Correctional Services Accreditation Panel. (2002). *Programme Accreditation Criteria*. London: Home Office.

Coxell, A., King, M., Mezey, G. & Gordon, D. (1999). Lifetime prevalence, characteristics and associated problems of non-consensual sex in men: cross sectional survey. *British Medical Journal, 318*, 846–850.

Craissati, J. (2003). *The relationship between developmental variables and risk*. Unpublished doctoral thesis, University of Birmingham, UK.

Crawford, P., Hueppelheuser, M. & George, D. (1996). Spouses of incest offenders: coaddictive tendencies and dysfunctional etiologies. *Sexual Addiction and Compulsivity*, 3(4), 289–312.

Crewdson, J. (1988). *By Silence Betrayed: Sexual Abuse Of Children In America*. Boston: Little Brown.

Daly, K. (1989). Rethinking judicial paternalism: gender, work-family relations and sentencing. *Gender and Society*, 3(1), 9–36.

Dandescu, A. & Wolfe, R. (2003). Considerations on fantasy use by child molesters and exhibitionists. *Sexual Abuse: A Journal of Research and Treatment*, 15(4), 297–305.

Davin, P. A., Hislop, J. C. R. & Dunbar, T. (1999). *Female Sexual Abusers*. Vermont: The Safer Society Press.

Deblinger, E., Hathaway, C. R., Lippman, J. & Stear, R. (1993). Psychological characteristics and correlates of symptom distress in non-offending mothers of sexually abused children. *Journal of Interpersonal Violence*, 8, 155–168.

De Jong, A. R. (1988). Maternal responses to the sexual abuse of their children. *Pediatrics*, 81(1), 14–21.

Demause, L. (1991). The universality of incest. *The Journal of Psychohistory*, 19(2), 123–164.

Denov, M. S. (2001). A culture of denial: exploring professional perspectives on female sex offending. *Canadian Journal of Criminology*, 43(3), 303–329.

Denov, M. S. (2003a). The myth of innocence: sexual scripts and the recognition of child sexual abuse by female perpetrators. *Journal of Sex Research*, 40(3), 303–314.

Denov, M. S. (2003b). To a safer place? Victims of sexual abuse by females and their disclosures to professionals. *Child Abuse and Neglect*, 27, 47–61.

Denov, M. S. (2004a). *Perspectives on Female Sex Offending*. Aldershot: Ashgate.

Denov, M. S. (2004b). The long-term effects of child sexual abuse by female perpetrators: a qualitative study of male and female victims. *Journal of Interpersonal Violence*, 19(10), 1137–1156.

De Young, M. (1994). Women as mothers and wives in paternally incestuous families: coping with role conflict. *Child Abuse and Neglect*, 18, 73–84.

Dietz, C. A. & Craft, J. L. (1980). Family dynamics of incest: a new perspective. *Social Casework*, 61, 602–607.

DiGiorgio-Miller, J. (1998). Sibling incest: treatment of the family and the offender. *Child Welfare*, 77, 335–346.

Dimock, P. T. (1988). Adult males sexually abused as children. *Journal of Interpersonal Violence*, 3(2), 203–221.

Dube, R. & Herbert, M. (1988). Sexual abuse of children under 12 years. A review of 511 cases. *Child Abuse and Neglect*, 12, 321.

Duncan, L. E. & Williams, L. M. (1998). Gender role socialisation and male-on-male vs. female-on-male child sexual abuse. *Sex Roles*, 39(9–10), 765–785.

Egeland, B. (1993). A history of abuse is a major risk factor for abusing the next generation. In R. J. Gelles & D. R. Loseke (Eds). *Current Controversies on Family Violence* (pp. 197–208). Newbury Park: Sage.

Eisenberg, N., Owens, R. G & Dewey, M. E. (1987). Attitudes of health professionals to child sexual abuse and incest. *Child Abuse and Neglect*, 11, 109–116.

Eldridge, H. (1993). Barbara's story – a mother who sexually abused. In M. Elliott (Ed.) *Female Sexual Abuse of Children: The Ultimate Taboo* (pp. 79–94). Chichester: John Wiley & Sons.

Eldridge, H. J. & Saradjian, J. (2000). Replacing the function of abusive behaviours for the offender: remaking relapse prevention in working with women who sexually abuse children. In D. R. Laws, S. M. Hudson & T. Ward (Eds). *Remaking Relapse Prevention with Sex Offenders: A Sourcebook*. (pp. 402–426). Thousand Oaks CA: Sage.

176

REFERENCES

Eldridge, H. J. & Saradjian, J. (in press a). *New Life Manual*. Thousand Oaks CA: Sage.

Eldridge, H. J. & Saradjian, J. (in press b). *Assessment, Treatment and Relapse Prevention with Women Who Sexually Abuse Children: A Therapist Guide*. Thousand Oaks CA: Sage.

Elliott, A. J. & Peterson, L. W. (1993). Maternal sexual abuse of male children: when to suspect and how to uncover it. *Postgraduate Medicine, 94*, 169–180.

Elliott, A. N. & Carnes, C. N. (2001). Reactions of nonoffending parents to the sexual abuse of their child: a review of the literature. *Child Maltreatment, 6*(4), 314–331.

Elliott, M. (1993a). What survivors tell us – an overview. In M. Elliott (Ed.) *Female Sexual Abuse of Children: The Ultimate Taboo* (pp. 5–14). Chichester: John Wiley & Sons.

Elliott, M. (1993b) (Ed.) *Female Sexual Abuse of Children: The Ultimate Taboo*. Chichester: John Wiley & Sons.

Etherington, K. (1997). Maternal sexual abuse of males. *Child Abuse Review, 6*, 107–117.

Faller, K. C. (1987). Women who sexually abuse children. *Violence and Victims, 2*(4), 263–276.

Faller, K. C. (1988). The myth of the "collusive mother". *Journal of Interpersonal Violence, 3*(2), 190–196.

Faller, K. C. (1990). *Understanding Child Sexual Maltreatment*. Newbury Park: Sage.

Faller, K. C. (1995). A clinical sample of women who have sexually abused children. *Journal of Child Sexual Abuse, 4*(3), 13–30.

Falshaw, L., Friendship, C. & Bates, A. (2003). *Sexual Offenders – Measuring Reconviction, Reoffending and Recidivism*. Research Findings no. 183. London: Home Office Research, Development and Statistics Directorate.

Featherstone, B. (1996). Victims or villains? Women who physically abuse their children. In B. Fawcett, B. Featherstone, J. Hearn & C. Toft (Eds). *Violence And Gender Relations: Theories And Interventions* (pp. 178–189). London: Sage.

Fehrenbach, P. A. & Monastersky, C. (1988). Characteristics of female adolescent sexual offenders. *American Journal of Orthopsychiatry, 58*(1), 148–151.

Ferree, M. C. (2003). Women and the Web: cybersex activity and implications. *Sexual and Relationship Therapy, 18*(3), 385–393.

Finkelhor, D. (1984). *Child Sexual Abuse*. New York: The Free Press.

Finkelhor, D. (1986). *A Sourcebook On Child Sexual Abuse*. Beverly Hills, CA: Sage.

Finkelhor, D. & Redfield, D. (1984). How the public defines sexual abuse. In D. Finkelhor (Ed.) *Child Sexual Abuse: New Theory And Research* (pp. 12–32). New York: Free Press.

Finkelhor, D. & Russell, D. (1984). Women as perpetrators: review of the evidence. In D. Finkelhor, (Ed.) *Child Sexual Abuse*. (pp. 171–187). New York: Free Press.

Finkelhor, D., Williams, L. M. & Burns, N. (1988). *Nursery crimes: Sexual Abuse in Day Care*. Newbury Park: Sage.

Finkelhor, D., Hotaling, G., Lewis, I. A. & Smith, C. (1990). Sexual abuse in a national survey of adult men and women: prevalence, characteristics and risk factors. *Child Abuse and Neglect, 14*, 19–28.

FitzRoy, L. (1998). Stepping into a feminist minefield: women sex offenders. *Australian Journal of Primary Health – Interchange, 4*(3), 185–191.

Fontes, L. A., Cruz, M. & Tabachnick, J. (2001). Views of child sexual abuse in two cultural communities: an exploratory study among African Americans and Latinos. *Child Maltreatment, 6*(2), 103–117.

Forbes, F., Duffy, J. C., Mok, J. & Lemvig, J. (2003). Early intervention service for non-abusing parents of victims of child sexual abuse. *British Journal of Psychiatry, 183*, 66–72.

Forbes, J. (1993). Female sexual abusers: the contemporary search for equivalence. *Practice, 6*(2), 102–111.

Freel, M. (1995). *Women who sexually abuse children*. Social Work Monographs 135. Norwich: University of East Anglia.

Freund, K., Watson, R. & Rienzo, D. (1988). Signs of feigning in the phallometric test. *Behavior Research and Therapy, 26*, 105–112.

Friedrich, W. N. (1988). Behaviour problems in sexually abused children: an adaptational perspective. In G. E. Wyatt & E. J. Powell (Eds). *Lasting Effects Of Child Sexual Abuse*. Beverly Hills, CA: Sage.

Friedrich, W. N. (1995). *Psychotherapy With Sexually Abused Boys: An Integrated Approach*. Newbury Park, CA: Sage.

Friendship, C., Falshaw, L. & Beech, A. R. (2003). Measuring the real impact of accredited offending behaviour programmes. *Legal and Criminological Psychology, 8*, 115–127.

Friendship, C. & Thornton, D. (2002). Risk assessment for offenders. In K. D. Browne, H. Hanks, P. Stratton & C. Hamilton, (Eds). *Early Prediction and Prevention of Child Abuse: A Handbook* (pp. 301–316). Chichester: John Wiley & Sons.

Fromuth, M. E. & Burkhart, B. R. (1989). Long-term psychological correlates of childhood sexual abuse in two samples of college men. *Child Abuse and Neglect, 13*, 533–542.

Fromuth, M. E. & Conn, V. E. (1997). Hidden perpetrators: sexual molestation in a nonclinical sample of college women. *Journal of Interpersonal Violence, 12*(3), 456–465.

Gallagher, B. (2000). The extent and nature of known cases of institutional child sexual abuse. *British Journal of Social Work, 30*, 795–817.

Gavin, H. (2005). The social construction of the child sex offender explored by narrative. *The Qualitative Report 10*(3), 395–415. Retrieved November 17, 2005 from the Web site: http://www.nova.edu/ssss/QR/QR10-3/gavin.pdf

Gelinas, D. J. (1983). The persisting negative effects of incest. *Psychiatry, 46*, 312–332.

Gelsthorpe, L. (1989). *Sexism And The Female Offender – An Organisational Analysis*. Aldershot: Gower Press.

Gibbens, T. C. N. (1971). Female offenders. *British Journal of Hospital Medicine, 6*, 279–286.

Glasser, M., Kolvin, I., Campbell, D., Glasser, A., Leitch, I. & Farrelly, S. (2001). Cycle of child sexual abuse: links between being a victim and becoming a perpetrator. *British Journal of Psychiatry, 179*, 482–494.

Graham, K. R. (1996). The childhood victimisation of sex offenders: an underestimated issue. *International Journal of Offender Therapy and Comparative Criminology, 40*(3), 192–203.

Grayston, A. D. & De Luca, R. V. (1999). Female perpetrators of child sexual abuse: a review of the clinical and empirical literature. *Aggression and Violent Behaviour, 4*(1), 93–106.

Green, A. H. & Kaplan, M. S. (1994). Psychiatric impairment and childhood victimization experiences in female child molesters. *Journal of the American Academy of Child and Adolescent Psychiatry, 33*(7), 954–961.

Green, J. (1996). Mothers in "incest families". *Violence Against Women, 2*(3), 322–348.

Greenberg, M. T. (1999). Attachment and psychopathology in childhood. In J. Cassidy & P. R. Shaver (Eds). *Handbook Of Attachment: Theory, Research And Clinical Implications* (pp. 497–519). London: The Guildford Press.

Grier, P. & Clark, M. (1987). *Female sexual offenders in a prison setting*. Unpublished manuscript, Behavioural Science Institute, Inc. St Louis.

Groth, A. N. (1979). Sexual trauma in the life histories of rapists and child molesters. *Victimology 4*, 10–16.

Groth, A. N., Longo, R. E. & McFadin, J. B. (1982). Undetected recidivism among rapists and child molesters. *Crime and Delinquency, 28*(3), 450–458.

Grubin, D. (1998). *Sex offending against children: understanding the risk.* Police Research Series Paper 99. London: Home Office.

Haley, J. (1990). *Strategies of psychotherapy,* 2nd edition. Rockville: Triangle Press.

Hall, L. A., Sachs, B. & Rayens, M. K. (1998). Mothers' potential for child abuse: the roles of childhood abuse and social resources. *Nursing Research 47*(2), 87–95.

Hamilton, C. & Browne, K. (2002). Predicting physical maltreatment. In K. D. Browne, H. Hanks, P. Stratton & C. Hamilton (Eds). *Early Prediction and Prevention of Child Abuse: A Handbook* (pp. 41–55). Chichester: John Wiley & Sons.

Hanson, R. K., Gordon, A., Harris, A. J. R., Marques, J. K., Murphy, W., Quinsey, V. L. & Seto, M. C. (2002). First report of the collaborative outcome data project on the effectiveness of psychological treatment for sex offenders. *Sexual Abuse: A Journal of Research and Treatment 14*(2), 169–194.

Harned, M. S. (2001). Abused women or abused men? An examination of the context and outcomes of dating violence. *Violence and Victims, 16*(3), 269–284.

Harnett, P. H. (1997). The attitudes of female and male residential care workers to the perpetrators of sexual and physical assault. *Child Abuse and Neglect, 21*(9), 861–868.

Harper, J. (1993). Prepuberal male victims of incest: a clinical study. *Child Abuse and Neglect, 17,* 419–421.

Harris, D. (2001). *Adolescent male and female sexual offending and treatment.* Unpublished Honours Thesis: Queensland University of Technology.

Harrison, H. & Cobham, C. (1993). Female abusers – what children and young people have told ChildLine. In M. Elliott (Ed.) *Female Sexual Abuse of Children: The Ultimate Taboo* (pp. 95–98). Chichester: John Wiley & Sons.

Hart, S. N., Binggeli, N. J. & Brassard, M. R. (1998). Evidence for the effects of psychological maltreatment. *Journal of Emotional Abuse, 1*(1), 27–57.

Hayashino, D. S., Wurtele, S. K. & Klebe, K. J. (1995). Child molesters: an examination of cognitive factors. *Journal of Interpersonal Violence, 10,* 106–116.

Hedderman, C. & Sugg, D. (1996). *Does Treating Sex Offenders Reduce Reoffending?* Research Findings no. 45. London: Home Office Research, Development and Statistics Directorate.

Heriot, J. (1996). Maternal protectiveness following the disclosure of intrafamilial child sexual abuse. *Journal of Interpersonal Violence, 11,* 181–194.

Hetherton, J. (1999). The idealisation of women: its role in the minimisation of child sexual abuse by females. *Child Abuse and Neglect, 23*(2), 161–174.

Hetherton, J. & Beardsall, L. (1998). Decisions and attitudes concerning child sexual abuse: does the gender of the perpetrator make a difference to child protection professionals? *Child Abuse and Neglect, 22*(12), 1265–1283.

Hickman, L. J., Jaycox, L. H. & Aronoff, J. (2004). Dating violence among adolescents: prevalence, gender distribution and prevention program effectiveness. *Trauma, Violence and Abuse, 5*(2), 123–142.

Hiebert-Murphy, D. (2000). Factors related to mothers' perceptions of parenting following their children's disclosures of sexual abuse. *Child Maltreatment, 5*(3), 251–260.

Higgins, D. J. & McCabe, M. P. (2001). Multiple forms of child abuse and neglect: adult retrospective reports. *Aggression and Violent Behaviour, 6,* 547–578.

Higgs, D. C., Canavan, M. M. & Meyer, W. J. (1992). Moving from defence to offence: the development of an adolescent female sex offender. *The Journal of Sex Research, 29*(1), 131–139.

Hill, A. (2001). "No-one else could understand": women's experiences of a support group run by and for mothers of sexually abused children. *British Journal of Social Work, 31,* 385–397.

Hilton, N. Z., Harris, G. T. & Rice, M. E. (2003). Adolescents' perceptions of the seriousness of sexual aggression: influence of gender, traditional attitudes and self-reported experience. *Sexual Abuse: A Journal of Research and Treatment, 15*(3), 201–124.

Hirschberg, D. & Riskin, K. (1994). *Female adolescent sexual offenders in residential treatment: characteristics and treatment implications.* Retrieved November 19, 2002 from the Web site: http://www.germainelawrence.org/web/fasort.html

Hirschberg, D. & Riskin, K. (1996). *Female juvenile sexual offenders: do gender differences require specialised treatment?* Retrieved November 19, 2002 from the Web site: http://www.germainelawrence.org/web/fjso.html

Holmes, W. C. & Slap, G. B. (1998). Sexual abuse of boys: definition, prevalence, correlates, sequelae and management. *The Journal of the American Medical Association, 280*, 1855–1865.

Home Office (2002). *Prison Statistics for England and Wales.* London: Her Majesty's Stationary Office.

Home Office (2002). *Statistics on Women and the Criminal Justice System.* Retrieved August 10, 2003 from the Web site: http://www.homeoffice.gov.uk/rds/pdfs2/s95women02.pdf

Hooper, C. (1989). Alternatives to collusion: the response of mothers to child sexual abuse in the family. *Educational and Child Psychology, 6*(1), 22–30.

Hooper, C. (1992). *Mothers Surviving Child Sexual Abuse.* London: Routledge.

Hooper, C. & Humphreys, C. (1998). Women whose children have been sexually abused: reflections on a debate. *British Journal of Social Work, 28*, 565–580.

Howitt, D. (1992). *Child Abuse Errors.* New York: Harvester Wheatsheaf.

Howitt, D. (1995a). *Paedophiles and Sexual Offences Against Children.* Chichester: John Wiley & Sons.

Howitt, D. (1995b). Pornography and the paedophile: is it criminogenic? *British Journal of Medical Psychology, 68*, 15–27.

Hunt, M. (1974). *Sexual Behaviour in the 1970s.* New York: Dell.

Hunter, J. A., Lexier, L. J., Goodwin, D. W., Browne, P. A. & Dennis, C. (1993). Psychosexual, attitudinal and developmental characteristics of juvenile female sexual perpetrators in a residential treatment setting. *Journal of Child and Family Studies, 2*(4), 317–326.

Hunter, M. (1990). *Abused Boys: The Neglected Victims of Child Sexual Abuse.* Lexington MA: Lexington Books.

Iowa Commission on the Status of Women, (1997). *Female juvenile justice report.* Retrieved October 18, 2002 from the Web site: http://www.infoiowa.state.ia.us/DHR/PDF/Public%20info/FemaleJuvJustice.pdf

Jackson, D. & Mannix, J. (2004). Giving voice to the burden of blame: a feminist study of mothers' experiences of mother-blaming. *International Journal of Nursing Practice, 10*, 150–158.

Jackson, L. A. (2000). *Child Sexual Abuse in Victorian England.* London: Routledge.

Jacobs, J. L. (1990). Reassessing mother blame in incest. *Signs: Journal of Women in Culture and Society, 15*(3), 500–514.

Jacobs, J. L. (1993). Victimised daughters: sexual violence and the empathic female self. *Signs: Journal of Women in Culture and Society, 19*, 126–145.

James, A. C. & Neil, P. (1996). Juvenile sexual offending: one year prevalence study within Oxfordshire. *Child Abuse and Neglect, 20*(6), 477–485.

Jennings, K. T. (1993). Female child molesters: a review of the literature. In M. Elliott (Ed.) *Female Sexual Abuse of Children: The Ultimate Taboo* (pp. 241–257). Chichester: John Wiley & Sons.

Johansson-Love, J. & Fremouw, W. (2006). A critique of the female sexual perpetrator research. *Aggression and Violent Behavior, 11*(1), 12–26.

Johnson, J. (1992). *Mothers Of Incest Survivors: Another Side Of The Story*. Indiana Press.

Johnson, R. L. & Shrier, D. (1987). Past sexual victimisation by females of male patients in an adolescent medicine clinic population. *American Journal of Psychiatry, 144*, 650–652.

Justice, B. & Justice, R. (1979). *The Broken Taboo: Sex In The Family*. New York: Human Sciences Press.

Kalders, A., Inkster, H. & Britt, E. (1997). Females who offend sexually against children in New Zealand. *The Journal of Sexual Aggression, 3*(1), 15–29.

Kalmus, E. & Beech, A. R. (2005). Forensic assessment of sexual interest: a review. *Aggression and Violent Behavior, 10*, 193–217.

Kaplan, M. S. & Green, A. (1995). Incarcerated female sexual offenders: a comparison of sexual histories with eleven female nonsexual offenders. *Sexual Abuse: A Journal of Research and Treatment, 7*(4), 287–300.

Kasl, C. D. (1990). Female perpetrators of sexual abuse: a feminist view. In M. Hunter (Ed.) *The Sexually Abused Male: Volume 1 – Prevalence, Impact and Treatment* (pp. 259–274). Lexington: Lexington Books.

Kaufman, J. & Zigler, E. (1993). The intergenerational transmission of abuse is overstated. In R. J. Gelles & D. R. Loseke (Eds). *Current Controversies on Family Violence* (pp. 209–221). Newbury Park: Sage.

Kaufman, K. L., Wallace, A. M., Johnson, C. E. & Reeder, M. L. (1995). Comparing male and female perpetrators' modus operandi: victims' reports of sexual abuse. *Journal of Interpersonal Violence, 10*, 322–333.

Kelley, S. J., Brant, R. & Waterman, J. (1993). Sexual abuse of children in day care centres. *Child Abuse and Neglect, 17*, 71–89.

Kelly, L. (1996). Pedophiles and the cycle of abuse. *Women in Action, 3*, 69–76.

Kelly, R. J., Wood, J. J., Gonzalez, L. S., MacDonald, V. & Waterman, J. (2002). Effects of mother–son incest and positive perceptions of sexual abuse experiences on the psychosocial adjustment of clinic-referred men. *Child Abuse and Neglect, 26*, 425–441.

Kemshall, H. (2004). Female sex offenders. In H. Kemshall & G. McIvor (Eds). *Managing Sex Offender Risk* (pp. 49–64). London: Jessica Kingsley.

Kemshall, H. & McIvor, G. (2004). Sex offenders: policy and legislative developments. In H. Kemshall & G. McIvor (Eds). *Managing Sex Offender Risk* (pp. 7–22). London: Jessica Kingsley.

Kendall-Tackett, K. A. & Simon, A. F. (1987). Perpetrators and their acts: data from 365 adults molested as children. *Child Abuse and Neglect, 11*, 237–245.

Kendrick, A. (2004). Managing children and young people who are sexually aggressive. In H. Kemshall & G. McIvor (Eds). *Managing Sex Offender Risk* (pp. 165–186). London: Jessica Kingsley.

Kilpatrick, D. G. & Himelein, M. J. (1986). Male crime victims, the most victimised, often neglected. *National Organisation for Victim Assistance Newsletter, 10*(12), 5–7.

King, M., Coxell, A. & Mezey, G. (2000). The prevalence and characteristics of male sexual assault. In G. C. Mezey & M. B. King (Eds). *Male Victims of Sexual Assault, 2nd Edition* (pp. 1–15). Oxford: Oxford University Press.

Kite, D. & Tyson, G. A. (2004). The impact of perpetrator gender on male and female police officers' perceptions of child sexual abuse. *Psychiatry, Psychology and Law, 11*(2), 308–318.

Koonin, R. (1995). Breaking the last taboo: child sexual abuse by female perpetrators. *Australian Journal of Social Issues, 30*(2), 195–210.

Krahé, B., Waizenhöfer, E. & Möller, I. (2003). Women's sexual aggression against men: prevalence and predictors. *Sex Roles, 49*, 219–232.

Kreklewetz, C. M. & Piotrowski, C. C. (1998). Incest survivor mothers: protecting the next generation. *Child Abuse and Neglect, 22*, 1305–1312.

Krug, R. S. (1989). Adult male report of childhood sexual abuse by mothers: case descriptions, motivations and long-term consequences. *Child Abuse and Neglect, 13*, 111–119.

Kubik, E. K., Hecker, J. E. & Righthand, S. (2002). Adolescent females who have sexually offended: comparisons with delinquent adolescent female offenders and adolescent males who sexually offend. *Journal of Child Sexual Abuse, 11*(3), 63–83.

La Fontaine, J. (1989). Child sexual abuse: an ESRC research briefing. In British Agencies for Adoption and Fostering. *After Abuse: Papers on Caring and Planning for a Child Who Has Been Sexually Abused.* London: British Agencies For Adoption and Fostering.

La Fontaine, J. (1990). *Child Sexual Abuse.* Cambridge: Polity Press.

Langevin, R. & Curnoe, S. (2004). The use of pornography during the commission of sexual offences. *International Journal of Offender Therapy and Comparative Criminology, 48*(5), 572–586.

Langevin, R., Lang, R. A. & Curnoe, S. (1998). The prevalence of sex offenders with deviant fantasies. *Journal of Interpersonal Violence, 13*(3), 315–327.

Långström, N. (2001). *Young sex offenders: a research overview.* Retrieved November 19, 2002 from the Web site: http://www.sos.se/fulltext/123/2001-123-17/2001-123-17.pdf

LaRocca, M. A. & Kromrey, J. D. (1999). The perception of sexual harassment in higher education: impact of gender and attractiveness. *Sex Roles, 40*(11–12), 921–940.

Lawson, C. (1993). Mother–son sexual abuse: rare or underreported? A critique of the research. *Child Abuse and Neglect, 17*, 261–269.

Leahy, T., Pretty, G. & Tenenbaum, G. (2004). Perpetrator methodology as a predictor of traumatic symptomatology in adult survivors of childhood sexual abuse. *Journal of Interpersonal Violence, 19*(5), 521–540.

Lee, D. (2000). Hegemonic masculinity and male feminisation: the sexual harassment of men at work. *Journal of Gender Studies, 9*(2), 141–155.

Leifer, M., Kilbane, T. & Grossman, G. (2001). A three-generation study comparing the families of supportive and unsupportive mothers of sexually abused children. *Child Maltreatment, 6*(4), 353–364.

Lewin, L. & Bergin, C. (2001). Attachment behaviours, depression and anxiety in nonoffending mothers of child sexual abuse victims. *Child Maltreatment, 6*(4), 365–375.

Lewis, C. F. & Stanley, C. R. (2000). Women accused of sexual offences. *Behavioral Sciences and the Law, 18*, 73–81.

Liem, J. H., O'Toole, J. G. & James, J. B. (1992). The need for power in women who were sexually abused as children. *Psychology of Women Quarterly, 16*, 467–480.

Lind, M. (1995). *Sexual abuse of girls by women.* Paper presented at the European Conference on Child Abuse and Neglect. Oslo, Norway.

Lisak, D. (1994). The psychological impact of sexual abuse: content analysis of interviews with male survivors. *Journal of Traumatic Stress, 7*(4), 525–548.

Longdon, C. (1993). A survivor's and therapist's viewpoint. In M. Elliott (Ed.) *Female Sexual Abuse of Children: The Ultimate Taboo* (pp. 50–60). Chichester: John Wiley & Sons.

Lovett, B. B. (1995). Child sexual abuse: the female victim's relationship with her nonoffending mother. *Child Abuse and Neglect, 19*(6), 729–738.

Lukianowicz, N. (1972). Incest: I Paternal incest, II other types of incest. *British Journal of Psychiatry, 120*, 301–313.

Lyon, E. & Kouloumpos-Lenares, K. (1987). Clinician and state children's services worker collaboration in treating sexual abuse. *Child Welfare, 67*, 517–527.

Maison, S. R. & Larson, N. R. (1995). Psychosexual treatment program for women sex offenders in a prison setting. *Nordisk Sexologi, 13*, 149–162.

Malamuth, N. M. (1989). The attraction to sexual aggression scale: part two. *Journal of Sex Research, 26*, 324–354.

Margolin, L. (1987). The effects of mother–son incest. *Lifestyles: A Journal of Changing Patterns, 8*(2), 104–114.

Margolin, L. (1991). Child sexual abuse by nonrelated caregivers. *Child Abuse and Neglect, 15*, 213–221.

Mars, D. (1998). A case of mother–son incest: its consequences for development and treatment. *Journal of Clinical Psychoanalysis, 7*(3), 401–420.

Marshall, W. L. & Serran, G. A. (2000). Improving the effectiveness of sexual offender treatment. *Trauma, Violence and Abuse, 1*(3), 203–222.

Martín, A. F., Vergeles, M. R., Acevedo, V., Sánchez, A. & Visa, S. L. (2005). The involvement in sexual coercive behaviours of Spanish college men. *Journal of Interpersonal Violence, 20*(7), 872–891.

Mathews, R., Hunter, J. A. & Vuz, J. (1997). Juvenile female sexual offender: clinical characteristics and treatment issues. *Sexual Abuse: A Journal of Research and Treatment 9*(3), 187–199.

Mathews, R., Matthews, J. & Speltz, K. (1990). Female sexual offenders. In M. Hunter (Ed.) *The Sexually Abused Male: Volume 1 – Prevalence, Impact and Treatment* (pp. 275–293). Lexington: Lexington Books.

Mathis, J. L. (1972). *Clear Thinking About Sexual Deviation*. Chicago: Nelson-Hall.

Matthews, J. K. (1993). Working with female sexual abusers. In M. Elliott (Ed.) *Female Sexual Abuse of Children: The Ultimate Taboo* (pp. 61–78). Chichester: John Wiley & Sons.

Matthews, J. K. (1998). An 11-year perspective of working with female sexual offenders. In W. L. Marshall, Y. M. Fernandez, S. M. Hudson & T. Ward (Eds). *Sourcebook of Treatment Programmes for Sexual Offenders* (pp. 259–272). New York: Plenum Press.

Matthews, J. K., Mathews, R. & Speltz, K. (1991). Female sexual offenders: a typology. In M. Q. Patton (Ed.) *Family Sexual Abuse: Frontline Research and Evaluation* (pp. 199–219). Newbury Park: Sage.

Mayer, A. (1992). *Women Sex Offenders: Treatment and Dynamics*. Holmes Beach: Learning Publications.

Maynard, C. & Wiederman, M. (1997). Undergraduate students' perceptions of child sexual abuse: effects of age, sex and gender role attitudes. *Child Abuse and Neglect, 21*(9), 833–844.

McCallum, S. (2001). Nonoffending mothers. *Violence against Women, 7*(3), 315–334.

McCarty, L. M. (1986). Mother–son incest: characteristics of the offender. *Child Welfare, 65*, 447–458.

McConaghy, N. (1993). *Sexual Behaviour: Problems and Management*. New York: Plenum Press.

McConaghy, N. (1998). Paedophilia: a review of the evidence. *Australian and New Zealand Journal of Psychiatry, 32*, 252–265.

McGuire, J. (2001). What works in correctional intervention? Evidence and practical implications. In G. A. Bernfield, D. P. Farrington & A. W. Leschied (Eds). *Offender Rehabilitation in Practice: Implementing and Evaluating Effective Programs* (pp. 25–43). Chichester: John Wiley & Sons.

Mendel, M. P. (1995). *The Male Survivor: The Impact of Sexual Abuse*. Thousand Oaks CA: Sage.

Messer, J., Maughan, B., Quinton, D. & Taylor, A. (2004). Precursors and correlates of criminal behaviour in women. *Criminal Behaviour and Mental Health, 14*, 82–107.

Meston, C. M., Heiman, J. R. & Trapnell, P. D. (1999). The relation between early abuse and adult sexuality. *Journal of Sex Research, 36*(4), 385–395.

Miccio-Fonseca, L. C. (2000). Adult and adolescent female sex offenders: experiences compared to other female and male sex offenders. *Journal of Psychology and Human Sexuality, 11*(3), 75–88.

Miller, D. L. (2003). *Research approaches and treatment protocols with female sexual perpetrators: going beyond gender-biased and gender-blind approaches.* Paper presented at the Association for the Treatment of Sexual Abusers Annual Conference, St Louis, Missouri, 8–11 October 2003.

Minasian, G. & Lewis, A. D. (1999). Female sexual abusers: an unrecognised culture. In A. D. Lewis (Ed.) *Cultural Diversity in Sexual Abuser Treatment: Issues and Approaches* (pp. 71–82). Brandon VT: Safer Society Press.

Mitchell, J. & Morse, J. (1998). *From Victims to Survivors.* Washington DC: Accelerated Development.

Morrel, T. M., Dubowitz, H., Kerr, M. A. & Black, M. (2003). The effect of maternal victimisation on children: a cross-informant study. *Journal of Family Violence, 1*, 29–41.

Muehlenhard, C. L. (1998). The importance and danger of studying sexually aggressive women. In P. B. Anderson & C. Struckman-Johnson (Eds). *Sexually Aggressive Women: Current Perspectives and Controversies* (pp. 19–48). New York: The Guilford Press.

Mullen, P. E., Martin, J. L., Anderson, J. C., Romans, S. E. & Herbison, G. P. (1993). Childhood sexual abuse and mental health in adult life. *British Journal of Psychiatry, 163*, 721–732.

Myhill, A. & Allen, J. (2002). *Rape and sexual assault of women: the extent and nature of the problem.* Home Office Research Study Number 237. Retrieved November 17, 2005 from the Web site: http://www.homeoffice.gov.uk/rds/pdfs2/hors237.pdf

Nagel, D. E., Putnam, F. W., Noll, J. G. & Trickett, P. K. (1997). Disclosure patterns of sexual abuse and psychological functioning at a 1-year follow up. *Child Abuse and Neglect, 21*(2), 137–147.

Nathan, P. & Ward, T. (2002). Female sex offenders: clinical and demographic features. *The Journal of Sexual Aggression, 8*(1), 5–21.

National Clearing House on Family Violence, (1990). *Adolescent sexual offenders.* Retrieved November 19, 2002 from the Web site: http://www.hc-.gc.ca/hppb/familyviolence/pdfs/adolsxo.pdf

Nelson, A. & Oliver, P. (1998). Gender and the construction of consent in child–adult sexual contact. *Gender and Society, 12*(5), 554–577.

Nelson, E. (1994). Females who sexually abuse children: a discussion of gender stereotypes and symbolic assaults. *Qualitative Sociology, 17*, 63–87.

Newberger, C. M. & White, K. M. (1989). Cognitive foundations for parental care. In D. Cicchetti & V. Carlson (Eds). *Child Maltreatment.* Cambridge: University of Cambridge Press.

Ng, M. (2001). Female Sexual Dysfunction. *Journal of Paediatrics, Obstetrics and Gynaecology, 27*(3), 45–48.

Noll, J. G. (2005). Does childhood sexual abuse set in motion a cycle of violence against women. What we know and what we need to learn. *Journal of Interpersonal Violence, 20*(4), 455–462.

O'Callaghan, D. & Print, B. (1994). Adolescent sexual abusers: research, assessment and treatment. In T. Morrison, M. Erooga & R. C. Beckett (Eds). *Sexual Offending against Children: Assessment and Treatment of Male Abusers* (pp. 146–177). London: Routledge.

O'Connor, A. A. (1987). Female sex offenders. *British Journal of Psychiatry, 150,* 615–620.

O'Keefe, M. (1997). Predictors of dating violence among high school students. *Journal of Interpersonal Violence, 12*(4), 546–568.

Office of Juvenile Justice and Delinquency Prevention (OJJDP), (2001). *Juveniles who have sexually offended.* Retrieved October 10, 2002 from the Web site: http://www.ncjrs.org/html/ojjdp/report_juvsex_offend/type.html

Ogilvie, B. & Daniluk, J. (1995). Common themes in the experiences of mother–daughter incest survivors: implications for counselling. *Journal of Counselling and Development, 73,* 598–602.

Olafson, E., Corwin, D. L. & Summit, R. C. (1993). Modern history of child sexual abuse awareness: cycles of discovery and suppression. *Child Abuse and Neglect, 17,* 7–24.

Olson, E. A. (1981). Socioeconomic and psycho-cultural contexts of child abuse and neglect in Turkey. In J. Korbin (Ed.) *Child Abuse And Neglect: Cross Cultural Perspectives* (pp. 96–119). Berkeley, CA: University of California Press.

Ong, B. N. (1985). Understanding child abuse, ideologies of motherhood. *Womens Studies Inc Forum, 8*(6), Pergamon Press.

Ovaris, W. (1991). *After The Nightmare: The Treatment Of Non-Offending Mothers Of Sexually Abused Children.* Holmes Beach: Learning Publications.

Parker, R. (1995). *Torn In Two: The Experience Of Maternal Ambivalence.* London: Virago.

Peluso, E. & Putnam, N. (1996). Case study: sexual abuse of boys by females. *Journal of the American Academy of Child and Adolescent Psychiatry, 35*(1), 51–54.

Pepi, C. L. (1997). Children without childhoods: a feminist intervention strategy utilising systems theory and restorative justice in treating female adolescent offenders. *Women and Therapy, 20*(4), 85–101.

Perrott, K., Morris, E., Martin, J. & Romans, S. (1998). Cognitive coping styles of women sexually abused in childhood: a qualitative study. *Child Abuse and Neglect, 22*(11), 1135–1149.

Peterson, K. D., Colebank, K. D. & Motta, L. L. (2001). *Female sexual offender recidivism.* Paper presented at the meeting for the Association for the Treatment of Sexual Offenders. San Antonio, TX.

Pierce, R. & Pierce, L. (1985). The sexually abused child: a comparison of male and female victims. *Child Abuse and Neglect, 9,* 191–199.

Pintello, D. & Zuravin, S. (2001). Intrafamilial child sexual abuse: predictors of post-disclosure maternal belief and protective action. *Child Maltreatment, 6*(4), 344–352.

Platts, H., Tyson, M. & Mason, O. (2002). Adult attachment style and core beliefs: are they linked? *Clinical Psychology and Psychotherapy, 9,* 332–348.

Polaschek, D. L. L. & Hudson, S. M. (2004). Pathways to rape: preliminary examination of patterns in the offence processes of rapists and their rehabilitation implications. *Journal of Sexual Aggression, 10*(1), 7–20.

Pothast, H. L. & Allen, C. M. (1994). Masculinity and femininity in male and female perpetrators of child sexual abuse. *Child Abuse and Neglect, 18*(9), 763–767.

Ray, J. A. & English, D. J. (1995). Comparison of female and male children with sexual behaviour problems. *Journal of Youth and Adolescence, 24,* 439–451.

Righthand, S. & Welch, C. (2001). *Juveniles who have Sexually Offended: A Review of the Professional Literature.* Retrieved November 19, 2002 from the Web site: http://www.ncjrs.org/pdffiles1/ojjdp/184739.pdf

Rind, B., Tromovitch, P. & Basuerman, R. (1998). A meta-analytic examination of assumed properties of child sexual abuse using college samples. *Psychological Bulletin, 124,* 22–53.

Ring, L. (2005). *Psychometric Profiles of female sexual abusers: a preliminary analysis into the differences between sexually abusive and non-offending females*. Unpublished MSc thesis: The University of Birmingham.

Robertiello, R. C. (1998). Effects of incestuous heterosexual childhood seduction on three men. *Journal of Contemporary Psychotherapy, 28*(3), 235–238.

Robinson, S. E. (1998). From victim to offender: female offenders of child sexual abuse. *European Journal on Criminal Policy and Research, 6*, 59–73.

Rowan, E. L., Rowan, J. B. & Langelier, P. (1990). Women who molest children. *Bulletin of the American Academy of Psychiatry and the Law, 18*(1), 79–83.

Rudin, M. M., Zalewski, C. & Bodmer-Turner, J. (1995). Characteristics of child sexual abuse victims according to perpetrator gender. *Child Abuse and Neglect, 19*(8), 963–973.

Ruscio, A. M. (2001). Predicting the child-rearing practices of mothers sexually abused in childhood. *Child Abuse and Neglect, 25*, 369–387.

Russell, B. L. & Oswald, D. L. (2001). Strategies and dispositional correlates of sexual coercion perpetrated by women: an exploratory investigation. *Sex Roles, 45*(1–2), 103–115.

Ryan, G. & Lane, S. (1991) (Eds). *Juvenile Sexual Offending: Causes, Consequences and Correction*. Lexington, MA: Lexington Books.

Ryan, G., Miyoshi, T. J., Metzner, J. L., Krugman, R. D. & Fryer, G. E. (1996). Trends in a national sample of sexually abusive youths. *Journal of the American Academy of Child and Adolescent Psychiatry, 33*, 17–25.

Salt, P., Myers, M., Coleman, L. & Sauzier, M. (1990). The myth of the mother as 'accomplice' to child sexual abuse. In B. Gomes-Schwartz, J. Horowitz & A. Cardarelli (Eds). *Child Sexual Abuse* (pp. 109–131). Newbury Park: Sage.

Salter, A. C. (1995). *Transforming Trauma*. Beverly Hills, CA: Sage.

Saradjian, J. (1996). *Women Who Sexually Abuse Children: From Research to Clinical Practice*. Chichester: John Wiley & Sons.

Saradjian, J. (1997). Factors that specifically exacerbate the trauma of victims of childhood sexual abuse by maternal perpetrators. *The Journal of Sexual Aggression, 3*(1), 3–14.

Sarrel, P. M. & Masters, W. H. (1982). Sexual molestation of men by women. *Archives of Sexual Behaviour, 11*(2), 117–131.

Scavo, R. R. (1989). Female adolescent sex offenders: a neglected treatment group. *Social Casework: The Journal of Contemporary Social Work, 70*(2), 114–117.

Scott, R. S. & Flowers, J. (1988). Betrayal by the mother as a factor contributing to psychological disturbance in victims of father–daughter incest. *Journal of Social and Clinical Psychology, 6*(1), 147–154.

Search, G. (1988). *The Last Taboo: Sexual Abuse of Children*. Harmondsworth: Penguin.

Sefarbi, R. (1990). Admitters and deniers among adolescent sex offenders and their families: a preliminary study. *American Journal of Orthopsychiatry, 60*, 460–465.

Sgroi, S. M. & Sargent, N. M. (1993). Impact and treatment issues for victims of childhood sexual abuse by female perpetrators. In M. Elliott (Ed.) *Female Sexual Abuse of Children: The Ultimate Taboo* (pp. 15–38). Chichester: John Wiley & Sons.

Shalhoub-Kevorkian, N. (1999). The politics of disclosing female sexual abuse: a case study of Palestinian society. *Child Abuse and Neglect, 23*(12), 1275–1293.

Shea, C. M. (1998). When the tables are turned: verbal sexual coercion among college women. In P. B. Anderson & C. J. Struckman-Johnson (Eds). *Sexually Aggressive Women: Current Perspectives and Controversies*. New York: Guildford Publications Inc.

Shumba, A. (2004). Male sexual abuse by female and male perpetrators in Zimbabwean schools. *Child Abuse Review, 13*, 353–359.

Silber, A. (1979). Childhood seduction, parental pathology and hysterical symptomatology: the genesis of an altered state of consciousness. *International Journal of Psychoanalysis, 61,* 109–116.

Silovsky, J. F. & Niec, L. (2002). Characteristics of young children with sexual behaviour problems: a pilot study. *Child Maltreatment, 7*(3), 187–197.

Sinason, V. (1994). Working with sexually abused individuals who have a learning disability. In A. Craft (Ed.) *Practice Issues in Sexuality and Learning Disabilities* (pp. 156–175). London: Routledge.

Sirles, E. A. & Franke, P. J. (1989). Factors influencing mothers' reactions to intrafamilial sexual abuse. *Child Abuse and Neglect, 13,* 131–139.

Smith, D. W. & Saunders, B. E. (1995). Personality characteristics of father/perpetrators and nonoffending mothers in incest families: individual and dyadic analyses. *Child Abuse and Neglect, 19*(5), 607–617.

Smith, G. (1989). Child sexual abuse: the power of intrusion. In British Agencies For Adoption and Fostering. *After Abuse: Papers on Planning and Caring for a Child Who has been Sexually Abused.* London: British Agencies for Adoption and Fostering.

Smith, R. E., Pine, C. J. & Hawley, M. E. (1988). Social cognitions about adult male victims of female sexual assault. *The Journal of Sex Research, 24,* 101–112.

Sorbello, L., Eccleston, L., Ward, T. & Jones, R. (2002). Treatment needs of female offenders: a review. *Australian Psychologist, 37*(3), 198–205.

Sorenson, S. B., Stein, J. A., Siegal, J. M., Golding, J. M. & Burnam, M. A. (1987). The prevalence of adult sexual assault: the Los Angeles Epidemiological Catchment Area Project. *American Journal of Epidemiology, 126,* 1154–1164.

Stephen, J. (1993). *The Misrepresentation of Women Offenders.* Probation Monographs 118. Norwich: University of East Anglia.

Stermac, L., Sheridan, P. M., Davidson, A. & Dunn, S. (1996). Sexual assault of adult males. *Journal of Interpersonal Violence, 11*(1), 52–64.

Still, J., Faux, M. & Wilson, C. (2001). *Thames Valley Sex Offender Groupwork Programme.* London: Home Office.

Strike, C., Myers, T., Calzavara, L. & Haubrich, D. (2001). Sexual coercion among young street-involved adults: perpetrators' and victims' perspectives. *Violence and Victims, 16*(5), 537–551.

Struckman-Johnson, C. (1988). Forced sex on dates: it happens to men, too. *The Journal of Sex Research, 24,* 234–241.

Struckman-Johnson, C. & Anderson, P. B. (1998). "Men do and women don't": difficulties in researching sexually aggressive women. In P. B. Anderson & C. Struckman-Johnson (Eds.) *Sexually Aggressive Women: Current Perspectives and Controversies* (pp. 9–18). New York: The Guildford Press.

Struckman-Johnson, C. J. & Struckman-Johnson, D. L. (1991). Men's and women's acceptance of coercive sexual strategies varied by initiator gender and couple intimacy. *Sex Roles, 25,* 661–676.

Struckman-Johnson, C. & Struckman-Johnson, D. (1994). Men pressured and forced into sexual experience. *Archives of Sexual Behaviour, 23*(1), 93–114.

Tamraz, D. N. (1996). Nonoffending mothers of sexually abused children: comparison of opinions and research. *Journal of Child Sexual Abuse, 5,* 75–104.

Tardif, M., Auclair, N., Jacob, M. & Carpentier, J. (2005). Sexual abuse perpetrated by adult and juvenile females: an ultimate attempt to resolve a conflict associated with maternal identity. *Child Abuse and Neglect, 29,* 153–167.

Thomas, A. (1999). *Treatment of female sexual offenders in custody: clinical and theoretical issues.* Paper presented at the VOTA conference, Melbourne, Australia.

Tomeo, M. E., Templer, D. I., Anderson, S. & Kotler, D. (2001). Comparative data of childhood and adolescence molestation in heterosexual and homosexual persons. *Archives of Sexual Behaviour, 30*(5), 535–541.

Travin, S., Cullen, K. & Protter, B. (1990). Female sex offenders: severe victims and victimisers. *Journal of Forensic Sciences, 35*(1), 140–150.

Truesdell, D. L., McNeil, J. S. & Deschner, J. P. (1986). Incidence of wife abuse in incestuous families. *Social Work, 31,* 138–140.

Tufts New England Medical Centre, Division of Child Psychiatry (1984). *Sexually Exploited Children: Service And Research Project.* Final report for the Office of Juvenile Justice and Delinquency Prevention. Washington, DC: Department of Justice.

Vandiver, D. & Kercher, G. (2002). *Registered female sex offenders in Texas: an oddity or an overlooked population?* Retrieved August 10, 2003 from the Web site: http://www.atsa. com/confpdfs/F-22.pdf

Vandiver, D. M. & Kercher, G. (2004). Offender and victim characteristics of registered female sex offenders in Texas: a proposed typology of female sexual offenders. *Sexual Abuse: A Journal of Research and Treatment, 16*(2), 121–137.

Veneziano, C. & Veneziano, L. (2002). Adolescent sex offenders: a review of the literature. *Trauma, Violence and Abuse, 3*(4), 247–260.

Viki, G. T., Massey, K. & Masser, B. (2005). When chivalry backfires: benevolent sexism and attitudes towards Myra Hindley. *Legal and Criminological Psychology, 10,* 109–120.

Ward, T., Day, A., Howells, K. & Birgden, A. (2004). The multifactor offender readiness model. *Aggression and Violent Behavior, 9*(6), 645–673.

Ward, T. & Hudson, S. M. (2000). A self-regulation model of relapse prevention. In D. R. Laws, S. M. Hudson & T. Ward, (Eds). *Remaking Relapse Prevention with Sex Offenders* (pp. 79–101). Thousand Oaks CA: Sage.

Ward, T. & Stewart, C. (2003). Criminogenic needs and human needs: a theoretical model. *Psychology, Crime and Law, 9*(2), 125–143.

Watkins, B. & Bentovim, A. (2000). Male children and adolescents as victims: a review of current knowledge. In G. C. Mezey & M. B. King (Eds). *Male Victims of Sexual Assault, 2nd Edition* (pp. 35–77). Oxford: Oxford University Press.

Weber, F. F. (1999). Coeducational sex offender therapy. *Sexual Addiction and Compulsivity, 6,* 311–315.

Weerman, F. M. (2003). Co-offending as social exchange: explaining characteristics of co-offending. *British Journal of Criminology, 43,* 398–416.

Welldon, E. V. (1988). *Mother, Madonna, Whore: The Idealization and Denigration of Motherhood.* New York: The Guildford Press.

Welldon, E. V. (1996). Female sex offenders. *Prison Service Journal, 107,* 39–47.

Wheeler, J. G., George, W. H. & Dahl, B. J. (2002). Sexually aggressive college males: empathy as a moderator in the "Confluence Model" of sexual aggression. *Personality and Individual Differences, 33,* 759–775.

White, C. (1992). Female sexual abusers are not rare. *British Medical Journal, 304,* 935–936.

Widom, C. S. (2000). Motivation and mechanisms in the "cycle of violence". *Nebraska Symposium on Motivation, 46,* 1–37.

Wilkins, R. (1990). Women who sexually abuse children. *British Medical Journal, 300,* 1153–1154.

Williams, C. (1995). *Invisible Victims: Crime and Abuse against People with Learning Disabilities.* London: Jessica Kingsley Publishers.

Williams, L. M. (1994). Recall of childhood trauma: a prospective study of women's memories of child sexual abuse. *Journal of Consulting and Clinical Psychology, 62,* 1167–1176.

Williams, L. M. & Farrell, R. A. (1990). Legal response to child sexual abuse in day care. *Criminal Justice and Behaviour, 17*(3), 284–302.

Williams, S. M. & Nicholaichuk, T. (2001). *Assessing Static Risk Factors In Adult Female Sex Offenders Under Federal Jurisdiction.* Paper presented at the 21st Research and

Treatment Conference of the Association for the Treatment of Sexual Abusers. San Antonio, Texas.

Woghiren, S. (2002). *An Exploration of Public Attitudes and Knowledge about Child Sexual Abuse and Those Who Perpetrate it in a Population-Based Study in Surrey.* Unpublished Masters dissertation: University of Surrey.

Wolfe, F. A. (1985). *Twelve Female Sexual Offenders.* Presentation to 'Next Steps in Research on the Assessment and Treatment of Sexually Aggressive Persons'. St Louis, MO.

Wolfers, O. (1992). Same abuse, different parent. *Social Work Today*, March 12, 1992, pp. 13–14.

Wolfers, O. (1993). The paradox of women who sexually abuse children. In M. Elliott (Ed.) *Female Sexual Abuse of Children: The Ultimate Taboo* (pp. 99–106). Chichester: John Wiley & Sons.

Woodward, C. & Joseph, S. (2003). Positive change processes and post-traumatic growth in people who have experienced childhood abuse: understanding vehicles of change. *Psychology and Psychotherapy: Theory, Research and Practice, 76,* 267–283.

Worrall, A. (1990). *Offending Women.* London: Routledge.

Wyatt, G., Notgrass, C. & Newcombe, M. (1990). Internal and external mediators of women's rape experiences. *Psychology of Women Quarterly, 14,* 153–176.

# INDEX